MORAL PROBLEMS IN HIGHER EDUCATION

D0986081

MORAL PROBLEMS IN HIGHER EDUCATION

EDITED BY Steven M. Cahn

TEMPLE UNIVERSITY PRESS
PHILADELPHIA

3692

KH

To my wife,
Marilyn Ross, M.D.

TEMPLE UNIVERSITY PRESS
Philadelphia, Pennsylvania 19122
www.temple.edu/tempress

Copyright © 2011 by Temple University
All rights reserved
Published 2011

Library of Congress Cataloging-in-Publication Data

Moral problems in higher education / edited by Steven M. Cahn.
   p. cm.
  ISBN 978-1-4399-0658-3 (cloth : alk. paper) — ISBN 978-1-4399-0659-0 (pbk. :
alk. paper)
1. Education, Higher—Moral and ethical aspects—United States. I. Cahn, Steven M.
LA227.4.M67 2011
  378'.014—dc22

                         2010047386

Printed in the United States of America
030813P

8/23/19

CONTENTS

PREFACE

Steven M. Cahn

During the late 1960s, American philosophers, spurred by debate over the morality of the Vietnam War, broadened their approach to the field of ethics. Until that time, the focus had been on exploring the meaning and justification of moral judgments and assessing the strengths and weaknesses of various moral theories. But once the War was deemed an appropriate subject for moral inquiry, so were other pressing issues, such as abortion, euthanasia, and world hunger.

Soon attention widened to include the ethical dimension of practices in various professions. The activities of physicians, nurses, lawyers, business managers, journalists, and engineers were all subjected to scrutiny, and serious questions were raised about the degree of moral sensitivity displayed in medical offices, courts, and boardrooms. Professional schools began to take such concerns seriously and even added ethicists to their faculties. Indeed, today the staff of a hospital is likely to include not only M.D.s practicing their specialties but also Ph.D.s focusing on questions of medical ethics.

Oddly, however, the moral issues inherent in the practices of one particular profession have for the most part escaped investigation. Few philosophers have shown much interest in examining the moral problems arising in their own bailiwick: higher education. Some scholars apparently believe that their professional activities and those of their colleagues raise no ethical concerns, while other potential inquirers are no doubt dissuaded from pursuing the subject by the discomfTable possibility of finding fault with the practices of their own institutions, their own colleagues, or even themselves.

Perhaps these philosophers realize that whereas hospital administrators and staff have welcomed inquiries by moral philosophers, no such warm greeting would be received from college administrators or faculty members asked to give researchers permission to visit classes or attend meetings in search of ethical lapses. Deans would likely reject such requests by appealing to the importance of confidentiality, while faculty members would seek refuge under the protection of academic freedom.

Thus while from the 1970s on, the literature in medical ethics flourished and studies in other types of professional ethics also grew, little scholarship developed in the field I dubbed "academic ethics." In 1986, however, Rowman & Littlefield published my *Saints and Scamps: Ethics in Academia*. Revised eight years later and recently reissued in an expanded 25th anniversary edition, this pioneering volume enumerates, explains, and emphasizes the most fundamental professorial obligations. I subsequently invited various colleagues across the country to write articles for a collection titled *Morality, Responsibility, and the University: Studies in Academic Ethics*, published in 1990 by Temple University Press. I was gratified that fourteen well-known professors contributed original essays covering a variety of topics, including academic freedom and tenure, sexual harassment, affirmative action, *in loco parentis* rules, and business–university partnerships.

In 1992, when Lawrence C. Becker edited the *Encyclopedia of Ethics*, brought out by Garland Publishing, I was pleased that an entry on "Academic Ethics" was thought worthy of inclusion. While I appreciated my having been invited to contribute the piece, I realized that a decade before the topic would not even have been recognized as appropriate.

The area, however, needed much further development, and so in the early 1990s I arranged with Rowman & Littlefield to publish a series titled *Issues in Academic Ethics*, each volume devoted to a different aspect of the subject. The first books appeared in 1994, and additional ones continued to be published through 2006. I list them here by title, author, and date:

Campus Rules and Moral Community: In Place of In Loco Parentis, David A. Hoekema (1994)

Ethics of Scientific Research, Kristin Shrader-Frechette (1994)

Neutrality and the Academic Ethic, Robert L. Simon (1994)

A Professor's Duties: Ethical Issues in College Teaching, Peter J. Markie (1994)

University–Business Partnerships: An Assessment, Norman E. Bowie (1994)

Academic Freedom and Tenure: Ethical Issues, Richard T. De George (1997)

Diversity and Community in the Academy: Affirmative Action in Faculty Appointments, Celia Wolf-Devine (1997)

The Moral Dimensions of Academic Administration, Rudolf H. Weingartner (1999)

Free Speech on Campus, Martin P. Golding (2000)

Sexual Harassment as an Ethical Issue in Academic Life, Leslie Pickering Francis (2001)

Moral Leadership; Ethics and the College Presidency, Paul J. Olscamp (2003)

Unionization in the Academy: Visions and Reality, Judith Wagner DeCew (2003)

Ethics and College Sports, Peter A. French (2004)

Peer Review: A Critical Inquiry, David Shatz (2004)

The Kindness of Strangers: Philanthropy and Higher Education, Deni Elliott (2006)

Each volume combines an original monograph with supplementary sources, such as philosophy articles, legal opinions, or university documents, chosen by the author to amplify the text.

While these books offer an inviting avenue to the study of academic ethics, what has been missing is a single anthology, suitable for completion in a single semester, that includes a collection of accessible essays covering a variety of topics. This volume fills that gap.

The selections offer defenses of competing positions. In these matters no one has the last word; discussion will continue. But what these writers have to say is understandable, and I hope their straightforwardness will serve to increase comprehension of the competing arguments that have been offered in disputes about these controversial matters.

A couple of these papers originally appeared in the 1990 Temple University collection, and several are drawn from books in the Rowman & Littlefield series. Others are reprinted from contemporary books or journals.

A single anthology cannot do justice to all the key issues in academic ethics, but I hope that the subjects and articles chosen will prove engaging and provocative. Note that while *Saints and Scamps* focuses primarily on professorial responsibilities, this work concentrates on institutional policies. Thus the two books are complementary.

I myself have offered a course devoted to academic ethics, and I hope others will do likewise. Some may opt, instead, to broaden existing courses in moral problems to include not only such subjects as genetic engineering, adultery, and animal rights but also speech codes, sexual harassment, and preferential admissions. After all, as Socrates taught, no inquiry is more important than the search for self-understanding.

My special thanks to Micah Kleit, executive editor at Temple University Press, for his unwavering support of the project. I also wish to express my gratitude to production editor Nancy Lombardi for her conscientiousness, and to the staff of Temple University Press for its kind assistance throughout production.

I

TENURE

A tenured professor holds a lifetime appointment, revocable only in rare instances of gross incompetence or moral turpitude. The purpose of the tenure system is to guarantee academic freedom: the right of professionally qualified people to discover, teach, and publish the truth as they see it within their fields of competence. Where academic freedom is secure, no one may dictate to professors that certain subjects are taboo, certain methods of inquiry illegitimate, or certain conclusions unacceptable.

But does the tenure system achieve its aim? How much autonomy should a tenured professor be granted? Can we assure professional conduct without undermining academic freedom? These questions are explored in Richard De George's essay.

He also warns that care needs to be exercised in granting tenure. In some cases, however, deciding whether to award a professor tenure is not easy. Paul J. Olscamp describes in detail two such instances.

1

The Justification
of Academic Tenure

RICHARD T. DE GEORGE

U niversities can exist without academic freedom and tenure, as they have done in many countries and for many years. Academic tenure as understood in the United States is of relatively recent origin when considered in the light of the history of the university as an institution.[1] Nonetheless, academic tenure as it has developed in the United States is a crucial part of the American academic scene, and its demise would be an enormous loss to colleges and universities as we have come to know them and as they now exist. This claim is not only not self-evident but it is being questioned increasingly by some powerful and influential voices both outside and, perhaps surprisingly, inside the walls of academe. The role, function, and justification of academic tenure are often simply equated with unnecessary, undeserved, and counterproductive job security for an elitist, self-serving group of overpaid and underworked college and university professors.

Because academic tenure has come under attack from both inside and outside the academy, I shall evaluate it to the extent possible on its merits, and see what sort of and how strong a case can be made for it. After providing an initial definition, I shall argue first that academic tenure is appropriate for a certain kind of university in a certain kind of society; second, that its justification in that sort of setting is based on the good of society,

Originally published in Richard T. De George, *Academic Freedom and Tenure: Ethical Issues*, pp. 3–28, 1997, Rowman & Littlefield. Reprinted by permission of Rowman & Littlefield.

not of individual faculty members; and third, that even in that setting there are certain norms to which the process must conform if it is to be justified. Attacks on academic tenure are based explicitly or implicitly on academic tenure's failure on one of these three counts.

I. What Is Academic Tenure?

The first task is to make clear what academic tenure is. Calling it *academic* tenure puts emphasis on the fact that it is a special kind of tenure, tied to a special rationale. Academic tenure in the United States is traditionally linked with institutions of higher education. Teachers on the primary and secondary levels of education may have job security or guaranteed reappointment or something else comparable either contractually negotiated or simply bestowed by the local school board or governing officials, but that is not the same as academic tenure.

Academic tenure, as the American Association of University Professors (AAUP) uses the term, and as I shall use it, is tenure held by members of a faculty at an institution of higher education, where this is defined as post-secondary education. The typical case is tenure held by a faculty member at a university or four-year college.

Academic tenure is explicitly tied to the academic function of faculty members. We can compare it to and distinguish it from other types of tenure. Judicial tenure is held by federal court judges. This is a guarantee that unless they fail to perform their functions, they have a guarantee of continued employment in their position as judges until they die or retire. The purpose of judicial tenure is to prevent the threat of dismissal from influencing their judicial decisions. Briefly stated, the argument is that for judges to make impartial judgments, they must feel free to make them on the basis of evidence, the arguments, and their best insights. If they could be fired for making unpopular judgments or if they had to worry about whether members of the executive branch of government liked or did not like their decisions, they would not be as free to render impartial decisions as otherwise.

Faculty members do not render judgments in the way judges do. Yet the kind of tenure appropriate to academics is tied to what they do in a way comparable to the way that judicial tenure is tied to what judges do. The claims of impartiality, of objectivity, and of lack of extraneous pressure are analogous in both cases.

Academic tenure is not the same as a guarantee of continuous employment, even though academic tenure may functionally be a guarantee of continuous employment. A guarantee of continuous employment may come about in many ways, for many reasons, in many different kinds of firms, organizations, or enterprises, and for many different reasons. It might be negotiated by a union for its members, or it might be bestowed by an employer on certain employees as a matter of principle or out of gratitude for long and excellent service. Usually the guarantee, just as with academic tenure, is contingent upon the financial viability of the entity guaranteeing the continuous employment and on the continued acceptable performance of the worker. Some civil service positions have the equivalent of guaranteed continuous employment as long as one's performance stays minimally satisfactory. Even though in some ways functionally equivalent to guaranteed continuous employment, academic tenure differs from these other cases by virtue of the ground on which it is bestowed and the function it is expected to play.

Academic tenure, considered as guaranteed continuous employment, was traditionally granted until the faculty member reached the mandatory retirement age set by the institution. With the demise of mandatory retirement ages, how long an institution guarantees continuous employment is no longer clear. Presumably it is until the faculty member dies, voluntarily retires, or is fired or otherwise relieved of his or her duties because of incompetence or failure to perform at an acceptable level.

Whether academic tenure is a right, and if so, what kind of right it is, are debated questions. As an approach to an answer, we can start by noting that no one has a right to any particular position. The doctrine of employment-at-will[2] still holds insofar as an institution has the right to hire certain individuals and not hire others. An institution may not ethically or legally discriminate against any candidate for a position on the basis of characteristics not related to the job, such as gender, race, national origin, and age. But an institution may describe its open positions as it wishes, and it may choose from among those applicants who satisfy the job requirements by any nondiscriminatory job-related criteria it wishes. No candidate can claim that he or she has a right to be hired by any given institution because of being the best or most qualified or for any other reason. The institution retains the right to hire whom it chooses, for the nondiscriminatory job-related reasons it chooses.

Initial hiring does not obligate the institution to grant continuous or even renewed annual employment. What ethics requires is that an institution make known to the applicant and to the newly hired faculty member the conditions of employment, including the terms and conditions of the initial contract, the possibility of a renewed appointment, the possibility of eventual tenure if that is the case, other conditions of employment, and the criteria that will be used in judging performance. Included in full disclosure of conditions of employment are the criteria that must be met for renewed appointment and, if appropriate, for academic tenure. Unless all this is clear upon the initial appointment, the agreement between the new appointee and the hiring institution is difficult to defend from an ethical point of view because the contract lacks the complete disclosure that is required if the contract is to be entered into and agreed upon knowingly and willingly. A binding contract from an ethical point of view requires that the contract be entered freely by both parties, and it requires that appropriate knowledge at least be available to both parties. For either party to hide something relevant to the contract is to knowingly deceive the other party, and so to undermine the ethical force of the agreement.

Tenure becomes a legitimate expectation when it is presented to a faculty member as something that may be earned and the conditions under which it may be earned are specified. To call tenure a right is to say that a faculty member who satisfies the stated criteria has a legitimate claim on it. But most institutions do not guarantee tenure or see it as something a faculty member can legitimately claim. Rather they see tenure as something bestowed by the institution and legitimately withheld by the institution for a wide variety of reasons. Tenure is rarely given automatically by an institution. It is usually granted only after an extensive review of the faculty member's performance by one or more committees and/or administrators. Some institutions have a formal or informal rule about the percentage of the faculty who may be tenured or who may be tenured in a given department. If such limits exist, that is pertinent information that affects the conditions of employment and that should be made known to faculty members upon initial appointment. An institution may also change its tenure policy, making it more or less strict because of growth or attrition in the number of students or because of financial reasons. This is permissible, as long as the policies are not ad hoc and are publicly defensible, and the affected faculty members are given adequate time to meet the new requirements.

If a right is a justifiable normative claim or entitlement, and if what we have said is correct, then untenured faculty members have no right to be granted tenure. What they have a right to is fair consideration for tenure in accordance with the criteria they have been told will apply. If they are refused tenure, they have a right to know why, providing they had a legitimate expectation that it would be awarded.

Just as no individual faculty member has a right to be awarded tenure, so no institution has an obligation to award tenure in a particular case or to have the practice of awarding academic tenure. It may be shortsighted of the institution not to have academic tenure, it may identify the institution as being of a certain kind or quality, and it may open it up to censure by the AAUP and other similar organizations or to boycott by potential faculty and by faculty elsewhere. But as long as the conditions of employment are clearly stated, those accepting appointment in such an institution cannot claim that they have a right to tenure since they were told from the start that the institution does not grant academic tenure.

Although tenure is not a right that one can claim, the granting of tenure confers certain rights on the faculty member, the principal one of which is guaranteed continuous employment, providing certain conditions are met on both sides. Once tenure is granted, the institution commits itself to certain conditions to which the faculty member has a legitimate claim or entitlement and so to which the faculty member has a right. The right is alienable, in that the faculty member may freely give up the claim. An institution that wished to phase out tenure, for instance, might offer large salary increases guaranteed for a specified number of years to faculty members who agree to give up any claim to tenure after the specified number of years. Faculty members at such an institution would be free to accept or reject such an offer. On the face of it, there is nothing unethical in either making or accepting such an offer, providing there is nothing unethical in undermining the institution of academic tenure once it has been established—a topic we shall discuss later.

Academic tenure is by definition academic. This means not only that it is held by people at postsecondary academic institutions, but that it is related directly and importantly to the academic mission and function of such institutions. Typically, academic tenure is not conferred by a college or university on administrators—not even the chief administrator or president or chancellor. Nor is it conferred on nonacademic appointees, such as clerical and support staff. It is restricted to those who teach and/or do research, although it is sometimes extended also to certain other classes of faculty-equivalent positions, such as librarians. These are the academic functions of the university, and it is to safeguard these that tenure was instituted and that it receives its clearest justification.

Although teachers in primary and secondary schools may be given guarantees of continuous employment, they do not usually receive academic tenure. The reason is that their relation to knowledge and to what they teach is considered importantly different from that of faculty at institutions of higher education. They are typically not expected to engage in research, or publish, or advance knowledge in the way that faculty members in postsecondary schools are expected to do. It may well be objected that what and how some high school teachers teach and what and how some junior college or college or university teachers teach is identical. Although this is true, the nature of the institutions in question and their function and role in society are different, and that difference makes the decisive difference with respect to academic tenure. What that difference is, we shall discuss shortly.

Academic tenure is defined by the AAUP as follows:

After the expiration of a probationary period, teachers or investigators should have permanent or continuous tenure, and their service should be terminated only for adequate cause, except in case of retirement for age, or under extraordinary circumstances because of financial exigencies.[3]

The 1940 document allows moral turpitude as a legitimate cause for dismissal. This is defined by the 1970 Interpretative Comments as violating a standard of "behavior that would evoke condemnation by the academic community generally."[4] Also generally included under adequate cause would be academic incompetence and failure to meet one's professional obligations.

Academic incompetence is often difficult to substantiate. Any faculty member who has earned a doctorate and successfully passed the requirements for tenure was at least at that time considered competent. Failure to keep up with developments in one's field does not constitute incompetence, much less does failure to contribute to the developments in one's field. Nor does failure to communicate effectively one's knowledge to students. Perhaps with the elimination of mandatory retirement ages senility might become a basis for declaring a faculty member incompetent. But incompetence is a seldom used justification for terminating a tenured faculty member, and this is understandably the case.

On the other hand, failure to meet one's professional obligations is in some cases clear. For instance, repeated failure to go to one's classes or to teach the subject of the course during one's classes or to grade one's students' work constitute quite clear failure to meet one's professional obligations. Yet failure to publish in one's field after attaining tenure is not clear evidence of failure to meet one's professional obligations, for many colleges consider publication an extra, deserving reward, but not a deficiency to be penalized.

The 1940 Statement of Principles does not specify what constitutes failure to meet one's professional obligations, nor should it, since obligations vary widely among departments, fields, and institutions. This does not mean that the faculty within an institution, together with the administrators, cannot agree on broad guidelines of what constitutes failure to meet one's professional obligations. Having such guidelines both informs the faculty of what is expected and provides criteria for possible dismissal of tenured faculty members.

The possibility of dismissal for cause is a legitimate part of the practice of academic tenure, and it is a necessary part of academic tenure, if it is to be justified. Nonetheless, academic tenure is difficult to attain and is awarded by an institution upon the evaluation and recommendation of one's peers. The onus of proving one's worth is on the faculty member. Academic tenure should be commensurably difficult to lose, if it is to have meaning and serve its function. A tenured faculty member should be fired only upon the evaluation and recommendation of one's peers, and the onus is on the institution to prove adequate cause. Dismissal of tenured faculty is appropriately rare and exceptional and difficult, but not impossible.

II. The Justification
of Academic Tenure

One of the arguments sometimes given for tenure is that it is justified in part because of the relatively poor salaries of most professors, given the years of study necessary for them to attain their positions.[5] It implies that relatively low salaries are justified for faculty members because they have tenure. That is, it implies that at some point faculty members traded job security for low salaries. This is historically inaccurate. Faculty salaries were low before academic tenure came on the scene. The other implication is that if faculty salaries were commensurate with the amount of study required to hold such a position, tenure would not be justified. But if, as I shall argue, and as the AAUP has consistently maintained, academic tenure is justified primarily because of its relation to academic freedom, then whether faculty members are well paid is beside the point. Academic tenure would be justified, if it is justified, even if faculty were relatively or even very well paid. If pay were a serious basis for tenure, then it is not clear why faculty should not be given a choice of either higher salaries without tenure or lower salaries with tenure. However, to offer any such choice is to imply that academic tenure is primarily a financial issue. It is not.

At best the financial argument is a justification given to some outside constituencies who do not understand the real basis for academic tenure, and to whom the claim that there is a trade-off between tenure and low salaries seems to make economic sense. There is an economic relation between job security and lower salaries. But this relation also serves as justification for keeping faculty salaries relatively low. To this extent academic tenure might well seem to some faculty members to be a disadvantage rather than an advantage. And certainly to some extent they would be correct. The argument for academic tenure is strengthened, not weakened, if accepting it brings with it a lower salary than faculty members would otherwise receive. For then the real reason for academic tenure becomes basic and overriding. What is that justification?

The justification is that academic tenure is the best means our society has devised to secure and preserve academic freedom.

In the former Soviet Union professors had job security, just as all workers did. The Soviet Constitution called for full employment and the government was the sole employer. Discharging any worker was very difficult under this system. Even though the professors in effect had guaranteed employment they did not have academic tenure because they could lose their positions if they attempted to publish or teach what was ideologically unacceptable. In 1924 over a hundred philosophers were removed from their positions and exiled. The only philosophers allowed to teach were Marxists. Some freedom of discussion among them was allowed until 1929. Then the leaders of the country stepped in and ruled against one of two competing factions. The winners in turn were replaced by a decree of the Central Committee of the Communist Party in 1931 for a list of ideological offenses. Thereafter, the leaders of the Communist Party were the ultimate authorities on what could and could not be taught. They were the defenders of the purity of Marxism and, in their minds, of the truth. Not without reason, they held that only the truth should and would be taught in all schools and universities.

In such a society the notion of academic freedom has no place. Since some group—in this case the leaders of the Communist Party—had both the truth and control over all the institutions of society, the task of those institutions was to promulgate the truth as defined by the leaders. Not only in philosophy, but in all other areas, these leaders—at least through 1951— were the final authority. Quantum mechanics and relativity theory were prohibited because they were bourgeois; Mendelian genetics was prohibited in favor of Lysenko's theories; non-Marxist philosophy could not be taught; only Marxist versions of history could be presented.[6]

Academic freedom involves the freedom to pursue one's research independent of outside political powers and pressures. Academic freedom loses its central meaning in a society in which the external powers that control the university decide what is true and what is not, and so what may be taught or published, and what may not be. In this situation, academic tenure also loses its meaning. At best what is provided is job security. But that is not academic tenure, since it is precisely for one's work in the academic area that one is most likely to lose one's position.

Academic tenure is closely linked to academic freedom. The main purpose of academic tenure is to prevent the possibility of a faculty member's being dismissed because what he or she teaches or writes about is considered by either administrators or some people outside the institution to be wrong or offensive. This is the basic claim in defense of academic tenure. The full argument requires spelling out and involves a discussion of academic freedom. But this rough statement suffices to see that academic tenure makes little sense in a society that does not allow academic freedom.

There are various models of a university. Only some of them are compatible with academic freedom, and hence only some of them are compatible with academic tenure.

One traditional model of a university goes back to its origins at the University of Paris in the thirteenth century. That model consists of a group of scholars banding together and gathering around them students interested in learning from the masters. The university claimed autonomy in the sense that it ran its own affairs and often even claimed independence from local authorities in the enforcement of laws and the punishment of student offenders. Debates and discussions proceeded without outside interference, even though sometimes certain theological doctrines would be condemned by the Catholic Church. As a model, however, the University of Paris was an autonomous faculty-run institution.

A second model is the student-run institution. Here students wish to be instructed in certain subjects in preparation for jobs of various sorts—law and medicine being the paradigms. The students hire faculty to teach them what they need to know. The faculty may have a voice in what they teach. But the students decide whether to retain the faculty, usually by whether they find their classes interesting enough to enroll in. The faculty in this model is not paid to do research, except insofar as they are expected to keep up with their field so that they can teach their students the latest knowledge.

A third model is the ideological model of the former Soviet Union in which the task of the faculty is to transmit the official state ideology as well as prepare students to fill the jobs society needs done. Here there is no autonomy of the university and it is completely subservient to the state.

A fourth model is the entrepreneurial model. Someone starts a university, hires administrators and faculty members, and pays them to teach students in such a way that students will pay to take their courses. The point is to make a profit, and the faculty are a means to that end.

A fifth model is the state university, which is a mixture of several of the above models. Typically the state university has some autonomy. Although the state supports the institution through tax dollars (and students support the institution through tuition) both the state officials and the students realize that they are not competent to decide what should be taught or how, and the academic part of the university is left primarily to the faculty, who are expected to have knowledge of their fields and of how to educate and train students for various kinds of work, including how to provide a liberal education.

Academic freedom may not be of much concern in models two and four and is of no concern in model three. Academic freedom is of central concern in model one, and it should be of central concern in model five, providing that society is of a certain type, the university is of a certain kind, and academic freedom is understood in a certain way. If the three are of the appropriate sort, then academic tenure is an important ingredient in the university, providing it is carried out in an appropriate manner. What are these types, and what is this manner?

A society should be interested in having a university to which it grants autonomy if the society receives something of benefit in return. The reason for granting autonomy is that those who wish to have a university and are not part of it believe that some people, whom they will hire as faculty, have specialized, systematic, and advanced knowledge. Unless the faculty have this specialized knowledge that others do not have, there would be little reason for letting them have much autonomy. It would make more sense simply to hire those willing and able to teach what they are told to teach. Typically that is what happens at the primary levels. Parents know they want their children to learn to read, write, calculate, and to know something about history, geography, their country, and a little about other parts of the world. School boards have a hand in developing and approving curricula.

Parents of would-be doctors, on the other hand, do not know what doctors should know, except generally that they should know anatomy and medicine. They must trust people trained in medicine to know what to prescribe for a curriculum and to teach the material and evaluate and certify the students. The same is true in law, engineering, mathematics, history, psychology, and the other areas covered at a university.

A society gives a university autonomy in the belief that the institution can achieve its results better if those who are competent in their fields run it than if people from outside with less knowledge try to run it. Primary among the tasks of a university are the education and training of students in their respective fields and professions. Not only do well-educated graduates fill the available jobs and keep the society functioning and productive, but they also make up an educated electorate, capable of voting intelligently, and of running government and keeping it from becoming a dictatorship, no matter how benign.

A second reason for granting a university autonomy is the belief that knowledge is not yet complete and that no one inside or outside the university knows all there is to know. If some group—a state, a political party, religious leaders—know the truth, then they would have little reason to grant autonomy to a university. At least in those domains in which they knew the truth, they would reasonably wish to ensure that the truth which they knew was taught accurately, that is, as they know it. On the other hand, if those who set up and fund a university believe that not all truth is known, then they would do well, if they also believed that it is worthwhile to pursue the truth and to learn more, to provide a place and to pay competent people to seek that truth. Since no one can say what will be discovered, no one can predict what will be discovered. Hence it would be a mistake to try to restrict the search for truth by establishing procedures or rules that might result in preventing investigators from finding the truth.

A third reason a society might wish to grant a university autonomy is if the society wished to have a place in which all aspects of the society could be freely examined and critiqued, without that examination and critique being expressed in a violent or destructive manner. If a society believes that it can be improved by having a place where debate takes place without immediate application in practice—as it is in a legislature, for instance—and where some distance from immediate results and politically motivated research can be carried on, then it would be reasonable to fund such an institution. Since it wants the investigations to be free of political partisanship, and at least to that extent to be objective, it can best achieve that result by granting the institution autonomy.

It is within a society such as this that a relatively autonomous university makes sense. The autonomy granted the university is justified not by the good of those within the university but by the good of the rest of society.

Within such an institution, the ends for which the university is given autonomy can in turn best be achieved by granting those within the university academic freedom. The same beliefs and arguments hold within the university as hold for the university. It is only if they do hold that the university can achieve the ends for which it is granted autonomy.

The final claim is that the best way to guarantee that faculty will pursue truth in their areas of competence freely and objectively is if they have no fear that they will be penalized if they break with tradition, try new approaches, or turn up unpopular results. One way to eliminate that fear and to reinforce the social and institutional desire for the advancement of knowledge is to guarantee that the teachers and researchers do not place their jobs in jeopardy by pursuing and reporting the truth as they discover it. That guarantee is what academic tenure provides, at least for those who have served a period of time to demonstrate their competence and their ability to pursue and advance knowledge and to communicate that to students and to pertinent others (colleagues, the general public, other specialists, as the case may be).

III. Academic Tenure
and Academic Freedom

Given the above analysis, it is primarily the good of society, not the good of individual faculty members, that is of greatest concern. The argument maintains that society is the loser if the practice of tenure disappears. Without tenure, the faculty members have no guarantee that they will not be penalized for presenting new ideas, for challenging accepted truths or ways of doing things, or for criticizing existing institutions, governments, mores, and morals. Without this guarantee some faculty members will still do all these things, and run the risk of being fired because of it. But many others will not, and will practice self-censorship. The chilling effect of the firing of just a few professors who present their views will be considerable on many, many others.

The result will be a less dynamic and bold faculty, with less in the way of new truths or techniques being developed. Without a free forum for critique and discussion the community and so the state as a whole become impoverished. Without the example and encouragement of teachers who are bold and seek the truth wherever it may lead them, students will in turn be taught by example to be conservative and safe. The detriment to society is a less critical citizenry. Some societies and some political leaders may relish these results. But a free, open society will not.

Although a society may grant a university autonomy based on the belief that it will get commensurable goods in return and that it will achieve more of what it wants by granting the institution autonomy than by not doing so, it does not and need not operate completely on blind trust. It can legitimately exercise some oversight and expect a certain accountability.

Students can tell whether they are learning something. Employers can tell whether their new hires are competent and whether they have learned in their college or university education enough to perform adequately in the positions for which they are presumably qualified because of their education. The members of society can tell whether the younger generation that emerges from college has learned to think clearly and critically. All these assessments are rough and do not imply that those making them have the knowledge or expertise that members of the faculty have. But they do not need that expertise to make their assessments. Patients can tell whether they are benefiting from their doctor's care without knowing medicine in the way that doctors do. People can assess results without knowing how to produce them. This is as true with respect to education as with a great many other areas in which expertise and knowledge are important in producing certain results.

This is not to say that education is a commodity or to be treated as if it were. The university is not a factory or business. Nonetheless, the university exists not primarily for the good of the faculty, but for the good of society.

The argument that I presented for academic tenure hinged on academic freedom. I argued that academic freedom was important to society, and that if academic tenure is the best way to protect academic freedom, then academic tenure is important to society. Yet academic freedom and hence academic tenure are defensible only if the good of society can be achieved thereby. And that means only if there is knowledge that is not yet known that can be pursued and found, and if the university is the place where this is done. If truth is already known, then it has only to be preserved, and those who know it can rightly demand that it be preserved and passed on in the universities over which they exercise control. Academic freedom makes sense only if those outside the university who fund and control it do not have any privileged access to the truth and stand to gain by its being pursued in a university.

If there is no truth to be pursued, if there is no knowledge to be gained, then once again there is little reason to grant faculty members academic tenure. If all that universities have is the opinion or personal belief of faculty members, none of which is demonstrably preferable to any other, then there is little sense in granting them academic tenure or in believing there is any benefit to society in granting academic freedom. Freedom of speech may benefit a society, but that is not the same as academic freedom.

IV. Academic Tenure and the American University

I have argued that academic tenure makes sense only in a certain kind of society and only under certain conditions. The United States is the kind of society in which academic tenure makes sense—it is a relatively free and open society, and one in which there is a widespread belief that knowledge is useful, and that not everything is known. It is a democracy in which an educated and critical citizenry can play an effective role. And it is a developed society in which creativity and originality have an important function. In such a society academic freedom can be and has been a crucial component in its college and university system. It has gone hand-in-hand with academic tenure.

If, as critics claim, academic tenure is an institution whose time has passed, is the same to be said of academic freedom? Might academic tenure be feasibly applied to only some faculty or restricted to only some departments or only to some colleges and universities?

Consider an institution that gives academic tenure only to some professors but not to others. Of course, this is already the case. Only some faculty members have tenure. Tenure is not held by beginning instructors or assistant professors who work full-time, nor by full-time faculty members who are on limited-term appointments, nor by part-time faculty. There can be no objection in principle, then, in advocating a system of selective tenure. The justification for tenure under the present system, however, is that those with tenure should guarantee the academic freedom of the institution as a whole and so the academic freedom of those who do not have or who do not yet have tenure. The test of whether selective academic tenure is justifiable is whether under such a system those with tenure will be both able and willing to guarantee the academic freedom of the institution and of those without tenure. There would be little reason to expect those with tenure to defend the academic freedom of those who might have opted for tenure but who, for instance, chose higher-paying term contracts. By choosing such contracts over tenured positions they have in fact indicated either that they do not care for or about academic freedom, or that, if they do, they expect those with tenure to protect them. The latter is an unreasonable expectation. Hence a system of this sort is unlikely to protect the academic freedom of the institution and of all those in it. And since it does not, the reason for granting academic tenure to any faculty would not exist.

Some faculty may claim that they would prefer to take higher-paying term contracts than lower-paying tenured appointments because they feel either that they work in areas in which academic freedom is not crucial or that their work is in an area or field in which knowledge is secure and unlikely to need challenge of the type for which academic freedom is important. They may also feel that if they are unjustly fired from one position they are talented enough to be able to find another position. They assume that there are other colleges or universities in which their views will be tolerated, even though not tolerated in their former institution. That is to assume more than may be justified if the attitude such people adopt toward tenure becomes widespread. Their view considers academic tenure a personal protection and one that they feel they can do without. They fail to understand that tenure exists and is conferred on individual faculty members not for the benefit primarily of that individual but for the benefit of the institution and of the larger society.

There is no area in a university that does not need academic freedom. If it deserves to be in a university, there is knowledge to be preserved and transmitted, critically developed, and potentially challenged. If academic freedom is not critical to it, it does not belong in a college or university. It is an accepted body of knowledge, developed by others, that needs only to be transmitted to students. That is characteristic of the knowledge taught on the primary and secondary levels, and that is one of the reasons why tenure is not typically given in such educational institutions, even though some sort of guaranteed renewable contracts may be given. Hence there is no academic area of the university to which tenure is not appropriate. And if the purpose of academic tenure is to protect academic freedom, then it is best protected if there are some tenured faculty in every area, the better to safeguard it.

Academic freedom cannot be given to some part of the university and not to other parts. To attempt to do so is to misunderstand that the institution as a whole is autonomous, not just parts of it. What is true from the outside is true as well from the inside.

That leaves us with the question of whether some institutions of higher education might claim autonomy, defend academic freedom, and grant their faculty tenure, while others do not. We have already seen that primary and secondary schools do not typically grant tenure. For an institution of higher education not to grant tenure is implicitly to say that it does not value academic freedom. To the extent that academic freedom benefits society, society is better off by having all or almost all of these institutions guaranteeing academic freedom. If only some do, then there is less chance of developing creative, new knowledge, and there are fewer students trained in the critical thinking fostered by the institutions that defend academic freedom. Just as the tenured faculty in an institution have the obligation to protect the academic freedom of all the faculty at their institution, so the tenured faculty members at each institution that values academic freedom should do what they can to protect academic freedom at all institutions. One institution typically does not put pressure on others. But it could do so. And faculty could apply pressure. That is the reason for the AAUP's censuring of institutions. The obligation of tenured faculty to support academic freedom in institutions other than their own is less strong than in their own institution. But since the reason for their tenure is the benefit not only of their own institution but of society as a whole, then they also have some obligation to do what they can to protect academic freedom wherever it is violated in the society.

Tenure has been misrepresented and misperceived both within and without the university. If understood as I have suggested, it is both defensible and of such benefit to society that it deserves to be continued.

V. Some Attacks on Academic Tenure

The attacks on tenure that have received the most public attention rarely mention academic freedom. Rather, the primary arguments are economic. I have already indicated that the economic arguments in favor of tenure are secondary and that the major line of defense is and should be the defense of academic freedom. But since the economic arguments get so much attention, they should be explored.

The most frequently heard argument is the "deadwood argument." There are various versions. The most extreme is that faculty members may work hard during their first six years in order to get tenure. But once they have attained tenure, they have little incentive to continue to work hard, and consequently do not. They tend to do as little as possible. They may teach, but they do not publish. They do not keep up in their fields. They spend as little time as possible in their offices or working with students. This is the claim. The basis for it is primarily imaginary, the result of the imaginations of those who are not in academe and assume that this is what must take place. There is no evidence that those who achieve tenure suddenly and en masse stop acting as they did before they got tenure. Any such broad claim is without substance. But the variation is that over the years after receiving tenure, some faculty members, perhaps a considerable number, find that they have little new to say and stop publishing, that they lose some of their energy and interest in teaching, that they perform at an adequate level but not more. And then they cannot be replaced because they have tenure.

Even this more modest charge is usually made without any evidence. But it would be equally unreasonable to claim this never happens. It happens in every profession and every area of work. And it is typical for burned-out employees to be kept on as long as they perform adequately. Those with civil service positions or union contracts usually cannot be fired. And even in areas where people can be fired they often are not. In cases of true incompetence, we have already seen that a college or university can fire a tenured faculty member. But in all these circumstances, whether at a university or in business, the proper first recourse is not termination but counseling and attention to rekindling the flame that once existed. Moreover, in the case of college and university faculty members, they have undergone longer periods of both training and probation than people in most other areas, and the chance of their becoming deadwood is correspondingly less than in other areas. Nonetheless, institutions do make mistakes, especially if they do not exercise the care they should in granting tenure. In such cases, the institution suffers the result of its mistake, just as in other cases. These bad effects are not a result of tenure. In fact the tenure process, with its requirement that one either get tenure or leave, is more likely than otherwise to help institutions terminate those who are not likely to continue to be productive. Without such a system it is very likely that marginal people would be kept on, perhaps indefinitely, one more year at a time. They become friends whom one does not want to hurt, and then they have been around so long that it feels unethical to dismiss them for acting as they have been acting for years.

The deadwood argument is exaggerated, and true deadwood can be terminated for incompetence or for failure to perform adequately. The problem, to the extent that it exists, is not with tenure but with the failure of institutions to counsel and help, and if necessary ultimately dismiss those deserving of dismissal.

The next charge is one of inefficiency. Corporations are engaged in downsizing and, in the process, getting rid of excess workers—executives as well as those in the ranks. The rationale is that the firms are becoming more efficient by becoming lean and mean. They can thus remain competitive. By contrast, it is claimed, universities are saddled with tenured faculty—perhaps too many or in the wrong areas as needs have changed. But because of tenure they are not able to get rid of them. They cannot become lean and mean. The institutions cannot become efficient. Because they are overwhelmingly not-for-profit organizations, they face no competition and have no incentive to cut costs or change with the times. Even if they wanted to, tenure makes it impossible for them to do so.

This charge is really multiple. The general charge of inefficiency is a difficult one to evaluate, because it is not entirely clear what efficiency means when applied to an institution of higher learning. "Efficiency" should not be equated simply with the number of degrees awarded or the number of courses or students taught. And in fact there is competition among colleges and universities. The costs of running a research institution are higher than those of running a primarily teaching institution. Tuition at prestigious institutions of higher education is typically much higher than tuition at a state-supported institution. Yet it is not clear that a school with a lower student/faculty ratio is more efficient than the reverse. American colleges and universities are still the envy of most countries, and these institutions attract students from around the globe, showing that they are competitive in the worldwide educational arena.

However, the important point is that the criterion of efficiency is not the appropriate one to apply. Universities should not be compared to factories, and the education of students is inappropriately considered comparable to the products turned out by factories. This does not mean that colleges and universities cannot be held accountable for what they do and how they use the funds they have or receive. But the criteria should be suitable to their mission, which is not the production of goods but the preservation, transmission, and development of knowledge.

The claim is rarely made that tenure makes it impossible or difficult or unlikely for universities and colleges to be run in such a way that when evaluated by the proper criteria they cannot or do not measure up. If it were made, then the difficulty would be to show that tenure is the culprit. But this is unlikely. It is in part tenure that helps keep the salaries of faculty members low in comparison to the training required. The economic value of tenure is factored into the salary structure. Since tenure is not something that a faculty member can opt out of, all faculty members pay in lower salaries for the job protection that tenure provides. Moreover, tenure provides a relatively stable faculty for an institution. It cuts down on the costs of constant recruiting and the training that takes place in the initial period on a new job.

Finally, unlike in many other positions, as faculty members grow older they can also grow in insight in their disciplines and they may gain wisdom with maturity. Wisdom is different from knowledge. It involves knowing not only a great deal but also how such knowledge fits together within a broader perspective. It also involves understanding the value of what is known and its place in a grander order of things. It involves as well the ability to make sound judgments that do not depend only on knowledge. Wisdom involves knowing not only what to do and how to do it but knowing what is worth doing. In a business in which the end is profit and the means available to a company are fairly well circumscribed, wisdom may play no important role. In a college or university setting in which the purpose is to train young minds, prepare them for the well functioning of a society, and counsel them in how to live, wisdom is an essential ingredient in the faculty. Older faculty are not the same drag on an institution that they might be considered in a business environment.

There are many other differences between a university and a business. A business arguably exists to make a profit. It downsizes in part to make it more likely to do so, and usually with an eye toward raising the value of its stock. Not only is a university usually a not-for-profit organization, but it has no unique end or bottom line by which it can be evaluated. It is multifaceted, and it exists to educate students, to increase knowledge, to preserve and interpret that knowledge, and to serve a number of different complex needs of the state or society in which it exists. Downsizing does not necessarily make the university more efficient (the same is true of corporations); nor does downsizing raise its value. On the contrary, downsizing faculty tends to diminish the university.

Corporations tend to be managed hierarchically. The CEO with or without the board of directors and with or without other senior managers can decide what or who is to go and what restructuring is to take place. A university is not typically structured in this way. Faculty members are not told what to do but help decide what to do. They are the authorities in their own area and they usually and appropriately have a strong voice in what the institution does and how. The president or board is not competent to direct the university as a CEO can, at least in theory, direct the corporation. In fact many companies are moving to a structure of shared responsibility and empowerment of lower-level managers and employees in order to improve morale, efficiency, and productivity. Such a structure of shared responsibility and empowerment is already present in the university and does not require that it be achieved by downsizing. Downsizing without faculty consultation is more likely to have precisely the opposite effect—lower morale, less efficiency, and decreased productivity. Loyalty to any institution on the part of those who work there is not automatically deserved or given but is appropriately the result of reciprocal consideration on both sides.

Finally, although some fields go out of favor and new ones emerge, such transitions take many years, and a well-managed institution will not find itself with faculty whose expertise is no longer needed. Before that happens the institution can help faculty members to retrain and move to neighboring fields to teach.

A third argument is not so much an economic one as it is an argument from supposed inequity, and more properly from a concealed sense of jealousy. Because many ordinary citizens live and work in an environment in which people are laid off due to no fault of their own—to downsizing or to technological changes—they ask why faculty members at colleges and universities should be treated differently from the mass of workers. When budgets become tight at universities the same question is often raised by those employed by the university who are not faculty or civil service or union-protected. These people are vulnerable in a way that tenured faculty are not. The reason is that they are not necessary to guarantee academic freedom. Once again the justification for academic tenure is not the good of the individual faculty member or even of the individual institution but the good of society as a whole. Those who attack tenure in this way ignore the fact that others, such as federal judges, also have tenure and that civil servants enjoy greater job security than those employed in the private sector. They also ignore the fact that faculty face a crucial period in which they either get tenure or are terminated, unlike those in other areas. The issue is not whether faculty with tenure are treated differently from other workers but whether such differential treatment is justified—an issue that the argument ignores.

In recent times a fourth argument against tenure has come from some medical schools. The salaries of clinical faculties at some medical schools have been extremely high even in comparison with the salaries of faculty members in medical schools who are not clinicians, much less with faculty not in a medical school.[7] The reason for the high salaries is that the faculty members, through clinical practices—especially expensive operations—bring in much more than the salary they receive. As HMOs became more competitive and other factors led to curbs on the income such faculty members were able to bring in, some of the schools proposed cutting the salaries of such doctors accordingly.[8] This seems like a reasonable proposal. But many faculty both in and out of the medical schools see this as a threat to tenure. If an institution can cut the salary of any tenured professor, and if this is not a violation of tenure, then what does tenure mean? Tenure ceases to have much meaning if the institution may cut one's pay to any level it chooses, and so force out those whose views someone in or out of the university disapprove of.

Some of the medical schools, conscious of this view, have proposed first that the salaries of those who already have tenure not be affected, and second that those who will receive tenure in the future be paid in two parts. One part of their salary will be comparable to that received by other non-clinical members of the medical school. This would be considered the regular salary and would not be subject to cuts except in cases of financial exigency. The other portion of the salary, in some cases the larger portion, would be tied to the income that the faculty member generates through clinical practice. The proposal has been condemned by some. It does create a dual salary structure for the time that two different salary systems are in place, and understandably new faculty members would prefer the old system. But it is arguably not unfair to new faculty members who come into the new system freely and completely informed. If they compare their positions not with senior clinical faculty but with all the other faculty, they would see they are not only being treated equitably but have the opportunity for much higher total salaries than most others. The solution respects the tenure system, and recognizes the importance of tenure and the principle of not cutting salaries, since that can rightly be seen as a means of undermining tenure. The proposal may have other defects. But from the point of view of tenure, it seems unlikely that the procedure would carry over into other areas. If it did, then it would make sense only in those areas in which faculty members generated large incomes for their institutions. And in those cases, granting tenure with a competitive guaranteed salary and additions based on income generated does not seem unreasonable.

At the present time it is not unusual for a tenured faculty member to be given a salary supplement when he or she takes on an administrative position in the university. Sometimes this is the change in appointment from nine months to twelve months. Since faculty members do not have tenure in administrative positions, when they leave administration and return to full-time teaching, they revert from a twelve-month appointment to a nine-month appointment, with the loss of two or three months' salary. This is not unusual or unfair, nor does it affect academic tenure in any way. A comparable case can be made for variable pay beyond a reasonable base in other cases with a comparably null effect on tenure.

Although the economic arguments receive the most attention, they are far from decisive, especially since I have argued that academic tenure is best justified as being beneficial to society rather than as being primarily beneficial to individual faculty members, even though individual faculty members who have academic tenure have guaranteed continuous employment. I have argued that the rationale for academic tenure is academic freedom. Once academic tenure is seen in this way, it is not something that is simply conferred on faculty members. It is conferred for certain reasons and carries with it certain obligations. When the obligations are not met, then the point of continuing the practice is correctly open to question.

Since the point of academic tenure is to allow faculty members to pursue the truth in their disciplines wherever it leads them, those who have tenure have the concomitant obligation in fact to pursue truth in their areas to the best of their ability. They have the obligation to be as objective as they can be, to be as critical as appropriate in their field, and to follow arguments and their data wherever they may take them. This is not a right they have because of their tenure, but an obligation that goes with tenure.

Similarly, since the point of academic tenure is the preservation of academic freedom, a second obligation of the tenured faculty is to protect academic freedom throughout the university. This means that they have the obligation to protect and promote academic freedom for their untenured faculty as well as for their students. Academic freedom solely for tenured faculty makes little sense. All members of the college or university must have academic freedom if the institution is to fulfill its mission. Since not all faculty are tenured, those who have tenure and hence cannot be fired except for cause—understood as incompetence or moral turpitude—are in a strong position to defend the academic freedom of those without tenure. This is another consequence of seeing that tenure is not solely or even primarily for the benefit of those to whom it is given but for the institution as a whole, and ultimately for the benefit of society. It is this perspective that allows us to develop the ethics of tenure, that is, not the ethical justification for tenure, but the ethical conditions that tenure imposes on institutions and on those members to whom it is given.

Academic tenure so understood allows us to evaluate and answer some of the noneconomic attacks on tenure. We shall look at four of the more prominent of them: (1) the deadwood argument, again; (2) the six-year conformity-training argument; (3) the postmodernist attack; and (4) the politicization attack.

(1) The deadwood argument, again. This version is noneconomic but also claims that some of those who get tenure use it as an excuse to do little, and eventually turn into deadwood. That is certainly an abuse of tenure, but there is little evidence that this is a widespread abuse. Academic tenure provides protection for faculty to pursue the truth. The guarantee of employment that is part of it is circumscribed and is not absolute. We have already noted that if a faculty member fails to perform his or her academic tasks, that is grounds for dismissal. Tenure does not prohibit continuous review for purpose of promotion and of salary increases. It does not relieve departmental chairpersons and deans and other university administrators from evaluating tenured faculty or from encouraging, counseling, and helping those who are not as productive as they once were or as the institution feels they should be. Tenure should not be an excuse for tolerating incompetence, laziness, or failure to perform at an acceptable level. If it is so used, then both the faculty member who so uses it and the institution that allows that abuse are at fault. But such failures do not show any intrinsic failure or weakness in the practice of awarding academic tenure.

(2) The six-year conformity-training argument. The second attack claims that young faculty are inculturated by the system to be safe rather than bold during their six or so years as faculty members without tenure. They spend six years conforming to the desires and views of their senior

colleagues, who hold the tenure decision in their hands. These senior colleagues are unlikely to vote tenure for new faculty who will challenge their views or undermine their authority with students. Hence the young faculty member conforms, perhaps thinking that after six years he or she will be free to be creative and really express individual views. But six years of repressed or constrained thought yield a habit of so thinking, and the habit of routine research takes over and typically replaces more creative tendencies. The result is a habit of safe research. Those who do not conform are weeded out prior to or in their sixth year.

This argument describes not the result of a tenure system but an abuse of the tenure system. If tenure is understood as I have portrayed it, then those with tenure have the obligation to protect the academic freedom of those without tenure. If their academic freedom is protected, then untenured faculty members will have little reason not to pursue truth and to follow their pursuit wherever it leads them. A university should in fact expect this in its new faculty members, and unless they do pursue truth in this way, they may not be deserving of receiving tenure. Hence tenure should not act as a deterrent to pursuing truth, but just the opposite. To the extent that this is not the case, those who have tenure can be faulted for not promoting the proper atmosphere of academic freedom in their institutions and for not demanding such pursuit of their new faculty.

(3) The postmodernist attack. According to postmodernists and others within the university, there is no such thing as objective truth, and all there is are opinions, points of view, and different stories. I argued that the rationale for academic tenure is academic freedom and that this presupposes that there is still knowledge to be developed and truth to be pursued. If there is no such truth and if there is only opinion, then the basis for academic tenure and academic freedom seems to disappear. This would indeed be the case if all one had was opinion and there were no objective criteria for deciding that one opinion is better than another. A complete answer to this objection is a long story.[9] The short answer is that in some fields—most clearly in the sciences—there is ample evidence that some theories are better than others because of the impressive results that are possible as a consequence of accepting those theories. Even in the humanities, which are most prone to the attack, sophisticated versions of the attack on objectivity redefine it and redefine truth so that not everything within the various disciplines is equally defensible or acceptable.[10] But if there were in fact no way to discern valid from invalid or true from false or better from worse claims, then it is not clear why those subjects are pursued at the university. The claim is not so much damaging to tenure as it is to the disciplines themselves. And if the disciplines are removed from the university, then those who teach them would have lit-

tle claim on tenure. But even defenders of the attack are reluctant to draw this conclusion. What they wish is not the abolition of the university or of certain departments within it, but an effective—preferably a dominant—voice within them.

(4) The politicization attack. The fourth attack is somewhat similar to the third. If universities are not places that search for truth but are the repository of positions of power in which certain political views are pressed on students, then academic freedom loses its rationale. And if academic freedom loses its rationale, so does academic tenure. Political correctness, some claim, is nothing new, but simply a new name given to the fact that the university is and always has been politicized.[11] The politicization of the university is inimical to academic freedom whether the politicization comes from without or from within—whether it is the tool of politicians or the tool of politicized faculty members.

The proper answer is that if the universities are politicized, they should be depoliticized. But if they cannot be, then the rationale for academic tenure dissolves.

In all these cases I have conceded that if the attacks are justified, then academic freedom is not justified. But in each case I have maintained that the charge is not an attack on the principle of academic tenure itself, but on some of the abuses to which it is amenable. Those who oppose academic tenure on these grounds do a service to academic tenure by pointing out abuses where they exist. Faculty and institutions interested in academic tenure have the obligation to use it properly and to police abuses. But abuses, unless they cannot be corrected, are not sufficient justification for eliminating tenure. And some of the objections we have briefly looked at have made this clear.

VI. COLLEGES AND UNIVERSITIES WITHOUT TENURE

The attacks on tenure have so far not seriously undermined the practice of tenure, although they have raised concern in many faculties and have led to increased attention on accountability. If the result of the attacks is a renewal of respect for the institutional and individual obligations that accompany tenure, they will have served a valuable function. But if they succeed in undermining tenure, they may achieve both less and more than their proponents intend.

What would happen if tenure were eliminated in all colleges and universities? The proper answer is that no one really knows what would happen. Tenure was eliminated in all English universities, and according to one commentator "English academic life so far appears unchanged."[12] He adds that the academic tradition in England is longer and different from that in the United States. So one guess is that little, if anything, would change immediately in academic life in the United States. It seems unlikely that many colleges or universities would suddenly fire their deadwood and replace them with bright, eager new faculty members. If those institutions have done nothing about faculty members the administration actually considers deadwood, it does not seem likely they have the nerve or inclination to take any drastic action if tenure were no longer required. If they had the nerve or inclination to do anything, they could have and would have done something about such faculty members—however few or many there are—under the tenure rules. Moreover, if tenure were abolished it is unlikely that it could legally or ethically be abolished retroactively. Those who were hired under conditions of tenure are entitled to tenure, even if it is abolished for those who start without any such expectation. Those on tenure-track appointments who have not been granted tenure had no assurance they would be granted it, and hence the institution's obligation to them is very different from those to whom it has granted tenure.

Without tenure would the pay of professors increase? This is difficult to predict. Since in the past decade or so there have been many more people applying for positions at colleges and universities than there have been openings, we can expect that the supply is still sufficient not to require any raise in pay. The abolition of tenure would not create any new positions. It would only make easier some reallocation of positions.

If there were no tenure, would young assistant professors be under pressure to publish and perform the way they are when on a tenure track, facing the requirement of receiving tenure or being dismissed? Would colleges and universities keep faculty on longer, and postpone any decisions about poor or mediocre performers, reappointing them year after year because the institution is not forced to make any decision? This would certainly happen at some institutions. It is not possible to guess whether it would happen at the majority of them. The abolition of tenure will not automatically produce better college or university administrators than we presently have, nor would it make any easier the kinds of value judgments required with respect to retaining faculty.

Would it mean a difference in the number or treatment of part-time faculty? Once again this is difficult to predict, but there seems to be little reason why the abolition of tenure would produce a change here. If part-time faculty are hired because they are paid less and do not have to be paid many fringe benefits, the presence or absence of tenure will not change this.

Would faculty change institutions more often? Once again there seems little reason to believe so. The number of openings will not change because of changes in tenure. Faculty members presently move, and if they have tenure they typically get it or get some assurance of it as a condition of their moving. If it is easier to fire faculty members, as it would be, more might be fired. But since the up-or-out requirement would no longer exist, it is not clear that more faculty on the whole in any given year would be let go from their positions.

The economic changes that would result are thus speculative. Those who attack tenure claim that the changes would be great, and those who defend tenure claim it would make little difference in the areas I have mentioned. The changes will probably on the whole be less than those who seek to abolish tenure envisage.

The big difference the abolition of tenure would make is the impact on academic freedom. And this is a loss that many of those who attack tenure fail to consider. I have argued that academic freedom is the central justification for tenure, and without tenure the status of academic freedom would certainly change. How quickly and how drastically, it is difficult to say. Tenure was abolished for new faculty at Bennington College in 1994 when the institution declared financial exigency and sent dismissal notices to twenty-seven faculty members, about two-thirds of them tenured. An AAUP investigating committee concludes its report by saying "Academic freedom is insecure and academic tenure is nonexistent today at Bennington College."[13] Tenure was evidently perceived as a hindrance not only to restructuring but to restructuring by the administration without faculty consultation. Without a tenure system there is a strong likelihood that safeguards for academic freedom will be seriously diminished. The university as a business, with authority coming from the top and faculty serving at the sufferance of the administration, is a model that some, perhaps many, colleges and universities would adopt. Once a college or university follows the model of business, it is likely that the movement toward faculty unionization would gain a momentum it has not yet had as the faculty members would attempt to provide some job security to make up for the tenure they had lost.

If not required to provide tenure, some institutions might still do so and might still commit themselves to something very much like academic tenure. But without the system's being widespread, there would almost certainly be a chilling effect on faculty teaching, research, and publication with respect to any area or topic that is at all controversial or possibly unpopular. And this will result in less critical students and less innovative and critical workers and citizens.

The major cost of the loss of tenure would not be to faculty members who would for the most part learn to protect themselves, to conform, and to secure their positions. The greatest loss would be to the fabric and quality of the society as a whole.

NOTES

1. For a history of the university, see Hastings Rashdall, *Universities of Europe in the Middle Ages*, F. M. Powicke, ed., and A. B. Emden, new ed. (Oxford: Clarendon Press, 1987), 3 vols. For a history of academic tenure in the United States, see Walter P. Metzger, "The 1940 Statement of Principles on Academic Freedom and Tenure," *Law and Contemporary Problems* 53, 2 (1990), pp. 2–77. Academic tenure as we know it is based on the 1940 Statement, coauthored by representatives of the American Association of University Professors (AAUP) and the Association of American Colleges (AAU). Interpretative comments were added in 1970.

2. The legal doctrine of employment-at-will states that an employer may hire whomever he or she wishes and fire that person whenever the employer wishes for any reason or even for no reason. An employee may accept any offered position he or she wishes and may quit whenever he or she wishes for any reason or even for no reason. The doctrine still applies in law, although it has been circumscribed in various ways by antidiscrimination, plant-closing, and other legislation.

3. "1940 Statement of Principles on Academic Freedom and Tenure With 1970 Interpretive Comments," *AAUP Policy Documents and Reports* (Washington, D.C.: American Association of University Professors, 1995), p. 4.

4. Ibid., p. 7.

5. The 1940 Statement states: "Tenure is a means to certain ends; specifically: (1) freedom of teaching and research and of extramural activities; and (2) a sufficient degree of economic security to make the profession attractive to men and women of ability" (ibid., p. 3).

6. See Richard T. De George, *Patterns of Soviet Thought* (Ann Arbor: University of Michigan Press, 1966), ch. X–XII.

7. The highest-paid professors are most often in medical schools, with some receiving salaries of over $400,000. *The Chronicle of Higher Education* (September 14, 1994, p. A25) lists a professor of cardiothoracic surgery at Cornell University Medical School as the highest paid for 1992–93, with a salary of $1,762,083. The average full professor's salary in a Category I institution in 1995–96 was $73,610 (*Academe*, March–April 1996, p. 26).

8. See, for example, the report on the University of Minnesota: "A Parlous Time for Tenure," *Chronicle of Higher Education* (May 17, 1996), A21–23.

9. For two arguments against this objection, see Ronald Dworkin, "Objectivity and Truth: You'd Better Believe It," *Philosophy and Public Affairs* 25, 2 (1996), 87–139, and John R. Searle, "Rationality and Realism, What Is at Stake?" *Daedalus* 122, 4 (1992), 55–84.

10. See Richard Rorty, "Does Academic Freedom Have Philosophical Presuppositions?" *Academe* (November–December 1994), 52–63, and Stanley Fish, *There's No Such Thing as Free Speech and It's a Good Thing, Too* (New York: Oxford University Press, 1994), 102–19.

11. "Political correctness" is the most recent version of the politicization argument. See "Two Views: Debating Political Correctness," by Elizabeth Fox-Genovese and Larry Scanlon, *Academe* (May–June, 1995), 8–15.

12. Ernest van den Haag, "Academic Freedom and Tenure," *Pace Law Review* 15, 1 (Fall 1994), 7.

13. "Report: Academic Freedom and Tenure: Bennington College," *Academe* (March–April 1995), 103.

STUDY QUESTIONS

1. If the practice of tenure disappears, is a free society the loser?
2. What is the "deadwood argument" against tenure, and what is the strongest reply to that argument?
3. In which respects is the university like a business, and in which respects is it not?
4. If academic positions were readily available, would tenure be less important?

The Tenure Decision:
Two Hard Cases

PAUL J. OLSCAMP

AN EXAMPLE OF TENURING
AND ACADEMIC POLITICS

Betty Smythe was a young assistant professor in the department of ethnic studies. She also taught frequently in the women's studies program. She had come to the faculty without her doctoral degree but had completed it during her second year. In her sixth year, she applied for tenure. She did not have much choice, for the university's policy followed the AAUP guidelines stipulating that if a faculty member has not earned tenure after six years, then the seventh year must be a terminal contract.

Dr. Smythe's academic record was acceptable but not outstanding. Her student evaluations of teaching were generally good, although spotty in places. She had taught a fairly broad range of courses but had not gained membership on the graduate faculty, which required a continuing and current record of scholarship, and the number and quality of her publications were questionable. She had recently contracted for the publication of a book, but an examination of the manuscript revealed that it was almost verbatim her doctoral dissertation, which was not about a particularly difficult or complex topic. No scholarly articles had been developed on the basis of the dissertation, and no evidence was presented of a serious work in progress. Smythe was strongly supported by peers at other institutions, but

Originally published in Paul J. Olscamp, *Moral Leadership: Ethics and the College Presidency*, pp. 35–47, 2003, Rowman & Littlefield. Reprinted by permission of Rowman & Littlefield.

upon examination these individuals all had some special relationship to her, which provided reason to question their objectivity. For example, her dissertation adviser wrote a laudatory review of her book manuscript, and as I have mentioned, the book was actually the dissertation, almost verbatim.

Dr. Smythe was strongly supported by her colleagues, at least publicly. Her female colleagues in particular were vociferous in her defense, and consequently the discussion surrounding the case was immediately personalized and politicized. To complicate matters further, the board of trustees at this time had a member who was a former faculty member, highly political in every way, and was a direct conduit of information that should have been confidential from discussions with other board members to faculty critical of the administration. Thus it was impossible to examine the case of Dr. Smythe in the careful and objective way these matters should always be handled.

Dr. Smythe's departmental tenure and promotion committee had voted to support her application, but the vote was not unanimous. The collegiate tenure and promotion committee had also voted to support her, but the vote again was not unanimous. The dean of the college did not support the collegiate committee and argued that Smythe should be denied tenure because of an insufficient scholarly record. The vice president supported the dean, and the president decided to deny Smythe tenure on the basis of the vice president's and dean's recommendations. The president had also been visited by a senior member of the departmental tenure and promotion committee who told him he regretted his affirmative vote and did not support Smythe. But he felt extremely pressured by female faculty who had made Smythe a cause célèbre. From other sources, reliable ones, it had also come to the president's private attention that Smythe had an alcohol problem and at least occasionally used cocaine. It should be noted that a faculty member cannot be dismissed for alcoholism, only for inadequate performance, which may or may not be related to that condition. The president consulted with the dean, the vice president, and the chair of the board before the public meeting, and they decided it would be unfair to Smythe to mention the informal contact with the senior faculty member who regretted his vote. The evidence of alcohol and cocaine use should also be concealed because in the former case incompetence because of the problem had not been alleged, and she had never been charged with a drug offense. But several people including board members knew of these facts, although not from the president or other administrators, and it seems impossible for this knowledge not to have influenced their opinions.

Because of the fairly widespread knowledge of the substance abuse problem, and also because Dr. Smythe had, willingly or unwillingly, become a symbol for causes having no essential connection to the facts of her tenure application, the president felt there was some justice to the claim that she could not receive a totally fair and objective hearing through the normal processes. The question was, What to do about this?

The trustee mentioned earlier now took up the Smythe case as a cause. Smythe was encouraged by the trustee and several faculty to demand a public hearing of her case before the board, and she did this. The president had no objection to the hearing but was concerned lest it become a spectacle used as a stage for women's issues at the university in general. And that is what happened. It was claimed that had she been male, her scholarly record would have been adjudged sufficient; that the tenure and promotion committees had been biased because both of them were preponderantly male, and that otherwise the committee votes would have been unanimous; that the dean was biased and opposed to both ethnic and women's studies programs; and that the president supported the dean because if he had not, the truth of the dean's critics' accusations would have been more obvious. The vice president, a woman, was accused of being a "yes person" for the president. Even certain outstanding female scholars on the faculty came to Smythe's defense, one of them openly arguing that the symbolism of the Smythe case for women on the campus was of such weight that this factor alone should determine that Smythe be given tenure. The trustee involved openly supported this view.

The president felt that the central issues were these:

- On the basis of the record over the last six years, how did Smythe's qualifications compare to others who had been granted tenure, without regard to gender?
- Had the process by which Smythe had been evaluated differed in any material way from others evaluated for tenure in that year or any other year, again without regard to gender?
- If, as had been found, her scholarly work was lacking, were there mitigating factors, such as unusual university service or unusual excellence in teaching, that might have had a bearing on this?
- Was there any evidence that those charged with evaluating her work had been biased in any way against her for nonacademic reasons?
- Had appropriate external evaluations of her work been sought?

Aside from these essential questions, the peculiar circumstances of the case had raised these further issues:

- If some particular case, for whatever reasons, comes to have serious symbolic implications for the sense of well-being of an important group on campus, should that fact have a bearing on a tenure or promotion decision?

- What would be the foreseeable impact in terms of campus well-being if tenure decisions were, from time to time, visibly influenced by factors other than academic ones?
- Is it possible to systematize (i.e., govern practice by rule) the consideration of nonacademic factors, assuming they were to be permitted in such a context?
- If Dr. Smythe were given tenure for reasons in addition to, or instead of, academic ones, would this serve her own true self-interest in the long run?
- Finally, but perhaps most importantly, what were the moral implications of the case for both individuals and the institution?

The president gave these matters serious thought and after appropriate consultation stated his answers to these questions at the public hearing.

It seemed clear to him that in those areas where it was possible to make comparisons, no one in the modern history of the university who had comparable qualifications to Smythe had been granted tenure at the university, nor, so far as could be discovered, at comparable institutions. An examination of these comparisons when gender was included as a variable revealed no bias. The process by which Smythe had been evaluated was identical to that of her recently tenured colleagues, and it was similar in all relevant respects to the tenuring process in other departments and at other similar universities; again, when gender was considered, no bias was found. These examinations were conducted by appropriately qualified faculty, including representatives from other universities.

Smythe did not have an unusual level of university service, nor an unusual teaching load, which might have partially explained her inadequate research and publication record. In fact, over the year prior to her evaluation, she had been given a lighter than average teaching load, and no service assignments, in order to free her to do more research. There was no evidence of any bias against her for nonacademic reasons on the part of those evaluating her work, although the department chair had spoken of his concern about the alcohol problem with her. He had supported her application for tenure, and according to him Dr. Smythe had promised to seek help for her alcoholism.

External evaluations of Dr. Smythe's work had been sought, and additional ones were solicited by the vice president's office when it was discovered that the initial evaluators had special relationships with her. These additional evaluators were chosen by experts in Smythe's field both within and without the university. They did not evaluate her work highly. On the basis of these findings, the president had no trouble recommending to the board that Dr. Smythe not receive tenure.

However, her case raised issues that far outweighed the Smythe case alone and the president felt these should be addressed as well. The entire campus community was discussing the issue of whether the symbolic importance of the Smythe decision for women ought to be a factor in the case, and a surprising number of faculty, men and women, thought that it should influence the outcome. The president and the board did not agree with this opinion, and their disagreement was based on three factors.

First, the symbolic factors were irrelevant from an academic viewpoint, and a decision to grant tenure was primarily, but not entirely, based on academic factors. They noted cases in which, for example, the applicant simply could not get along with any other members of the department and was a constant source of friction. There is no policy in any handbook of which I am aware that addresses this issue, yet such material facts certainly play a role. But in the present instance such other concerns were not material. And it would not be possible to formulate any policy that purported to allow symbolic issues to be counted that did not result in arbitrary and capricious behavior, the very antithesis of what fair and objective evaluation is supposed to be.

Second, if the symbolism of the decision were allowed to carry the day, the foreseeable impact on any university campus would be devastating, for no one would have any confidence in a process of selection that, by common knowledge, could be manipulated by political and sectarian maneuvering. Since it would be impossible to institutionalize such practices with any consistency, they would by definition be arbitrary and capricious, and thence random. A fundamental principle of morality is that justice must be equitable, and by definition randomness is the opposite of equitability. A president who allowed factors that created such random conditions would therefore be violating the basic moral principle of justice and would a fortiori be committing immoral acts.

Third, it is foreseeable that such institutional behavior would result in chaos and/or authoritarian administration, and it certainly would cause pain and suffering to individuals. It would also obviously leave any university wide open to legal suit.

The moral issues involved here were clear. First, there was the principle that every individual has the right to be treated justly and fairly, and with due regard to her personal dignity. Smythe had been so treated. Indeed, extraordinary efforts had been exerted to ensure that this was visibly so. Second, the moral obligation to preserve a process of integrity with respect to the distribution of justice within the institution was material. That is, if rewarding excellence through granting tenure is not merely a matter of prudence but of justice, then the processes through which this is accomplished must be such as to preserve the trust of the faculty and others in their fairness and thoroughness. Extraordinary efforts were taken to ensure that was the case. Third, given that the negative decision with respect to Smythe inevitably caused her some distress, the president felt that he had an obligation to "go the extra mile" to comfort and advise her. He did this to the best of his ability. This last point is not, strictly speaking, a matter of moral principle, falling as it does under the first principle given above, but it is a subsidiary obligation.

CHANGING VALUES
AND VAGUE STANDARDS

The second tenure case involved a classic conflict over the operational meaning of standards for tenure and promotion. In most faculty handbooks at most universities, the language governing the process by which tenure is granted is fairly standard. In general, most universities stipulate three areas of performance in which acceptable standards must be met in order for a candidate to stand for tenure: teaching, research, and service. I have never seen a handbook in which the three types of service were explicitly ranked in order of importance, nor have I ever seen more detailed delineation of the expectations with respect to quality or level of service, except that in some policies with respect to tenure, it is stated that in general, promotion to the rank of associate professor is anticipated at the time of tenuring. Also, it is not uncommon for language to be used indicating that tenure and promotion to associate professor ought not to be given unless the quality of performance gives reason to believe that the faculty person will be able to achieve the rank of full professor in the future. Because of the breadth of academic disciplines, however, it is hard to be more specific about performance in documents intended to be used by the entire university.

In spite of the absence of more specific language, there is an unwritten ranking of the three areas of service, depending on the type of college or university being considered. At smaller liberal arts colleges, teaching at a high level of excellence and repute is essential. Service to the college is also expected and is valued highly in the process although not anything like teaching excellence. Whether there is a research and publication expectation at such an institution often depends on the individual understandings reached at the time of hiring with the new faculty. For example, the new faculty member might have a lighter teaching load than normal but in return understands that he or she will be judged, when the time comes, on the basis of research performance at a much higher level of expectation than others with whom no such expectations have been established.

Such arrangements are quite common in transitional schools—those evolving from regional state colleges to universities, for example.

At major research institutions, it is understood from the time of hiring that research and publication or their equivalents (i.e., performance, exhibition of works, etc.) are the sine qua non for gaining tenure. Teaching skill is appreciated, but an "acceptable" level is sufficient provided that research and publication occur at a high level. Service ranks as a distant third in the triumvirate of evaluation areas, and at many research universities younger faculty are discouraged from serious service commitments such as membership on the faculty senate until after they have achieved tenure so they will have more time to devote to research and the improvement of teaching. None of this is to say that teaching is unimportant at these flagship institutions. A faculty person probably would not achieve tenure even with a fairly high level of research performance if his teaching was very poor, particularly since in recent times there has been a resurgence of emphasis on undergraduate education and teaching at the expense of research. But even today, it would be unlikely in the extreme for an excellent teacher to achieve tenure with a very poor research and publication record.

These variant practices between research universities and small liberal arts schools have long been the norm, and they are well understood and accepted in their respective environments. But there is a large set of institutions between these two types of school where the picture is not so clear. This third kind of university generally developed from the old "normal school" and state college traditions, which concentrated almost exclusively on the preparation of teachers for the lower grades at the turn of the century, plus a basic liberal arts education in the colleges. As college-age populations expanded and the demand for broader educational experiences rose, and with the passage of GI legislation after World War II, the majority of the normal schools became four-year colleges, often by first becoming colleges of education with a curriculum somewhat broader than the normal school, and then, beginning in the late 1920s and continuing until the present, colleges of arts and science.

For the last thirty-five years or so, there has been a progressive trend throughout the country for these colleges to develop graduate programs, first at the master's and certificate levels and then often doctoral work, and this has been followed by efforts to reclassify these middle-level institutions as universities. These sorts of institutions constitute the majority of universities in the United States today, and they enroll more than 20 percent of all the undergraduate students in the country. Since more than four hundred of them belong to the American Association of State Colleges and Universities (AASCU), I shall refer to them as AASCU institutions.

At this third sort of institution, expectations for tenure and promotion are often not as clear as they are at the other two. For one thing, it is still true that older faculty from the "college" days remain, who were hired with a very different set of performance expectations but now serve at senior levels within the infrastructure, including positions such as chair of tenure and promotion committees. Frequently they are now asked to judge their new colleagues by standards that they themselves would not have met. There is resentment by both parties in such a context. Often the institution as a whole does not have a clear role and mission statement, and the limitations on and purposes of research efforts and development of graduate programs are not very clear. Furthermore, almost all of the younger faculty standing for tenure or promotion received their advanced degrees from research universities. The doctoral degree almost always qualifies the holder to do research in the discipline of the degree. These faculty are not being trained to teach in an atmosphere that does not also require them to do research. Inevitably, the pressures in such an environment are to become more like the research institutions that trained the faculty in the first place. Even where the university has done a fairly good job of distinguishing selective disciplines in which it wishes to establish a "niche" reputation, it is very hard to dampen the aspirations of other departments that might not receive the same level of resources. The net effect is that the "new university" aspires to become a research university, and this overall effort creates and/or emphasizes the fractures between older faculty, teaching-oriented faculty, research faculty, graduate schools, and undergraduate programs. The frequent victim at AASCU universities is the young faculty person standing for tenure who is not sure that the expectations of his or her department are supported, or even understood, by collegiate and central administrative decision makers who may have developed in much earlier and different times.

An Example of a Transitional Victim

Dr. Sally Morse (a fictitious name) found herself standing for tenure and promotion to associate professor in just such a context. Her department was targeted by her university as a "niche" discipline—a discipline or set of disciplines in a single department that the university wished to develop into a major player in the state's research environment. There were reasonable hopes that a consistently excellent national and even international reputation would evolve from the work of the younger faculty. Expectations, and rewards, were higher for this department than for all others in the university except for the few other "niche" programs in which a similar investment of resources was being made. The hopes for Morse's university so far as ranking as a nationally important university was concerned seemed to rest on the development of these niche programs more than anything else. Dr. Morse's department had undertaken a broad variety of steps to enhance the department's quality: heavily recruiting graduate students from schools that already excelled in their fields and enhancing enrollment requirements for their undergraduate programs. They had raised private endowments and provided scholarships for National Merit Scholars to study with them, and they had combined faculty "lines" (i.e., money for new positions to create endowed chairs for "stars" with already established national and international reputations).

Morse submitted her application in her sixth year as a faculty member. Her teaching evaluations were excellent. This is significant because of the way in which teaching returns inform evaluators after a sufficient number of returns for all courses taught at all levels have been received. The evaluations do not give a lot of information at the middle levels of competence: they identify your "superstar" teachers and the ill-prepared and boring instructors. Dr. Morse was a superstar teacher.

Morse's service record was barely adequate, but the department informed the collegiate-level tenure and promotion committee that this was because the department discouraged her service activities and encouraged research in its place. Dr. Morse's research and publication record was clearly good enough to have earned her tenure in almost all of the university departments not designated as "niche" departments. But it was average in comparison to the records of similar applicants from other "niche" programs. In a split vote within her department (I believe it was 6–4 with one abstention), she was recommended for tenure and promotion. Included within her file was a letter from the chair noting that Morse's research protocol was proceeding on schedule, and that the majority of the published work expected from her project could not be expected until her work was complete. It was also noted that Morse had not attracted significant outside funding from either government or private sources.

On the basis of the departmental split vote, and including the letter about Morse's grant funding record, teaching evaluations, and service component, the collegiate-level tenure and promotion committee voted 5–4 to deny her tenure and promotion. The committee noted that this decision was particularly difficult for them, because in most other departments her record would have qualified her for tenure and promotion. They also noted the systematic vagueness in the university's standards of excellence with respect to the three evaluative criteria (teaching, research, and service). In effect, they said, there were no qualitative criteria other than those used by the individual peers and outside evaluators who were expert in Morse's field of study to help the university committee decide that an individual, call him or her "A," had work that was either more excellent or less excellent than another applicant "B" because no standards for excellence within the individual categories to be evaluated (teaching, research, and service) were part of the handbook guidelines. Only where such measurable information as scores of student evaluations for teaching was available could intracategorical comparisons be identified. But such information was almost impossible to find in the area of research, other than counting the number of publications, which tells one little about the quality of the work, just that peers who referee the publishing journals think it worth presenting. In Morse's case, she had few refereed publications, although the ones she had were in journals of high repute.

The dean of the college recommended that Morse be given tenure but that promotion to associate professor be withheld pending further publication of her research. In his recommendation, the dean noted the split vote of the collegiate committee and their comments on the vagueness of the evaluative criteria. He stated that if "niche" programs were to have higher standards, then the departmental policies should say that and define them; they should be approved by the collegiate and central administrations, the faculty senate, and the trustees.

The university-level tenure and promotion committee overturned the dean's recommendation, agreeing with the collegiate committee, but once again by a split vote, and with the same reservations expressed by the dean. The recommendations then came to the vice president for academic affairs, the Senate Committee on Faculty Welfare and Grievances having already announced that regardless of the final outcome, the issues raised by the case justified a senate investigation.

Theoretically, the vice president should make his or her recommendation to the president based on an objective evaluation independent of the president, since if there is an appeal it always goes to the chief executive of the institution. In fact, when recommendations were positive from the vice president, it was almost a certainty that the president would support them, save in those rare instances where extra scrutiny was warranted because of heavily split opinion early in the process. In this case, however, it seemed that university-wide issues of major importance having to do with role and mission, the place and function of niche programs, and the use of different criteria of excellence by different academic units, as well as the absence of criteria of excellence within the published handbook criteria for tenure and promotion, made it imperative for the chief academic officer and the president to have a common understanding of these issues and their relevance before she made her recommendation in the particular case of Morse.

We began by agreeing on certain factual and general principles essential to the university. (1) We agreed that the university's resources would not now or in the foreseeable future permit the achievement of the highest levels of excellence in research in every department on campus. (2) We agreed that the role and mission of the university entailed the achievement of research excellence in selected fields, with the approval of the board of trustees and the state board of regents if this entailed the development of new degree programs. (3) We agreed that (1) and (2) implied that the university's resources should be distributed differentially and according to the expectations laid down for each department and college. (4) We agreed that if (1), (2), and (3) were given, then, costs per unit being otherwise equal, the higher the funding and resource levels, the higher the faculty performance levels we could justifiably expect. (5) If performance levels were to vary by resource allocation and department or program, then all faculty in those programs had a right to know what would define the higher performance levels expected of them, how much time they had to meet the higher levels, and how it would be determined whether they had met these higher standards.

Having agreed on these for the most part essentially normative principles, we now had to face certain matters of fact, both about the institution and about the Morse case itself. The principle of the differential distribution of resources had been practiced for many years but was nowhere enunciated as university policy. The "niche" programs, all of them granting the doctoral degree, which now received higher funding than the norm, had, with but two notable exceptions, initially been identified for additional support after they had already achieved levels of renown at the university. In the two notable exceptions, the programs had raised millions of dollars from private sources before having supplementary funds allocated by the institution. Enforcement of higher standards for promotion and tenure in these programs had evolved within the departments from the ground up, as it were, and not by use of funding pressure through administrative channels.

But in no case, so far as we were aware, had these higher standards of excellence been articulated in departmental or collegiate handbooks or in other policy documents, and certainly they had not been approved centrally or by the board. Although it was assumed that the higher standards had been communicated initially to all new hires in the concerned departments, and that thereafter they had been regularly counseled by their senior peers, there was no evidence save the anecdotal to confirm this. This was true in the Morse case as well, although she had been told to ignore service for the most part and to concentrate on her research. Nor was there any place where an exception in expectations for promotion and tenure standards from the university handbook had been noted. This was what had concerned the tenure and promotion committees so keenly, as well as the absence of criteria defining "excellence" as opposed to acceptable or satisfactory performance.

It was clear that the expectations of Morse were much higher than the average for tenure and promotion applicants for the university as a whole. It was also clear that the higher criteria she had to meet were nowhere clearly defined in university policy; there were split votes on whether she had met the undefined higher criteria; and there was general agreement that if she were being considered according to general handbook criteria, she would have been granted tenure and promotion. Given her record to date, it was reasonably foreseeable that Dr. Morse would continue to develop in her research, as well as in other professional categories. It seemed equally clear that confusion about the higher standards for "niche" departments might also have victimized her through no fault of her own, and that the general faculty were upset by the vagueness of the situation as well. Were Morse to be denied tenure, the university at best would be viewed as having done a clumsy job of evaluation, and at worst would be seen as having acted unjustly to a well-qualified person. Its essential processes would be brought under serious doubt.

Dr. Sally Morse was given tenure and promoted. She is today one of the most widely respected and well-known teachers and scholars at the university, and her work is internationally respected. The policies and procedures manuals were and are being revised to correct the deficiencies noted by the committees. This work is still in progress, having proven much more difficult than was anticipated.

The moral principles at issue here are similar to those in the Smythe case. Clearly we had an obligation to treat Morse honestly, fairly, and with dignity. We also had an obligation to ensure that the process by which she was given or denied tenure was fair and was worthy of respect and trust on the part of the university's constituencies. The first principle concerns the rightness or wrongness of actions, the second the distribution of justice. It was virtually impossible to demonstrate the fairness of the process of distribution in this case, for the reasons given above. In such a case, it was felt that treating the individual honestly, fairly, and with dignity should supervene on the broader obligation to distribute justice fairly. Not ensuring this would bring both principles into disrepute and might cause irreparable institutional harm and harm to other individuals in the future. This was not as difficult a decision as it might seem, given the promising nature of Morse's research efforts to date.

There was, however, another moral principle operative here, which was the commitment the university had made about the quality of its teaching to parents and students. The university is a doctorate-granting one, but not a major research university. Although graduate work and research were important and becoming more so as the institution matured, it had a fundamental commitment of principle to unusual excellence in teaching and had advertised that fact widely. Morse was a superstar teacher, and even in a niche department the school could not afford to lose such a fine instructor without violating its promises to students and their parents. The university kept that commitment.

STUDY QUESTIONS

1. Should Smythe's alcohol problem or her promise to seek help for it have been a factor in the decision about her tenure?
2. If Smythe's record had included an unusually high level of university service, should she have been awarded tenure?
3. Given that the expectations and rewards were higher for Sally Morse's department than for most others in the university, and that after having been told to ignore service and concentrate on her research, she had published few refereed papers and had not attracted outside funding, should she have been granted tenure?
4. What criteria should be used to determine whether someone is a "superstar" teacher or just a good one, and, without a strong publication record, how effective in the classroom does a professor need to be to deserve tenure?

II

FREE SPEECH
ON CAMPUS

The maintenance of free inquiry requires that all points of view be entitled to a hearing. As long as an individual remains civil, no one at a university, whether professor, student, or guest, should ever be prevented from stating beliefs. No matter how noxious some opinions may be, the greater danger lies in stifling them. For when one person's opinion is silenced, no one else's may be uttered in safety.

Yet those seeking the truth need not be shielded from error. Quite the opposite. We fully understand our own views only after they have been subjected to challenge. As John Stuart Mill wrote in his classic treatise On Liberty, *"He who knows only his own side of the case knows little of that."*

But what if a speaker violates civility by resorting to epithets and slurs? Should a speech code be in place to prevent such vilification of individuals and groups? Charles R. Lawrence III believes so. Martin P. Golding does not.

3

Regulating Racist Speech on Campus

CHARLES R. LAWRENCE III

M uch recent debate over the efficacy of regulating racist speech has focused on the efforts by colleges and universities to respond to the burgeoning incidents of racial harassment on their campuses. At Stanford, where I teach, there has been considerable controversy over whether racist and other discriminatory verbal harassment should be regulated and what form any regulation should take. Proponents of regulation have been sensitive to the danger of inhibiting expression, and the current regulation (which was drafted by my colleague Tom Grey) manifests that sensitivity. It is drafted somewhat more narrowly than I would have preferred, leaving unregulated hate speech that occurs in settings where there is a captive audience, but I largely agree with this regulation's substance and approach. I include it here as one example of a regulation of racist speech that I would argue violates neither first amendment precedent nor principle. The regulation reads as follows:

Fundamental Standard Interpretation: Free Expression
and Discriminatory Harassment

1. Stanford is committed to the principles of free inquiry and free expression. Students have the right to hold and vigorously defend and promote their opinions, thus entering them into the life of the University, there to flourish or wither according to their merits. Respect for this right requires that students tolerate even expression of opinions which they find abhorrent. Intimidation of

Originally published as "If He Hollers Let Him Go," *Duke Law Journal* 1990:3; pp. 431–483. Reprinted by permission of Duke Law Journal and Charles R. Lawrence III.

students by other students in their exercise of this right, by violence or threat of violence, is therefore considered to be a violation of the Fundamental Standard.

2. Stanford is also committed to principles of equal opportunity and nondiscrimination. Each student has the right to equal access to a Stanford education, without discrimination on the basis of sex, race, color, handicap, religion, sexual orientation, or national and ethnic origin. Harassment of students on the basis of any of these characteristics tends to create a hostile environment that makes access to education for those subjected to it less than equal. Such discriminatory harassment is therefore considered to be a violation of the Fundamental Standard.

3. This interpretation of the Fundamental Standard is intended to clarify the point at which protected free expression ends and prohibited discriminatory harassment begins. Prohibited harassment includes discriminatory intimidation by threats of violence, and also includes personal vilification of students on the basis of their sex, race, color, handicap, religion, sexual orientation, or national and ethnic origin.

4. Speech or other expression constitutes harassment by vilification if it:

   a) is intended to insult or stigmatize an individual or a small number of individuals on the basis of their sex, race, color, handicap, religion, sexual orientation, or national and ethnic origin; and

   b) is addressed directly to the individual or individuals whom it insults or stigmatizes; and

   c) makes use of "fighting" words or non-verbal symbols.

   In the context of discriminatory harassment, "fighting" words or nonverbal symbols are words, pictures or symbols that, by virtue of their form, are commonly understood to convey direct and visceral hatred or contempt for human beings on the basis of their sex, race, color, handicap, religion, sexual orientation, and national and ethnic origin.[1]

This regulation and others like it have been characterized in the press as the work of "thought police," but the rule does nothing more than prohibit intentional face-to-face insults, a form of speech that is unprotected by the first amendment. When racist speech takes the form of face-to-face insults, catcalls, or other assaultive speech aimed at an individual or a small group of persons, then it falls within the "fighting words" exception to first amendment protection. The Supreme Court has held that words that "by their very utterance inflict injury or tend to incite an immediate breach of the peace"[2] are not constitutionally protected.

Face-to-face racial insults, like fighting words, are undeserving of first amendment protection for two reasons. The first reason is the immediacy of the injurious impact of racial insults. The experience of being called "nigger," "spic," "Jap," or "kike" is like receiving a slap in the face. The injury is instantaneous. There is neither an opportunity for intermediary reflection on the idea conveyed nor an opportunity for responsive speech. The harm to be avoided is both clear and present. The second reason that racial insults should not fall under protected speech relates to the purpose underlying the first amendment. The purpose of the first amendment is to foster the greatest amount of speech. Racial insults disserve that purpose. Assaultive racist speech functions as a preemptive strike. The racial invective is experienced as a blow, not a proffered idea, and once the blow is struck, it is unlikely that dialogue will follow. Racial insults are undeserving of first amendment protection because the perpetrator's intention is not to discover truth or initiate dialogue, but to injure the victim.

The fighting words doctrine anticipates that the verbal slap in the face of insulting words will provoke a violent response, resulting in a breach of the peace. When racial insults are hurled at minorities, the response may be silence or flight rather than a fight, but the preemptive effect on further speech is the same. Women and minorities often report that they find themselves speechless in the face of discriminatory verbal attacks. This inability to respond is not the result of oversensitivity among these groups, as some individuals who oppose protective regulation have argued. Rather it is the product of several factors, all of which evidence the nonspeech character of the initial preemptive verbal assault. The first factor is that the visceral emotional response to personal attack precludes speech. Attack produces an instinctive, defensive psychological reaction. Fear, rage, shock, and flight all interfere with any reasoned response. Words like "nigger," "kike," and "faggot" produce physical symptoms that temporarily disable the victim, and the perpetrators often use these words with the intention of producing this effect. Many victims do not find words of response until well after the assault, when the cowardly assaulter has departed.

A second factor that distinguishes racial insults from protected speech is the preemptive nature of such insults—words of response to such verbal attacks may never be forthcoming because speech is usually an inadequate response. When one is personally attacked with words that denote one's subhuman status and untouchability, there is little, if anything, that can be said to redress either the emotional or reputational injury. This is particularly true when the message and meaning of the epithet resonates with beliefs widely held in society. This preservation of widespread beliefs is what makes the face-to-face racial attack more likely to preempt speech than other fighting words do. The racist name caller is accompanied by a cultural chorus of equally demeaning speech and symbols. Segregation and other forms of racist speech injure victims because of their dehumanizing and excluding message. Each individual message gains its power because of the cumulative and reinforcing effect of countless similar messages that are conveyed in a society where racism is ubiquitous.

The subordinated victims of fighting words also are silenced by their relatively powerless position in society. Because of the significance of power and position, the categorization of racial epithets as fighting words provides an inadequate paradigm; instead one must speak of their functional equivalent. The fighting words doctrine presupposes an encounter between two persons of relatively equal power who have been acculturated to respond to face-to-face insults with violence: The fighting words doctrine is a paradigm based on a white male point of view. It captures the "macho" quality of male discourse. It is accepted, justifiable, and even praiseworthy when "real men" respond to personal insult with violence. (Presidential candidate George Bush effectively emulated the most macho—and not coincidentally most violent—of movie stars, Clint Eastwood, when he repeatedly used the phrase, "Read my lips!" Any teenage boy will tell you the subtext of this message: "I've got nothing else to say about this and if you don't like what I'm saying we can step outside.") The fighting words doctrine's responsiveness to this male stance in the world and its blindness to the cultural experience of women is another example of how neutral principles of law reflect the values of those who are dominant.

Black men also are well aware of the double standard that our culture applies in responding to insult. Part of the culture of racial domination through violence—a culture of dominance manifested historically in thousands of lynchings in the South and more recently in the racial violence at Howard Beach and Bensonhurst—is the paradoxical expectation on the part of whites that Black males will accept insult from whites without protest, yet will become violent without provocation. These expectations combine two assumptions: First, that Blacks as a group—and especially Black men—are more violent; and second, that as inferior persons, Blacks have no right to feel insulted. One can imagine the response of universities if Black men started to respond to racist fighting words by beating up white students.

In most situations, minorities correctly perceive that a violent response to fighting words will result in a risk to their own life and limb. This risk forces targets to remain silent and submissive. This response is most obvious when women submit to sexually assaultive speech or when the racist name caller is in a more powerful position—the boss on the job or a member of a violent racist group. Certainly, we do not expect the Black woman crossing the Wisconsin campus to turn on her tormentors and pummel them. Less obvious, but just as significant, is the effect of pervasive racial and sexual violence and coercion on individual members of subordinated groups, who must learn the survival techniques of suppressing and disguising rage and anger at an early age.

One of my students, a white, gay male, related an experience that is quite instructive in understanding the fighting words doctrine. In response to my request that students describe how they experienced the injury of racist speech, Michael told a story of being called "faggot" by a man on a subway. His description included all of the speech-inhibiting elements I have noted previously. He found himself in a state of semishock, nauseous, dizzy, unable to muster the witty, sarcastic, articulate rejoinder he was accustomed to making. He was instantly aware of the recent spate of gay bashing in San Francisco and that many of these incidents had escalated from verbal encounters. Even hours later when the shock subsided and his facility with words returned, he realized that any response was inadequate to counter the hundreds of years of societal defamation that one word—"faggot"—carried with it. Like the word "nigger" and unlike the word "liar," it is not sufficient to deny the truth of the word's application, to say, "I am not a faggot." One must deny the truth of the word's meaning, a meaning shouted from the rooftops by the rest of the world a million times a day. The complex response "Yes, I am a member of the group you despise and the degraded meaning of the word you use is one that I reject" is not effective in a subway encounter. Although there are many of us who constantly and in myriad ways seek to counter the lie spoken in the meaning of hateful words like "nigger" and "faggot," it is a nearly impossible burden to bear when one is ambushed by a sudden, face-to-face hate speech assault.

But there was another part of my discussion with Michael that is equally instructive. I asked if he could remember a situation when he had been verbally attacked with reference to his being a white male. Had he ever been called a "honkey," a "chauvinist pig," or "mick"? (Michael is from a working-class Irish family in Boston.) He said that he had been called some version of all three and that although he found the last one more offensive than the first two, he had not experienced—even in that subordinated role—the same disorienting powerlessness he had experienced when attacked for his membership in the gay community. The question of power, of the context of the power relationships within which speech takes place, and the connection to violence must be considered as we decide how best to foster the freest and fullest dialogue within our communities. Regulation of face-to-face verbal assault in the manner contemplated by the proposed Stanford provision will make room for more speech than it chills. The provision is clearly within the spirit, if not the letter, of existing first amendment doctrine.

The proposed Stanford regulation, and indeed regulations with considerably broader reach, can be justified as necessary to protect a captive
audience from offensive or injurious speech. Courts have held that offensive speech may not be regulated in public forums such as streets and
parks where listeners may avoid the speech by moving on or averting their
eyes,[3] but the regulation of otherwise protected speech has been permitted when the speech invades the privacy of unwilling listeners' homes or
when unwilling listeners cannot avoid the speech.[4] Racist posters, flyers,
and graffiti in dorms, classrooms, bathrooms, and other common living
spaces would fall within the reasoning of these cases. Minority students
should not be required to remain in their rooms to avoid racial assault.
Minimally, they should find a safe haven in their dorms and other common rooms that are a part of their daily routine. I would argue that the
university's responsibility for ensuring these students receive an equal educational opportunity provides a compelling justification for regulations
that ensure them safe passage in all common areas. Black, Latino, Asian,
or Native American students should not have to risk being the target of
racially assaulting speech every time they choose to walk across campus.
The regulation of vilifying speech that cannot be anticipated or avoided
would not preclude announced speeches and rallies where minorities and
their allies would have an opportunity to organize counterdemonstrations
or avoid the speech altogether.

NOTES

1. Interpretation of the Fundamental Standard defining when verbal or nonverbal abuse violates the student conduct code adopted by the Stanford University Student Conduct Legislative Council, March 14, 1990. *SCLC Offers Revised
Reading of Standard, Stanford Daily*, Apr. 4, 1990, §1, col. 4.
   It is important to recognize that this regulation is not content neutral. It prohibits "discriminatory harassment" rather than just plain harassment, and it regu-
lates only discriminatory harassment based on "sex, race, color, handicap, religion,
sexual orientation, and national and ethnic origin." It is arguably viewpoint neutral with respect to these categories, although its reference to "words . . . that, by
virtue of their form, are commonly understood to convey direct and visceral hatred
or contempt" probably means that there will be many more epithets that refer to
subordinated groups than words that refer to superordinate groups covered by the
regulation.
2. Chaplinsky v. New Hampshire, 315 U.S. 568, 572 (1942).
3. *See* Cohen v. California, 403 U.S. 15, 21 (1971) (holding that the state
could not excise, as offensive conduct, particular epithets from public discourse);
Erznoznik v. City of Jacksonville, 433 U.S. 205, 209 (1975) (overturning a city
ordinance that deterred drive-in theaters from showing movies containing nudity).
4. *See* Kovacks v. Cooper, 336 U.S. 77, 86 (1949) (right to free speech not
abridged by city ordinance outlawing use of sound trucks on city streets); Federal
Communications Comm'n v. Pacifica Found., 438 U.S. 726, 748 (1978) (limited

first amendment protection of broadcasting that extends into privacy of home); Rowan v. United States Post Office Dep't, 397 U.S. 728, 736 (1970) (unwilling recipient of sexually arousing material had right to instruct Postmaster General to cease mailings to protect recipient from unwanted communication of "ideas").

STUDY QUESTIONS

1. Do you find any problems with the Stanford code?
2. Are racist ideas more acceptable than racist epithets?
3. Should slurs against men and majorities be treated the same as slurs against women and minorities?
4. Should a university allow lecturers on campus who use racist speech?

Campus Speech Restrictions

Martin P. Golding

The Stanford code is tightly drafted, and it represents a noble effort on Professor Grey's part to protect campus speech to the extent it is compatible with the aim of eliminating discriminatory harassment. The code is *almost*, but not quite, acceptable to me. For even a tightly drafted code can have a chilling effect on speech.

Part of the reason I do not find it entirely acceptable is expressed in the Duke University Law School's "Rules, Policies, and Procedures":

When students have allowed standards of civility to slip seriously in ways repeatedly hurtful to others entitled to share the campus equally with themselves the response at some universities to such recurrently offensive activities has been more rules. Such requests have been made to us to make more rules, but this is not an undertaking welcomed by us [the law school's administration] or by the faculty. We want you to know why this is so.

Regulation of student expression, whether of particular viewpoints, or even of the circumstances or manner of their utterance, is a very tricky undertaking. Such rules often convey their own intolerance without meaning to do so. However artfully drawn, they can chill a good deal of provocative expression that is altogether desirable, especially within a lively professional school. They also convey the message that those who carry unpopular messages are being

Originally published in Martin P. Golding, *Free Speech on Campus*, pp. 60–64, 69, 2000, Rowman & Littlefield. Reprinted by permission of Rowman & Littlefield.

told to be quiet. The business to "judicialize" academic life and our relationships is often also a sign of mutual failure to operate within the common sense notions discussed earlier [good judgment, self-restraint, and civility].[1]

The crucial sentences occur in the second paragraph: "Such rules often convey their own intolerance without meaning to do so. However artfully drawn, they can chill a good deal of provocative expression that is altogether desirable. . . ."

It seems to me that a prohibition on some forms of racist or sexist speech may easily be seen as a general viewpoint-based restriction; certain speech is condoned and other speech is proscribed. It conveys the broader message that speech that doesn't fit in with the official, underlying viewpoint is better not spoken.

Aside from this general concern, to which I shall return, there are other difficulties. Exactly what does Stanford's phrase (4c), "commonly understood to convey direct and visceral hatred or contempt for human beings on the basis of their sex, race," etc., cover? Would a black calling a white a racist offend against the code? Or is this an instance of "victim's privilege"? . . .

Consider the infamous "water buffalo" affair at the University of Pennsylvania, which stretched out over a number of months. On the night of January 13, 1993, a group of women from a black sorority were very loudly singing, chanting, and stomping under Eden Jacobowitz's dormitory window. He was working on a paper for a course. Jacobowitz shouted out, "Please be quiet." The noise continued and he shouted out, "Shut up, you water buffalo." Jacobowitz was then charged with a violation of Penn's policy on racial harassment. While Penn's policy is not identical to Stanford's, it is close to it. Our question is whether Stanford's provision covers this case. It shouldn't, but one doesn't really know.[2]

The Stanford policy is not problem free for people unfairly *charged* with the offense of discriminatory harassment by vilification. There are numerous reports of people, students and faculty, who have been perceived to vilify or harass someone and who were, as a result, put through the wringer. Sometimes they were vindicated in the end, but often the proceedings ended inconclusively, and they ended up being stigmatized as racists, sexists, and so on.[3] Perhaps even more than in the public realm, merely being accused of a "speech offense" on campus can be quite serious.

A good noncampus example of the problem occurred in January 1999 in Washington, D.C. David Howard, the mayoral ombudsman, who is white, said the following at a budget meeting with two coworkers, one of whom was black: "I will have to be niggardly with this fund because it's not going to be a lot of money." The black coworker became incensed;

Howard apologized and submitted his resignation, which was quickly accepted by the mayor. The word "niggardly," however, has no connection to the racial slur, which entered English about 1700, from the Latin "niger," or "black." According to etymologists the word "niggardly" goes back to the fourteenth-century Scandinavian term "niggard," meaning "miser," and some speculate that it goes back earlier to a Middle English word. Howard said that he learned the word for his S.A.T. test in high school. His problem was that the word *sounded* like the slur.[4] The indignation industry seems to have been at work here, and many people thought that the mayor did right to accept Howard's resignation immediately rather than rise to his defense; Howard should have watched his language.

But what protection does the Fundamental Standard Interpretation offer someone who is accused of using a word that *sounds* like a term "commonly understood to convey direct and visceral hatred or contempt for human beings on the basis of their sex, race," etc.? It might be answered that it is, first of all, unlikely that such an accusation will be made. After all, what we do want to get at are the egregious cases of verbal harassment, and how else get at them except with a speech code? But what about a male's deliberately calling a female student a "witch" rather than a "bitch," or a white calling a black a "chigger" rather than a "nigger"? Does that get him off the hook? Or are these terms the "equivalent" of an epithet? . . .

I don't mean to be nitpicking here; no code is perfect, and all codes need to be interpreted. However, in order to determine whether some given term has been used as the equivalent of an epithet, we would have to look at the intention of the speaker. But it is precisely this kind of inquiry, once we go beyond a definite list of words, that leads to the fear that "however artfully drawn, [codes] can chill a good deal of provocative expression that is altogether desirable," and "that those who carry unpopular messages are being told to be quiet," as the Duke Rules put it.

Now, one does hope that the Stanford community is knowledgeable enough to make proper distinctions, that enforcement of the policy will be intelligent, and that problem cases, if they arise, will be handled sagaciously. But the opportunity for misunderstanding is present, unfortunately, even for a code that is as finely drawn as Stanford's, and how much more so for more loosely formulated codes! There is little protection afforded by any code against overzealous administrators.

Granted, the Interpretation does require that the speaker "*intended* to insult or stigmatize," in order to hold him or her guilty of harassment by vilification. In contrast to some other campus speech codes, strict liability is rejected. But intent is difficult to prove. More than likely, though, it is the accused who will be put in the difficult position of establishing that he had no such intent.[5] As a number of cases show, and as cases told to me by those involved indicate, a presumption of innocence does not always hold and the disciplinary procedures are not always fair.[56] And even if the accused is found innocent, or the charges are eventually dropped, he will have gone through a terrible ordeal. . . .

Slurs, epithets, and vulgarity—no matter to whom they may be directed, and whether or not face-to-face—should be condemned, and maintaining a positive message of civility is important. But more crucial than the outlawing of single words—which is *almost* acceptable to me—is the general effect on the expression of ideas.

What, then, about *ideas* that stigmatize a group? Ideas, too, can "convey direct and visceral hatred or contempt," for instance, the idea that blacks are intellectually inferior to others. Plainly, a statement to this effect, with or without a gutter epithet, can be as wounding as racial slurs alone. If one wants to penalize "wounding words" it makes no sense to single out gutter epithets, as the African American academic Henry Louis Gates says.

Professor Grey takes up this question. Imagine, he says, this scenario:

[A] student's habit of loudly proclaiming his admiration for *The Bell Curve* around the dormitory becomes the target of protest by African-American students, who say it is aimed at (and certainly has the effect of) making them feel unwelcome in the university and making it more difficult to do their work. He refuses to stop, and the dispute gets into the campus newspaper, which quotes the offending student as saying that he has no intention of letting "a bunch of affirmative action morons" silence him, and that he hopes "what I'm saying will get some of them to think about whether they are really qualified to be here. . . ."

Under the Stanford policy that was invalidated, the result would be clear: the white student could be freely criticized, but he would not be in violation of University disciplinary standards. No racial epithet or its equivalent has been addressed to a targeted individual.[7]

Grey's claim is reassuring for those who want controversial ideas to be protected, although his remarks make it plain that the Stanford policy doesn't get to the heart of forestalling "wounded identity." Why shouldn't the student's assertions, "wounding words," after all, be regarded as the equivalent of a racial epithet? True, there was no targeted individual in Grey's example, but we can imagine a case in which there is such a one. . . .

I conclude, so far, that campus speech codes, even one as good as Stanford's, have serious formulation and enforcement problems. . . . I am not happy with this result, though. In any event, demeaning assertions should be combated by counterargument, not by punitive sanctions.

There is little doubt, on the other side, that racist speech may have a distorting effect on the operation of the marketplace of ideas. . . . However, it is not only racist speech that distorts the market. And the attempt to police all speech that might adversely affect the marketplace of ideas would be infeasible and intolerable.

I further admit that the face-to-face use of fighting words and racial slurs, in particular, may have a "silencing" effect on their recipient that impedes free trade in ideas, which trade is the work of the university, because they can impede discussion. ("More speech" will not always immediately work against a targeted attack.) This is true generally of uncivil discourse. Of course, many academic exchanges are quite heated, and the line is sometimes crossed. Again, though, it is the role of teachers to educate students on what the boundaries are and to show them by example that civil debate promotes the search for truth.

NOTES

1. Duke University Law School's "Rules, Policies, and Procedures," www.law.duke.edu/general/info/s11.html#policy11-5 (Dean's Statement on Freedom of Expression in the Law School).

2. See the quotation from Grey, at n. 7 ("a racial epithet or its *equivalent*"). The water buffalo incident is described in detail in A. C. Kors and H. A. Silvergate, *The Shadow University: The Betrayal of Liberty on America's Campuses* (New York: Free Press, 1998), 9–33. The Penn code is quoted at p. 11. The charges generated a body of scholarship on whether "water buffalo" is a racial epithet.

3. See, e.g., the case of Cornell Professor James Maas at the Web site of the Center for Individual Rights, www.wdn.com/cir/maas.htm. Cornell maintained a secret file on his alleged harassment, to which Maas was not given access. See, also, a lengthy account in Craig L. Hymowitz, "The Locked Box," *Heterodoxy* (May 1995), beginning on p. 1. Of course, I am in no position to vouch for the complete accuracy of these accounts.

4. See *New York Times*, January 29, 1999, A8 ("Race Mix-Up Raises Havoc for Capital"). A similar incident is reported from Chicago. While presenting a bill to a Jewish patient, a dentist said, "Don't be afraid of chewing down on it." At his two-day hearing before the city human rights committee, the dentist kept lamely trying to argue that he was talking about the patient's new filling, not about a bargaining trait often attributed to Jews by their detractors. *Herald Sun* (Durham, N.C.), February 3, 1999, A10.

5. "Stigmatize" is a vague term and I am not clear on its scope. Someone who uses a "fighting word," as understood in the Interpretation, is likely to have the burden of showing lack of intent to stigmatize.

6. See Kors and Silvergare, and Nat Hentoff, *Free Speech for Me—But Not for Thee* (New York: HarperCollins, 1992), passim.

7. Thomas C. Grey, "How to Write a Speech Code Without Really Trying: Reflections on the Stanford Experience," 29 *U.C. Davis L. Rev.* 924 (1996). Professor Grey is at this point arguing that the Stanford code is more protective of free speech than an alternative harassment code that very likely would have been upheld, but which would have had the flaw of the potentially chilling vagueness of

hostile-environment discrimination. . . . Richard J. Hernstein and Charles Murray, *The Bell Curve: Intelligence and Class in American Life* (New York: Free Press, 1994) is the subject of much debate.

STUDY QUESTIONS

1. Does a speech code imply that some points of view are better unspoken?
2. Should a university permit the expression of ideas that stigmatize a group?
3. How do you assess the "water buffalo" affair?
4. Should a university discipline any person who calls another a "moron"?

III

SEXUAL HARASSMENT

Faculty members ought to care about the progress of each student, but they should also remain able to deliberate, judge, and act without thought of personal interest. Even the appearance of partiality is likely to impair the learning process by damaging an instructor's credibility, causing students to doubt that standards are being applied fairly.

Thus every teacher should be scrupulous in ensuring that no student receives, or even appears to receive, preferential treatment. An obvious implication of this principle of equal consideration is that romance between teacher and student is inappropriate.

Nancy Tuana argues that students can be coerced into sexual activity under circumstances in which no threats are made. Leslie Francis Pickering defends a ban on even consensual faculty-student relationships so long as the student is under the direct supervision of the professor. In her view such relationships distract from teaching, learning, and research; threaten equality of educational opportunity; and too often proceed without informed consent.

5

Sexual Harassment:
Offers and Coercion

Nancy Tuana

Sexual harassment has as its central meaning the coercion of sexual activity. Charges of sexual harassment are most generally raised when an employee or student feels that his or her employer, supervisor, or instructor has used his or her institutional authority to coerce sexual favors. However, current analysis of coercion rejects the possibility of offers being coercive. Such analysis thus calls into question the status of attempts to procure sexual favors by offers of rewards. Are we to classify such actions as cases of sexual harassment?

The Case against Coercive Offers

The main attack on the possibility of coercive offers was developed by Michael Bayles who argued that only actions that involve threats can be viewed as coercive. By claiming that offers do not involve threats, he was able to conclude that offers cannot be coercive. His attempt to illustrate this position is directly applicable to the issue of sexual harassment. In his rejection of Virginia Held's position that inducements can be coercive, Bayles offers the following example to illustrate his position:

> Assume there is a mediocre woman graduate student who would not receive an assistantship. Suppose the department chairman offers her one if she goes to bed with him, and she does so. In what sense has the graduate student acted against her will? She apparently preferred

Originally published as "Sexual Harassment in Academe," *College Teaching* 1983:33; pp. 53–63. Reprinted by permission of Taylor & Francis Ltd.

having an assistantship and sleeping with the chairman to not sleeping with him and not having an assistantship. So it would appear that she did what she wanted in the situation. Held may mean that the woman acted against her will in that she would rather have had the assistantship and not slept with the chairman; that is, there was a consequence of her choice which she found undesirable. But the fact that a choice has an undesirable consequence does not make it against one's will. One may prefer to have clean teeth without having to brush them; nonetheless, one is not acting against one's will when one brushes them.

From this analysis, Bayles would have us conclude that offers to students by instructors (or by extrapolation, to employees by employers) do not involve sexual harassment if sexual harassment is viewed as involving coercion. In fact, Bayles would have us believe that in such situations, students and employees experience no impairment of their freedom of choice.

Such an analysis of offers or rewards in return for sexual favors does not fit well with the experiences of students and employees who have been in such situations. A classification of the results of a 1978 study of sexual harassment at the University of California at Berkeley, in which students who felt that they had been harassed were asked to describe that harassment, includes sexual bribery as one of the self-reported types of sexual harassment. A number of students, in reporting the events they perceived to constitute harassment, described grade offers in exchange for affairs. A survey conducted at the University of California at Santa Barbara in 1981, which consisted of student reactions to a series of vignettes, revealed that the inclusion, within such a vignette, of the instructor indicating that sexual cooperation would improve the student's grade dramatically, increased the sexual harassment rating of that vignette. In fact, the survey revealed that the addition of sexual bribery to a vignette increased the sexual harassment rating of a vignette more that did the addition of a warning by the instructor that the student's success in the class could be affected if he or she did not consent to sexual activity with the instructor.

Thus we see a clear tension between philosophical analyses that reject the possibility of coercive offers and the experiences of students and employees. In order to reconcile the tension between these two positions, it would be helpful to look at the standard analysis of coercion.

THE STANDARD ANALYSIS OF COERCION

According to the accepted analysis of coercion, there are six criteria that must be satisfied to classify an action as coercive. The analysis of a person, X, having coerced another person, Y, to do an action, A, would be the following:

1. X intends that Y do A
2. X further intends to harm Y if Y does not do A
3. X threatens Y with harm if Y does not do A
4. Y does A
5. Y would have done otherwise had Y so chosen
6. Y would have chosen otherwise had Y not been threatened by X.

Given this analysis of coercion, it becomes clear why one might reject the possibility of offers being coercive. If we examine the illustration given above, we can see that Bayles is claiming that the offer merely makes the action of sex with the chair more desirable or less undesirable to the student than it had been prior to the offer, or makes available a choice not previously available to the student. Such an offer then, according to this analysis, presents no harm to the recipient. It would seem to follow from this that if in order for there to be coercion, there must be a person (or group of people) who threatens to harm the coerced individual and intends to so harm her or him, then it would appear that offers could not be coercive. In order for an action to be threatening, that act must make a victim's choice situation less desirable or more undesirable, and this is done either by adding some undesirable consequence to, or removing a desirable consequence from, one of the victim's alternative choices, which will result in harm to him or her if he or she refuses to act as is desired. Bayles claims that the offer made by the chair made the student's choice situation more desirable by providing her the option of an assistantship that would not otherwise have been available. If sexual harassment is defined as involving coercion, one could use the analysis above to deny that solicitation of sexual favors by promise of rewards falls under the category of sexual harassment.

It is my contention that the attempt to procure sexual contact through the promise of rewards can be and often is coercive when the person who makes the offer is in a position of authority over the person to whom he or she makes the offer. I believe that the above illustration could be classified as coercive even though there is no threat to harm the student and the chair has no intention of harming the student should she refuse. I will therefore show that the standard analysis of coercion is not complete, for it omits a very important and common type of coercion.

OFFERS AND COERCION

Let us look again at the above illustration of solicitation of sexual favors. Bayles spends no time considering the context in which the offer was made nor does he consider the beliefs or reactions of the student to whom the offer was made. I will show that this is a significant omission that, when rectified, will demonstrate the possibility of coercive offers.

In this case the person who has made the offer is the chairperson of the department. The chairperson of this department has a variety of powers, including the ability to offer or refuse assistantships. Given typical department politics it would be fair to assume that the chairperson also has the power to make other very important decisions that could affect the career of this graduate student, such as assigning the members of her dissertation committee, deciding on the jobs for which she will receive a departmental recommendation, and the like. In other words, the chair has the power to make it very difficult for this student to receive her degree and to succeed in her career. We have to add to this the fact that this graduate student is "mediocre." What this means is that if the chairperson wishes to, he would have a less difficult time getting this student dropped out of the program than he would if she had been a star student. Given her record, there are probably no instructors who are willing to support her case should she complain, for it would be difficult to make a case for her given her less than excellent record. Also, as all of us who have been a part of academia know, the decisions of retention or expulsion in borderline cases are difficult and anything but objective. It would be very easy for the chairperson of a department to recommend against retention when the student's record is reviewed, using her mediocre performance as the sole reason for this recommendation, and probably not raise anyone's suspicions in so doing. Had the student an excellent record it would be more difficult for the chairperson to recommend against retention without casting suspicion on his motives. But given her mediocre record, should she protest such an action or claim that it was the result of her refusal to grant sexual favors, most people would tend to discredit her complaint as "sour grapes." Now let us assume that the student believes all of this.

In addition to the above beliefs about the power of the chairperson of one's department, given that the chairperson has offered this student a position better than she deserves in return for sexual favors, she now knows that the chairperson of her department feels neither morally nor legally obliged to promote fairly. The very fact that the chairperson was willing to give her a position for which she did not qualify is good reason to believe that he might be the type of person who would be willing to abuse a student who displeases him. So the student now knows that the chairperson is the type of person who is willing to misuse his power to obtain what he wants, and thus has good reason to believe that this misuse of power might extend to penalizing a student who gets in the way of his wants.

An additional aspect of this situation that must be taken into consideration is the nature of the action being requested by the chair and the social attitudes surrounding such an action. We live in a culture in which people are often very sensitive about another person's response to their request for sexual contact. People generally have very fragile egos concerning rejections of sexual advances. A very common response to a refusal of a sexual proposition is to feel hurt and upset. Furthermore, many people who experience such hurt then develop the desire to retaliate. The graduate student will be well aware of this and will probably start thinking about all the instances she has heard of in which instructors retaliated against students who refused their sexual advances by misusing their authority to hurt the student.

So the graduate student accepts the chairperson's offer. Notice that Bayles' explanation is that she did so because "she apparently preferred having an assistantship and sleeping with the chairman to not sleeping with him and not having an assistantship." If that was all there was to the situation (the student was quite willing to have sex with the chairperson in order to acquire the assistantship), then I would be willing to say that there was no coercion and that the situation involved no sexual harassment, though I would want to fault the chairperson for immoral and unprofessional conduct. But it is not acceptable to assume that this explanation will fit all cases. I would like to suggest another plausible scenario, which happens quite frequently, which does involve coercion and should be classified as sexual harassment.

Given the context of the situation as I have spelled it out in the above paragraphs, the student finds herself in a situation where she is very vulnerable to being harmed by the chairperson, well knowing that there is a very good chance that if she rejects his proposition, he will be upset enough to want to hurt her in turn. The student has no desire to have any sexual contact with the chairperson, and she does not think that getting the assistantship is a good reason for having the sexual contact. However, being aware of the power of the chairperson and the vulnerability of her position in the department, she fears that a refusal of the offer will upset and anger the chairperson, making him want to retaliate. Furthermore, she believes that such retaliation could result in her being failed out of the program, thus ending her hopes of an academic career. Because of her fear of such harm, the student accepts the offer.

If we were to analyze this case based on the above model, where X is the chair, Y the student, and A the act of sexual involvement, the result would be the following:

1. X intends that Y do A
2. Y does A
3. Y would have done otherwise had Y so chosen
4. Y would have done otherwise had he or she not feared that Y would harm him or her if he or she did not do A.

It is important to notice that this analysis is significantly different from the standard analysis of coercion. There is no initial intention to harm on the chairperson's part, nor does the student think that the chair has the intention to harm her when the chair makes the offer. Also there is no threat made by the chairperson, nor does the student think that the chairperson has threatened her. One cannot thus object that the case that I am describing is a case of a mixed offer and threat where the student is offered an inducement for submitting to the sexual involvement, and threatened with a harm if she refuses. I have no doubt that such situations do occur, but such an analysis does not fit the above situation in that it is not the case, nor does the student believe that it is the case, that the chair has the *intention* to threaten the student with harm, or to harm the student should she refuse *when the offer is made.*

Despite the absence of a threat or any intention to harm on the part of the chair, what makes this action coercive and thus a case of sexual harassment is that the student's choice situation is made less desirable or more undesirable because of her fear of harm if she refuses to act as is desired. What is significantly different about this case, and what the standard analysis of coercion misses completely, is that a person can reasonably believe that her refusal of an offer, like the one above, would result in a situation in which she would be harmed. As I am describing it, the above situation is one in which the student believes that there is a very high probability that her rejection of the offer will *cause* the chairman to have the desire to harm her. So the situation is one in which the threat of harm that the student fears is not made prior to or at the time of the offer, but will *come into existence* as a result of her refusal. One thing that is overlooked on the standard analysis of coercion is a person's reaction to having his or her offer rejected. Some offers are so loaded that a refusal may cause a desire to retaliate. In the words of a lawyer who was a junior member of a law firm, regarding the sexual proposition of one of the senior members of that firm:

> . . . I also recognized I was in a compromising and extremely dangerous position. I definitely didn't want to have an affair with Mr. Scott . . . however, Mr. Scott's ego was on the line. Terribly frightened of offending him and possibly ruining my chances for success in the firm, I knew I was treading on thin ice . . . Mr. Scott had a reputation for extreme ruthlessness when crossed.

What my depiction of the "offer" scenario illustrates is that in certain situations, a student's situation after an offer can be worse than it was before the offer. Accounts that consider offers noncoercive deny that even unwelcome offers are coercive, ". . . for one would not have done or chosen otherwise had they not been made. Nor are they turned into threats, for they do not make any of the alternative choices less desirable or more un-desirable." I have, on the contrary, shown that this need not be the case. In the present situation, if the student consents to a sexual involvement in order to avoid the harm in which she thinks a refusal will result, *then the offer does modify her choice.* The offer also makes alternative choices less desirable, for the student reasonably believes that the choice of rejecting the offer will result in harm that she would not have experienced had the offer never been made. Hence, I conclude that the above described situation is an offer situation involving coercion, and is the type of situation that we would want to classify as sexual harassment.

What I have shown is that the standard analysis of coercion is inad-equate in that it omits sufficient reference to the context, the situation in which the action is performed. Once this omission is remedied, it can be shown that offers can be coercive whenever the background context is such that it is reasonable for the victim to believe that her refusal to accept the offer will result in harm.

STUDY QUESTIONS

1. Are inducements less coercive than threats?
2. Do you accept Tuana's four-criteria analysis of coercion?
3. If a student seeks a romance with an instructor, how should the instruc-tor respond?
4. Could an instructor be the victim of sexual harassment by a student?

6

Consensual Sex on Campus

Leslie Pickering Francis

Joan is a graduate student at a top-tier university in her field. She is about to take her comprehensives and begin work on a cutting-edge dissertation. She's highly regarded by the faculty in her department: their rising star. The department is recruiting a new faculty member in her field; the top candidate is a man who, the professional gossip goes, just has been unfairly denied tenure at unquestionably the best department in the country. Joan meets the candidate during the interviews and they hit it off, both intellectually and socially. Joan learns that he is in the process of a painful divorce; he is sad because the tenure denial and move prevent him from remaining as involved in the lives of his two young children. Joan looks forward eagerly to his arrival and to her ability to work with him. This story has many beginnings, but it also has many endings.

Ending One. The candidate arrives on campus and becomes Joan's dissertation chair. Although it's clear that under other circumstances they might have become romantically involved, it remains unspoken between them that this would not be a good idea because of their professional relationship. Her chair publishes a brilliant book and becomes the object of much professional attention. When Joan goes on the job market, however, she finds herself fighting the suspicion that she and her chair have been having an affair, which is the reason she is so highly regarded by her depart-

Originally published in *Sexual Harassment as an Ethical Issue in Academic Life*, pp. 99–112, 263, 2000, Rowman & Littlefield. Reprinted by permission of Rowman & Littlefield.

ment. The suspicions are based on what has by now become professional gossip that her chair's departure from his first institution was clouded by an affair with a student. Joan gets a series of temporary jobs and eventually leaves the field. (Or Joan gets a job at a small school too far away to have heard the professional gossip. Or, Joan gets a job at another research university, at a department willing to ignore the gossip. . . .)

Ending Two. Joan and her professor fall in love and are married within six months after his arrival on campus. At first, they experience domestic bliss; Joan works excitedly on her dissertation, gives department dinner parties, and enjoys her status as almost-peer. Their mutual interest in the field and the particular topics on which they are working give the pair subjects for endless hours of conversation. The professor publishes a brilliant book that makes him famous; although no one else knows this, Joan is the author of at least half the book. One child later, Joan finishes her dissertation and reconsiders her professional future. Her institution does not hire its own graduates and her husband does not want to move. After three years of teaching on a temporary basis for the university's extension program, Joan goes to law school. (Or Joan takes a job at the community college down the road. Or Joan goes on the job market, receives the job of her dreams, and she and her husband commute between universities one thousand miles apart. Or another top research university in the field offers them both "real" jobs, Joan on tenure track and her husband with tenure, and they live happily ever after. . . .)

Ending Three. Joan and her professor begin a passionate affair. At first it is wonderful. Joan makes great progress on her dissertation. Then the affair goes sour. The professor becomes very critical of Joan's work. It's hard to tell which happened first, the end of the affair or the dissatisfaction with Joan's work. Joan herself begins to lose confidence in her abilities. Joan seeks a replacement as her dissertation chair, and finds someone who is interested in the area but not an expert. At first, things improve and Joan believes she is beginning to do good work again. Then the new chair becomes very critical of her work, and Joan suspects it is because of derogatory remarks by Joan's first chair. Joan eventually is told that it is unlikely she will be able to complete a dissertation that meets the standards of her department. (Or after the relationship sours, Joan files a complaint of sexual harassment with the university's office of equal opportunity. The complaint charges that the relationship had been unwelcome from the beginning, that Joan had felt pressured to enter into it and had been afraid that the professor would refuse to work with her unless she gave into his demands. The complaint is investigated but found to have no merit because the relationship was voluntary and the EEOC office defers to the judgment of departments about the academic qualifications of their students. Or the complaint is investigated and the story comes out that the reason the professor was not given tenure at his former institution is that he had been notorious for having sex with graduate students. Joan is vindicated, but with a reputation as a troublemaker has great difficulty finding a job in the field. . . .)

These stories are all true enough, based on composites of the lives of people I have known, the backgrounds of many academic marriages, and the sad stories of failed careers and acrimonious litigation. What do they show about sexual relationships between faculty and students from varying moral points of view? What do they show about other sexual relations on campus: faculty-staff relations, faculty-faculty relations, staff-student relations, or student-student relations? Viewpoints here range from the position that Joan and the professor are both adults with rights to enter into relationships of their own choosing, to the position that all faculty-student relationships and many other relationships should be prohibited because of the power imbalance and opportunity for exploitation they embody. In this chapter, I defend the moderate view that sexual relationships within universities should be prohibited when one of the parties has direct supervisory authority over the other and should be strongly discouraged when there are significant power imbalances between the two. Moreover, the overt expression of consensual sexual relationships on campus—fondling in the library or intercourse in the dorm, for example—should not be treated as special but should follow other campus policies, such as those involving gender harassment or social life in dormitories.

Consensual Relations: The Case for a Permissive Policy

. . . [Sexual] assaults, threats, and even offers are wrong because they interfere with choice about important, intimate relationships. A policy that seriously limited consensual sexual relationships on campus also would interfere significantly with the liberty to enter into relationships. How, then, could such a policy be defended in the context of a commitment to autonomy about intimate relationships? Joan and her professor, for example, have the moral and the legal right to their intimate associations.[1] As the policy from Wellesley College—interestingly enough, an undergraduate institution—puts it: "When there is no supervisory relation between students, or between faculty members; or between faculty and staff members, or between staff members—any recommendations by the College concerning sexual relations would constitute an intolerable invasion of privacy." . . . Privacy and associational liberty are the core of the argument for a permissive policy about sexual relationships on campus, but several other moral considerations also lend support to such a policy.

A corollary of the value of autonomy is opposition to paternalism. The critique of consensual sexual relationships between professionals and those who receive their services typically invokes paternalism, as demonstrated in the following way. The professional has experience and skills not possessed by those seeking his services: patients or clients. He is in a position of trust; they are in a position of reliance and dependency, often exacerbated by the life events—an illness, a divorce—that led them to seek professional services in the first place. The best way to protect vulnerable clients from abusive professionals is a prophylactic ban on sexual relationships, even apparently consensual relationships. This critique is, quite frankly, paternalistic in its assumptions about the recipients of professional services. . . . My fictitious graduate student, Joan, for example, might argue that a ban on professor-student relationships is an insult to her independence; she is perfectly able to make decisions about her personal relationships without any help from authoritarian protectionism. She might add that to the extent that such bans are seen as protecting her from her professors, rather than her professors from her, they are particularly demeaning to her.

A further, related concern about any bans on consensual relationships on campus is that they affect women unequally. . . . If faculty demographics are largely male and graduate-student populations increasingly female, bans may preclude women students from a particularly desirable source of satisfying relationships. Or they may force women already in relationships to choose schooling at a different institution or in a different field. At the very least, a ban on consensual relationships between faculty and the students they supervise would force Joan to a hard choice: either seeking a new, possibly less intellectually appropriate advisor or sacrificing the relationship.

These considerations make the case for a permissive policy a very powerful one. It is supported by respect for the autonomy and the equality of women in the academic community. Why, then, have the calls for bans on consensual relationships, in the academy and in other professional relationships, been so persistent and so increasingly accepted? Are any of the arguments powerful enough to override the case for permissiveness?

The insistence of these questions can be understood by viewing the problem of whether consensual relations are sexual harassment as a problem of ethics under less than ideal circumstances. In *A Theory of Justice*, published nearly thirty years ago, John Rawls distinguished between ideal theory and partial compliance theory.[2] Rawls's point was that the principles of justice that apply under nonideal circumstances might differ from those that apply under ideal circumstances. Rawls's own view of ideal justice was that basic liberties, when they can be exercised effectively, take priority over the principle of equal basic opportunity. The argument for a permissive policy then could be viewed as a reflection of the priority of a basic liberty, the liberty to enter into intimate, consensual relationships. Critics of such a permissive policy, by contrast, might argue that in a less than ideal world, basic liberties do not take priority over values such as equality of educational opportunity.

In answering the ethical questions about consensual relationships in a university setting, it also is important to bear in mind the wide variety of such possible relationships on campus: faculty-student, faculty-staff, faculty-faculty, student-student, staff-staff, and staff-student. Yet another set of permutations appears if visitors are considered part of the university community: alumni, donors, guest speakers, patients at university hospitals or clinics, sports fans, theatergoers, and casual visitors. These permutations can be doubled if they are classified by the initiator of the relationship: faculty-student or student-faculty, for example. An additional complication is that groups on campus may not fit neatly into one or another of these categories. Should all students be classified together, the most senior of graduate students with the entering freshman, the oldest of nontraditional students with the early-entry sixteen-year-old? Are professionals in training programs, such as post-docs or medical residents, more like students or like faculty? What about staff members who are also students, possibly part-time students? What about alumni who return to campus for continuing education courses? What about teaching or laboratory assistants who are graduate students? Are instructors and research and part-time faculty like regular faculty? These permutations alone suggest powerfully that a "one size fits all" policy cannot be defended for consensual relations on campus and as well that different policies may be appropriate for universities that serve very different populations. With all of these differences in mind, I turn now to the reasons offered in support of restricting at least some types of sexual relations on campus. Although questioning the adequacy of consent is the predominant reason offered for regulating relationships, it does smack of paternalism. I begin, therefore, with two other concerns: quality of education and equality of opportunity. In assessing each of these concerns, my goal will be to see whether they are of sufficient moral importance to override the general argument for a permissive policy just presented.

CONSENSUAL SEXUAL RELATIONSHIPS AND EDUCATIONAL QUALITY

The University of Iowa's consensual relationship policy begins with the observation that "the University's educational mission is promoted by professionalism in faculty-student relationships. Professionalism is fostered by an atmosphere of mutual trust and respect." The Iowa policy continues by linking the lack of professionalism to the abuse of power and failure of genuine consent, but educational aspects of the lack of professionalism also are important.

The first problem of consensual sexual relationships is distraction from teaching, learning, and research. Such distraction may affect the parties to the relationship and those who observe it. Any student who has sat next to other students fondling each other in class may recognize the difficulties such behavior poses for the overall success of the class. Even faculty may be distracted by the side show. (I once tried to lecture to a class when two students, sitting in the center of the front row, were quite obviously fondling each others' genitals. I didn't know whether it would be more distracting to try to ignore the situation or to ask them to desist. I tried to conduct the class as though nothing were happening, but I am certain that it was one of my less successful efforts.) The atmosphere in a research laboratory can deteriorate quickly when a major source of interest is figuring out who matches up sexually with whom. These distractions are manifest even when the relationships in question are entirely consensual and harmonious—in fact, too amorous, at least if they spill over actively in more serious contexts such as the laboratory. And imagine the intrigue that might follow if there were competitors for relationships among members of the same small group such as members of the same lab group.

Such problems in mixing the personal and the professional are commonplace, both within and without the university. Their effects are manifest, whatever the power levels of the involved parties: An overt sexual relationship between two students in a class can affect significantly both what they and what others learn. The effects are exacerbated, moreover, as the context becomes more intimate. An overt sexual relationship between two students in a small seminar or in an intense laboratory setting could be more distracting than a relationship among two students in a large lecture class. Ironically, because smaller settings within research universities are likely to be the province of more advanced students, these distractions may be more intense when the apparent need for paternalism is less.

These educational effects of romantic relationships also are exacerbated when one of the parties is the centerpiece of the setting: the senior professor in a laboratory or the instructor in a class. Even apart from the conflicts of interest and power imbalances discussed below, romantic interest on the part of a professor might take his or her own mind away from instruction. The student who is the object of affection might find it more difficult to concentrate. Other students also might be distracted if the relationship is in any way obvious or even known. It is more likely that educational quality would suffer in a small discussion section, a seminar, or a smaller research setting than it would in a large lecture. Both small and large settings might be negatively affected when one of the participants occupies a privileged position vis-à-vis the instructor. Behavior that overtly indicates a sexual relationship in an instructional or research setting is problematic because it interferes with core functions of the academy, the development and transmission of knowledge. Overt expression of a sexual relationship in class is inappropriate and should be regulated by the university in the same way that the university should restrict sexualization as a form of gender harassment.

Another difficulty with consensual sexual relations on campus is that a romantic relationship can create a conflict of interest that impairs the quality of professional services. At universities the most likely conflict is with evaluative functions: grading, awarding fellowships or scholarships, or making decisions about tenure or promotion. In other professions, the case for prohibition rests centrally on the nexus between the delivery of the professional services and the sex. Psychiatrists cannot treat their lovers. Dermatologists can, maybe, if the professional relationship is short-lived and does not involve confidences that could be exploited. Divorce lawyers should not become romantically involved with their clients during the divorce proceedings: Romantic involvement gives the lawyer a personal stake in the outcome and may compromise the client's position as well.[3] In education, it seems that there is a nexus between evaluation and affection. The teacher who is also a lover will both want his beloved to do well and be obligated to judge work impartially. He may find it very difficult to demand excellence from his lover—or, bending over backward trying to be fair, he may judge his lover too harshly. In either case, other students may reasonably fear that evaluations of their work are compromised by the professorial confusion. Such conflicts will be worse when evaluative judgments are highly subjective—as many in academe are—and less severe when evaluation is relatively mechanical, such as when processing a machine-scored multiple-choice exam.

Jane Gallop[4] argues that education is sexy. Her point, put in a pedestrian way, is that there is no conflict of interest between sex and learning—indeed, there is a felicitous marriage of the two, in the style of Plato's *Symposium.* Perhaps the reason her joking remark, "My sexual passion is graduate students," fell flat is the evaluative aspect of contemporary higher education. Other graduate students may not have seen the sexiness of the learning when it was not directed to them. And the graduate student who was the immediate target of the remark also may have felt compromised. As a graduate supervisor of one of the students, after all, Gallop was in the position to make extremely important, but subjective, judgments about the quality of her student's work. From the perspective of other students, what Gallop was defending could seem more like massive self-indulgence than like a serious supervisory relationship.

Ironically, the impact of such conflicts of interest is probably the worst at the highest academic levels, where relationships are likely to occur; arguably taking an introductory logic class with machine-graded exams is more like filing routine legal documents or taking off a wart than like psychiatry. Such tasks are more mechanical, and so the difficulties raised by a mixture of personal and professional involvement might be less severe. One of the features of academic life, particularly at the graduate-student level and beyond, however, is the mixture of the personal and the professional. Small departments or laboratories become the centers of social lives. Although, there certainly are advantages to this mixture, the conflicts of interest generated where there are direct supervisory relationships seem highly likely to impair the quality of the professional judgments rendered in important academic matters.

In sum, educational quality can be impaired in several ways by consensual relationships. First, if the relationships are overt enough to be distracting, quality may suffer. Such distractions are most likely in smaller settings or where one of the parties to the relationship is the focus of educational attention, such as a professor. Second, if the relationships create conflicts of interest because of the supervisory or evaluative responsibilities of one of the parties, the relationship has the potential to impair the quality of the resulting judgments that affect all students. In either case, the knowledge functions of the academy are impaired.

EQUALITY OF OPPORTUNITY

The second problem of consensual sexual relations is their potential impact on equality of educational opportunity. These concerns are more likely to be raised by others outside the relationship, but the parties to the relationship also may find their opportunities are affected.

First, overt expression of sexual relationships in educational settings may make others feel uncomfortable, compromising their opportunity to participate in the class, laboratory, or other educational activity. This discomfort may arise whether those romantically involved are faculty members or students. To be sure, some people may be oversensitive to such relationships just as they are when sexuality of any kind is introduced into an educational setting. . . . [T]he treatment of such behavior should be judged by the relevance of the sexuality to the educational topic at hand. It is hard to see what the relevance of an individual sexual relationship would be to a classroom or research setting. Nor are sexual relationships burdened very much by requiring that their overt expression should be confined to more private settings. Thus, making out in class is inappropriate and could be banned.

A harder question is posed by the occurrence of consensual sex in areas on campus that are not primarily academic in function, because the conflicts between the relationship and opportunity may be more or less severe. Consider Jane . . . [who, with her roommate,] had worked out a mutually acceptable accommodation between their sexual lives and their abilities to function as students: Whoever had a guest got the bedroom. In cramped dormitories, it may be difficult to make such arrangements. Moreover, roommates may be assigned relatively randomly and may not share common views about the appropriateness of sex. Suppose, for example, two freshmen share a double room; one falls madly in love and her boyfriend, in effect, moves in. The other roommate both disapproves of the relationship and finds it very difficult to study when the boyfriend is around. The relationship is very important to the one roommate, but the other roommate's learning and grades suffer. This conflict should be treated like many other social conflicts that occur between roommates, over music, television, or even art on the walls. There is nothing special about sex here, unless dormitories are still to be viewed as an area where the enforcement of morality is appropriate. Sex is just one of many behaviors that can affect roommates' comfort, happiness, and, ultimately, educational performance. If there are nonsexual reasons for the university to prohibit aspects of sexual relationships or to otherwise make accommodations between roommates, they should be followed. An example would be one roommate's boyfriend moving in. There are general reasons to limit the length of time guests can stay in dormitories, whether or not the reason for the stay is romantic. For a start, students who pay for a space in a dormitory are paying for their own living space, not for someone else's. One's roommate's young sister—or mother, for that matter—living in a dormitory room intended for two may cause as many problems as a boyfriend. And colleges should make every effort to reassign roommates when incompatible preferences— whether over music or sex—threaten to make life particularly difficult for one of them. Otherwise, the college is not ensuring that all of its students receive maximum educational opportunities. The college should make sure that one roommate does not impose his or her preferences on the other, be it over sex or music, if reassignment proves impossible. Just as roommates should accommodate other differences, so should they accommodate differences in romantic relationships; at the least cooperative, this might mean one roommate gets the room one night until a reasonable time for sleep, the other gets the room the next night, and so on.

The most serious concerns about how someone else's consensual relationship affects the educational opportunities of others occur with evaluation. If one of those being evaluated has a romantic relationship with the evaluator, others may believe that they are unlikely to receive fair evaluations. Even if these perceptions are inaccurate, because the evaluator bends over backward to be fair or because the evaluation is entirely mechanical (as with a machine-graded test), these students' beliefs may still affect their opportunity, because they may not think their hard work will be rewarded and their motivation may suffer as a result. These perceptions are not unreasonable, because there are many ways beyond the actual moment of evaluation in which someone may benefit by a romantic relationship with a superior. My fictional Joan, for example, will have many opportunities to share wisdom about the field with her mentor. To he sure, students vary immensely in their ability to interact with faculty, as employees vary greatly in their ability to seek out and receive mentoring. Such differences are inevitable and probably should be left unregulated because of the importance of mentoring relationships, unless they fall into patterns under which identified groups find it very difficult to receive mentoring (women, for example, finding that men hold all of the powerful positions and will only mentor other men). But the problem here is not inequality in mentoring generally. It is the inequality resulting from the fact that the mentor, in a position of authority, has chosen to enter a romantic relationship with someone he is charged to evaluate. The whole evaluative process may be tarnished as a result.

This effect on the evaluative process, as it is and as it is perceived, also explains why the parties to the relationship cannot decide on their own to take the risks of a compromised evaluation. The concern here is not merely a paternalistic one. Joan might object, "I'm willing to take the risks that my supervisor will bend over backward to be hard on me, because I value the relationship. I'm also willing to take the risk that others in the field will believe I got ahead because I slept with my mentor. That's my choice, to conclude that the relationship means more to me than untarnished professional success." But the choice is not Joan's alone to make. If it becomes known that evaluations in a department take place despite romantic connections between the evaluator and student, observers may raise red flags about other evaluations, affecting the overall confidence in the evaluative judgments and hence compromising the opportunities of all those being evaluated. Equality of opportunity is a second reason for the university to restrict consensual relationships when those involved have positions of direct supervision and evaluation.

IMPAIRED CONSENT

A third issue about consensual relationships on campus is the genuineness of the consent. Many writers argue that either the characteristics of one of the parties to the relationship (a gullible student) or the structure of the relationship (a powerful professor importuning a powerless student) mean that even a clear "yes" is not what it seems. This argument is most likely to be made about faculty-student sex, but it might also be made about other relationships in which there is an imbalance of power. Arguing that such a "yes" does not mean "yes" requires an account of what makes consent genuine. Medical ethics literature contains significant discussion of the nature of genuinely informed consent. There are important analogies between the physician-patient relationship and the professor-student relationship for purposes of analyzing problems with consent: the potential vulnerability of the student or patient, the power structure of the relationship, and even possibly the major life-significance of the choice at issue. The medical analogy therefore, is an appropriate framework for analyzing consent in romantic relationships on campus.

Writers in medical ethics focus on a number of factors in deciding whether consent is genuine: the patient's level of understanding, the patient's preferences, the patient's ability to link understanding with preferences and give an account of why s/he decided as s/he did, possible impairment of the patient's decision-making capacities, and features of the circumstances that might be regarded as coercive.[5]

For consent to be informed, the patient's level of understanding must be such that she can give an account of the options available to her and what their likely consequences would be. A student considering entering a romantic relationship, by analogy, would need to know what her choices are (enter the relationship, do not enter the relationship, or possibly delay entering the relationship). She also would need to understand what the likely consequences are of each of these options: Is the professor married? Is the relationship likely to be a fling or a long-term affair? How will she feel if the relationship ends despite her wishes to continue it? Because it involves difficult-to-predict factors—how will the relationship develop? how will she feel if things go badly from her perspective? what will be the effects on her education?—levels of understanding are likely to be limited, especially for students who have not had previous serious romantic relationships.

A second factor important to informed consent is an understanding of preferences. For patients, this includes an understanding of which kinds of risks are more or less troublesome—for example, risks of loss of mobility or risks of pain. For someone considering a romantic relationship, many kinds of preferences might be relevant: preferences for a long- or short-term relationship, for a relationship that is primarily sexual or that is satisfying in other ways, or for a given balance between a relationship and a career. In some respects, it is unrealistic to expect such preferences to be mapped out clearly in advance: To an important extent, what one wants in life is developed along the way. At the same time, to the extent that a student has less clear preferences about the direction of her life, she is less congruent with the model of rational choice that underlies informed consent in medicine. For young undergraduates particularly, there are difficult questions about what autonomy means in a context of growing up. Colleges are places where people explore relationships, learn to make and reject overtures, try out different partners, and even find mates. To conclude that because her preferences are relatively unformed, an undergraduate does not have the capacity to consent would be to short-circuit much that is socially important on campus. On the other hand, to assume that younger students are rational consumers of romantic relationships in the way they might be rational consumers of products would be too simplistic. A tentative conclusion to draw here is that where students are less mature and have less self-knowledge of likely outcomes or how their preferences will be affected, there is more reason to be cautious about whether other aspects of the relationship also are problematic.

A third concern raised in medical ethics about consent is whether the patient is able to process information to realize satisfaction of his or her preferences. For example, suppose that a patient understands that a given diagnostic procedure (such as a spinal tap) will establish whether she suffers from a readily treatable condition (such as meningitis), expresses that she does not want to die, but refuses the procedure for no accountable reason (religion, fear of pain or needles, and so on). We might be inclined to question whether her refusal was genuine or whether some other factors, as yet unarticulated, were in play. Perhaps her understanding of the medical indications for the procedure was flawed, or perhaps she was angry at the medical professionals involved in her care, or perhaps she was suffering from an undiagnosed depression. Rather than accepting the refusal immediately, medical professionals would search for the as-yet unidentified grounds for the refusal. In the end, of course, defenders of autonomy would respect the patient's refusal, but only after being especially careful to understand whether it was the product of other problematic factors. The academic analogy would be a student who has expressed goals that have not changed, realizes that a particular romantic relationship puts all of those goals at risk (including goals for relationships), and yet persists in the relationship without giving any further explanation (even "love conquers all"). Perhaps love does conquer all, but perhaps other unidentified factors are also at work that would make it questionable as to whether the student is fully processing the information that she has.

In medicine, another of the problematic factors about consent is impairment of the patient's decision-making capacities as a result of illness. Temporary physical factors such as medication or fatigue can impair decision-making capacities. Treatable depression could alter decision making, as could other forms of mental illness, such as schizophrenia. It is not unlikely that college students would be fatigued or depressed. If they were medical patients making a momentous decision to refuse care, medical professionals would likely ascertain whether the students suffered from treatable conditions of this kind and at least offer the opportunity for therapy. This is not to say that college students should be offered treatment for depression before they enter romantic relationships with faculty. It is to say that attention to the possibility that a student may have impaired decision-making capacities is at least another reason for caution about across-the-board acceptance of all romantic relationships involving faculty and students.

Another set of problematic factors in medicine is the coercive aspects of the patient's situation. The overwhelming nature of illness can make patients particularly vulnerable and is a reason for caution in making important decisions. Students too may feel overwhelmed by the life-decisions they face about fields of study, jobs, or careers. Another aspect of patient vulnerability is being torn from familiar surroundings and familiar systems of support; patients in hospitals or nursing homes may suffer particularly from the effects of dislocation. Students also may be dislocated; an undergraduate, living away from home for the first time, faces new responsibilities and decisions without familiar landmarks. The comparative powerlessness of patients in medical institutions is another noteworthy concern; feminist bioethics writers point out the disparities in information, understanding, and dependency that affect a patient's medical decision making.[6] Although they are not physically dependent in the way patients are, students are powerless vis-à-vis faculty in some ways analogous to the powerlessness of patients vis-à-vis physicians. There are imbalances in information between students and faculty. Faculty can manipulate information, for example, about the nature or importance of courses or fields of study. Faculty who have the power to evaluate students literally can make or break careers. Although colleges are not institutions in the same way hospitals are,[7] they may feel like them sometimes; particularly at small, residential campuses, students' lives may be spent in a confined setting for long periods. There even may be analogies between economic coercion in medicine and in education. Medical expenses may be more catastrophic, less predictable, and less voluntary than educational expenses, but educational expenses in today's world are comparatively huge. A student who fears that continued scholarship support or job recommendations are dependent on the good opinion of faculty may feel just as vulnerable as a patient who faces major medical expenses.

None of these five factors—understanding, preferences, reasoning ability, physical or mental condition, or circumstances—are sufficient grounds for concluding that faculty-student relationships cannot be consensual. They are all reasons for caution, however. When they are combined, as they are most likely to be in the case of an undergraduate at a traditional small college, with having a relationship with a professor who has supervisory authority, then the case for prohibition is strongest.

CONCLUSION

Consensual relationships on campus should be permitted when they do not threaten the educational or opportunity mission of the campus. However, there are three basic reasons for concern about consensual sexual relationships on campus: educational quality, educational opportunity, and the quality of consent. All are particularly weighty where a student is under the direct supervision of a faculty member. In such cases, therefore, consensual relationships should be prohibited. This would mean the prohibition of consensual relationships while a student is in the faculty member's class; while the faculty member has responsibility for the student in an extramural program (such as a study-abroad program); and while the faculty member serves on a supervisory committee, awards committee, or as a program director.

Some of these prohibitions will be relatively short-lived and hence minimally burdensome on relationships; quarters or semesters do end eventually. Others, such as Ph.D. supervision, are typically lengthy and may place significant burdens on relationships. Others, even though short-lived, may be unavoidable, as when a spouse in a program needs to take a required course taught by her spouse. Because of these burdens, universities should strive to help the people in the relationship make alternative arrangements so that one party is not supervising the other, such as appointing a new committee for a graduate student, reassigning evaluative functions, or even granting a special exception for a student to take a required course pass-fail if there is simply no other choice.

The university should also prohibit such relationships in other types of campus sexual relationships, involving those in supervisory positions over their partners. Faculty should not be able to vote on the tenure or promotion of those with whom they are romantically involved. Nor should employment supervisors be involved with those whose work they directly evaluate. These prohibitions are typically in force in nonacademic employment relationships, because of the potential for unfairness. As with faculty-student relationships, universities should strive to arrange alternatives in these cases; tenure decisions can be made in the absence of the department member with a conflict, and workplace lines of evaluation can sometimes be reconfigured.

Finally, other consensual relationships on campus should be permitted. Personal relationships are important, and such relationships do not threaten the educational or the opportunity mission of the academy. Caution is appropriate, particularly where there are imbalances in power, as with a faculty member and an undergraduate not in the faculty member's class or a student whom the faculty member mentors. When there are such imbalances, there may be reason for concern about the quality of the consent, and relationships that are not genuinely consensual are impermissible harassment on this basis. Those in the more powerful positions who are able to recognize these risks, should enter into such relationships with particular caution.

NOTES

1. For a discussion of how the constitutional right to privacy applies to regulation of consensual amorous relationships in public colleges and universities, see Elizabeth Keller, "Consensual Amorous Relationship between Faculty and Students: The Constitutional Right to Privacy," *Journal of College and University Law* 15:21–42 (1988).

2. John Rawls, *A Theory of Justice*. Cambridge, MA: Harvard University Press, 1971, especially section 53.

3. Several state bar associations prohibit any sexual relationships between a lawyer and a client that did not predate the lawyer-client relationship; see Minnesota Rule 1.8(k), Oregon DR 5-110, West Virginia Rule 1.8(g), Wisconsin Rule 1.8(k). Florida establishes a rebuttable presumption that sexual relationships with a client are exploitative and subject the lawyer to discipline. Florida Rule 4-8.4(1). California, the first state to address sexual relationships between lawyers and clients, prohibits coercive relationships or relationships that compromise the quality of legal services. California Rule 3-120.

4. [See Jane Gallop, *Feminist Accused of Sexual Harassment*. Durham, NC: Duke University Press, 1997.—S.M.C.]

5. For a particularly good account of autonomy and informed consent in medicine, see Allen Buchanan and Dan W. Brock, *Deciding for Others: The Ethics of Surrogate Decisionmaking*. Cambridge and New York: Cambridge University Press, 1989.

6. See, for example, Susan Sherwin, *No Longer Patient: Feminist Ethics and Health Care*. Philadelphia: Temple University Press, 1992.

7. For a discussion of the concept of a total institution, see Erving Goffman, *Asylums: Essays on the Social Situation of Menial Patients and Other Inmates*. Garden City, NY: Anchor Books, 1961.

STUDY QUESTIONS

1. Can you imagine a fourth ending to the story of Joan that is more plausible than the three given?

2. Does the physician-patient relationship offer a useful analogy to the professor-student relationship?

3. Is a prohibition on consensual relationships between a professor and a student in the professor's class significantly different from a prohibition on consensual relationships between a judge and a party to a case the judge is deciding?
4. If, as Francis says, a faculty member should be cautious in having a relationship with a student not in the professor's class, what steps would constitute sufficient caution?

IV

PREFERENTIAL STUDENT ADMISSIONS

When a college or university chooses among applicants for admission, is taking a student's race into account unethical? William G. Bowen and Derek Bok maintain that it is not. Indeed, they claim that long-term societal needs require that an applicant's race ought to be considered. In particular, they point to the history of discrimination against African Americans, and argue that race-sensitive admissions are needed to continue the progress that has been made in narrowing black-white gaps in earnings, and increasing more balanced representation of the races in top-level positions.

Stephan Thernstrom and Abigail Thernstrom disagree. They argue that in the effort to create a certain racial mix on campus, intellectual standards should not be sacrificed. They also urge that our society, rather than instituting or maintaining racial preferences in higher education, should strive to provide much better schooling at the elementary and secondary levels.

7

The Meaning of "Merit"

WILLIAM G. BOWEN AND DEREK BOK

"Merit," like "preference" and "discrimination," is a word that has taken on so much baggage we may have to re-invent it or find a substitute.

Still, it is an important and potentially valuable concept because it reminds us that we certainly do not want institutions to admit candidates who lack merit, however the term is defined. Most people would agree that rank favoritism (admitting a personal friend of the admissions officer, say) is inconsistent with admission "on the merits," that no one should be admitted who cannot take advantage of the educational opportunities being offered, and that using a lottery or some similar random numbers scheme to choose among applicants who are over the academic threshold is too crude an approach.

One reason why we care so much about who gets admitted "on the merits" is because . . . admission to . . . selective schools . . . pays off handsomely for individuals of all races, from all backgrounds. But it is not individuals alone who gain. Substantial additional benefits accrue to society at large through the leadership and civic participation of the graduates and through the broad contributions that the schools themselves make to the goals of a democratic society. These societal benefits are a major justification for the favored tax treatment that colleges and universities enjoy and for the subsidies provided by public and private donors. The presence of

Originally published in William G. Bowen, *The Shape of the River*, pp. 276–286, 1998, Princeton University Press. © Princeton University Press; reprinted by permission.

these benefits also explains why these institutions do not allocate scarce places in their entering classes by the simple expedient of auctioning them off to the highest bidders. The limited number of places is an exceedingly valuable resource—valuable both to the students admitted and to the society at large—which is why admissions need to be based "on the merits."

Unfortunately, however, to say that considerations of merit should drive the admissions process is to pose questions, not answer them. There are no magical ways of automatically identifying those who merit admission on the basis of intrinsic qualities that distinguish them from all others. Test scores and grades are useful measures of the ability to do good work, but they are no more than that. They are far from infallible indicators of other qualities some might regard as intrinsic, such as a deep love of learning or a capacity for high academic achievement. . . . Moreover, such quantitative measures are even less useful in answering other questions relevant to the admissions process, such as predicting which applicants will contribute most in later life to their professions and their communities.[1]

Some critics believe, nevertheless, that applicants with higher grades and test scores are more deserving of admission because they presumably worked harder than those with less auspicious academic records. According to this argument, it is only "fair" to admit the students who have displayed the greatest effort. We disagree on several grounds.

To begin with, it is not clear that students who receive higher grades and test scores have necessarily worked harder in school. Grades and test scores are a reflection not only of effort but of intelligence, which in turn derives from a number of factors, such as inherited ability, family circumstances, and early upbringing, that have nothing to do with how many hours students have labored over their homework. Test scores may also be affected by the quality of teaching that applicants have received or even by knowing the best strategies for taking standardized tests, as coaching schools regularly remind students and their parents. For these reasons, it is quite likely that many applicants with good but not outstanding scores and B+ averages in high school will have worked more diligently than many other applicants with superior academic records.

More generally, selecting a class has much broader purposes than simply rewarding students who are thought to have worked especially hard. The job of the admissions staff is not, in any case, to decide who has earned a "right" to a place in the class, since we do not think that admission to a selective university is a right possessed by anyone. What admissions officers must decide is which set of applicants, *considered individually and collectively*, will take fullest advantage of what the college has to offer, contribute most to the educational process in college, and be most successful in using what they have learned for the benefit of the larger society. Admissions processes should, of course, be "fair," but "fairness" has to be understood to mean only that each individual is to be judged according to a consistent set of criteria that reflect the objectives of the college or university. Fairness should not be misinterpreted to mean that a particular criterion has to apply—that, for example, grades and test scores must always be considered more important than other qualities and characteristics so that no student with a B average can be accepted as long as some students with As are being turned down.

Nor does fairness imply that each candidate should be judged in isolation from all others. It may be perfectly "fair" to reject an applicant because the college has already enrolled many other students very much like him or her. There are numerous analogies. When making a stew, adding an extra carrot rather than one more potato may make excellent sense—and be eminently "fair"—if there are already lots of potatoes in the pot. Similarly, good basketball teams include both excellent shooters and sturdy defenders, both point guards and centers. Diversified investment portfolios usually include some mix of stocks and bonds, and so on.

To admit "on the merits," then, is to admit by following complex rules derived from the institution's own mission and based on its own experiences educating students with different talents and backgrounds. These "rules" should not be thought of as abstract propositions to be deduced through contemplation in a Platonic cave. Nor are they rigid formulas that can be applied in a mechanical fashion. Rather, they should have the status of rough guidelines established in large part through empirical examination of the actual results achieved as a result of long experience. . . .

Above all, merit must be defined in light of what educational institutions are trying to accomplish. In our view, race is relevant in determining which candidates "merit" admission because taking account of race helps institutions achieve three objectives central to their mission—identifying individuals of high potential, permitting students to benefit educationally from diversity on campus, and addressing long-term societal needs.

Identifying Individuals of High Potential

An individual's race may reveal something about how that person arrived at where he or she is today—what barriers were overcome, and what the individual's prospects are for further growth. Not every member of a minority group will have had to surmount substantial obstacles. Moreover, other circumstances besides race can cause "disadvantage." Thus colleges and universities should and do give special consideration to the hardworking son of a family in Appalachia or the daughter of a recent immigrant from Russia who, while obviously bright, is still struggling with the English language. But race is an important factor in its own right, given this nation's history and the evidence presented in many studies of the continuing effects of discrimination and prejudice. Wishing it were otherwise does not make it otherwise. It would seem to us to be ironic indeed—and wrong—if admissions officers were permitted to consider all other factors that help them identify individuals of high potential who have had to overcome obstacles, but were proscribed from looking at an applicant's race.

BENEFITING EDUCATIONALLY FROM DIVERSITY ON THE CAMPUS

Race almost always affects an individual's life experiences and perspectives, and thus the person's capacity to contribute to the kinds of learning through diversity that occur on campuses. This form of learning will be even more important going forward than it has been in the past. Both the growing diversity of American society and the increasing interaction with other cultures worldwide make it evident that going to school only with "the likes of oneself" will be increasingly anachronistic. The advantages of being able to understand how others think and function, to cope across racial divides, and to lead groups composed of diverse individuals are certain to increase.

To be sure, not all members of a minority group may succeed in expanding the racial understanding of other students, any more than all those who grew up on a farm or came from a remote region of the United States can be expected to convey a special rural perspective. What does seem clear, however, is that a student body containing many different backgrounds, talents, and experiences will be a richer environment in which to develop. In this respect, minority students of all kinds can have something to offer their classmates. The black student with high grades from Andover may challenge the stereotypes of many classmates just as much as the black student from the South Bronx. . . .

ADDRESSING LONG-TERM SOCIETAL NEEDS

Virtually all colleges and universities seek to educate students who seem likely to become leaders and contributing members of society. Identifying such students is another essential aspect of admitting "on the merits," and here again race is clearly relevant. There is widespread agreement that our country continues to need the help of its colleges and universities in building a society in which access to positions of leadership and responsibility is less limited by an individual's race than it is today. . . .

Fundamental judgments have to be made about societal needs, values, and objectives. When a distinguished black educator visited the Mellon Foundation, he noted, with understandable pride, that his son had done brilliantly in college and was being considered for a prestigious graduate award in neuroscience. "My son," the professor said, "needs no special consideration; he is so talented that he will make it on his own." His conclusion was that we should be indifferent to whether his son or any of the white competitors got the particular fellowship in question. We agreed that, in all likelihood, all of these candidates would benefit from going to the graduate school in question and, in time, become excellent scientists or doctors. Still, one can argue with the conclusion reached by the parent. "Your son will do fine," another person present at the meeting said, "but that isn't the issue. *He may not need us, but we need him!* Why? Because there is only one of him."

That mild exaggeration notwithstanding, the relative scarcity of talented black professionals is all too real. It seemed clear to a number of us that day, and it probably seems clear to many others, that American society needs the high-achieving black graduates who will provide leadership in every walk of life. This is the position of many top officials concerned with filling key positions in government, of CEOs who affirm that they would continue their minority recruitment programs whether or not there were a legal requirement to do so, and of bar associations, medical associations, and other professional organizations that have repeatedly stressed the importance of attracting more minority members into their fields. In view of these needs, we are not indifferent to which student gets the graduate fellowship.

Neither of the authors of this study has any sympathy with quotas or any belief in mandating the proportional representation of groups of people, defined by race or any other criterion, in positions of authority. Nor do we include ourselves among those who support race-sensitive admissions as compensation for a legacy of racial discrimination.[2] We agree emphatically with the sentiment expressed by Mamphela Ramphele, vice chancellor of the University of Cape Town in South Africa, when she said: "Everyone deserves opportunity; no one deserves success." But we remain persuaded that present racial disparities in outcomes are dismayingly disproportionate. At the minimum, this country needs to maintain the progress now being made in educating larger numbers of black professionals and black leaders.

Selective colleges and universities have made impressive contributions at both undergraduate and graduate levels. To take but a single illustration: since starting to admit larger numbers of black students in the late 1960s, the Harvard Law School has numbered among its black graduates more than one hundred partners in law firms, more than ninety black alumni/ae with the title of chief executive officer, vice president, or general counsel of a corporation, more than seventy professors, at least thirty judges, two members of Congress, the mayor of a major American city, the head of the Office of Management and Budget, and an assistant U.S. attorney general. . . . If, at the end of the day, the question is whether the most selective colleges and universities have succeeded in educating sizable numbers of minority students who have already achieved considerable success and seem likely in time to occupy positions of leadership throughout society, we have no problem in answering the question. Absolutely.

We commented earlier on the need to make clear choices. Here is perhaps the clearest choice. Let us suppose that rejecting, on race-neutral grounds, more than half of the black students who otherwise would attend these institutions would raise the probability of acceptance for another white student from 25 percent to, say, 27 percent at the most selective colleges and universities. Would we, as a society, be better off? Considering both the educational benefits of diversity and the need to include far larger numbers of black graduates in the top ranks of the business, professional, governmental, and not-for-profit institutions that shape our society, we do not think so.[3]

How one responds to such questions depends very much, of course, on how important one thinks it is that progress continues to be made in narrowing black-white gaps in earnings and in representation in top-level positions. As the United States grows steadily more diverse, we believe that Nicholas Katzenbach and Burke Marshall are surely right in insisting that the country must continue to make determined efforts to "include blacks in the institutional framework that constitutes America's economic, political, educational and social life." This goal of greater inclusiveness is important for reasons, both moral and practical, that offer all Americans the prospect of living in a society marked by more equality and racial harmony than one might otherwise anticipate.

We recognize that many opponents of race-sensitive admissions will also agree with Katzenbach and Marshall, but will argue that there are better ways of promoting inclusiveness. There is everything to be said, in our view, for addressing the underlying problems in families, neighborhoods, and primary and secondary schools that many have identified so clearly. But this is desperately difficult work, which will, at best, produce results only over a very long period of time. Meanwhile, it is important, in our view, to do what can be done to make a difference at each educational level, including colleges and graduate and professional schools.

The alternative seems to us both stark and unworthy of our country's ideals. Turning aside from efforts to help larger numbers of well-qualified blacks gain the educational advantages they will need to move steadily and confidently into the mainstream of American life could have extremely serious consequences. Here in the United States, as elsewhere in the world, visible efforts by leading educational institutions to make things better will encourage others to press on with the hard work needed to overcome the continuing effects of a legacy of unfair treatment.

NOTES

1. Martin Luther King, Jr., now regarded as one of the great orators of this century, scored in the bottom half of all test takers on the verbal GRE.

2. Justice Thurgood Marshall made such an argument in the *Bakke* case in urging his colleagues on the Supreme Court to uphold the racial quotas provided by the University of California Davis School of Medicine; in his view, such programs were simply a way "to remedy the effects of centuries of unequal treatment. . . . I do not believe that anyone can truly look into America's past and still find that a remedy for the effects of that past is impermissible" (438 U.S. at p. 402). Understandable as this argument may seem against a historical background of slavery and segregation, it did not prevail because the remedy is not precise enough to be entirely just in its application. Not every minority student who is admitted will have suffered from substantial discrimination, and the excluded white and Asian applicants are rarely responsible for the racial injustices of the past and have sometimes had to struggle against considerable handicaps of their own. For these reasons, a majority of justices in the *Bakke* case rejected Marshall's reasoning, although similar arguments continue to be heard.

3. This emphasis on the consequences of rejecting race-neutral policies will seem misplaced to some of the most thoughtful critics of affirmative action, who will argue that their objection to race-based policies is an objection in principle: in their view, no one's opportunities should be narrowed, even by an iota, by reference to the individual's race. We respect this line of argument. However, we do not agree, "in principle," that colleges and universities should ignore the practical effects of one set of decisions or another when making difficult decisions about who "merits" a place in the class. The clash here is principle versus principle, not principle versus expediency. As we argued earlier in the chapter, in making admissions decisions, what is right in principle depends on how one defines the mission of the educational institution involved. For us, the missions of colleges and universities have strong educational and public policy aspects and do not consist solely of conferring benefits on particular individuals.

STUDY QUESTIONS

1. Should the racial diversity of the student body be considered more important than diversity of students by gender, religious affiliation, economic class, regional background, and sexual orientation?

2. Is rejection of the principle of proportional representation by race consistent with claiming that present racial disparities are disproportionate?

3. Is the aim of narrowing gaps in earning between members of different races as important as the aim of narrowing gaps in earnings between rich and poor?

4. Would Bowen and Bok agree with President Obama's statement that his children should not be beneficiaries of affirmative action?

8

Does Your "Merit" Depend
upon Your Race?
A Rejoinder to Bowen and Bok

STEPHAN THERNSTROM
AND ABIGAIL THERNSTROM

In his *Reflections of an Affirmative Action Baby,* Stephen Carter tells us that his academic record as an undergraduate at Stanford was strong, but not good enough to win him admission to Harvard Law School. Shortly after he got a rejection letter from Harvard, though, he received a telephone call informing him that there had been a mistake in the review of his application. The admissions committee had somehow failed to notice that Mr. Carter was an African American, and that made all the difference. As an ordinary applicant, Carter did not make the grade. But Harvard Law School had a lower standard for black applicants, so it was eager to have him.

Stephen Carter felt patronized and demeaned by Harvard Law School, and chose to go elsewhere for his law education. He recognized that his race may well have given him a boost at the other schools that admitted him, but he could not be sure how much. Only Harvard made it crystal clear, inadvertently making the racial basis of its judgment completely transparent. He was not being admitted because of his personal achievements; he was not unequivocally outstanding, but merely outstanding compared with other African-American applicants.

Originally published in Steven M. Cahn, ed., *The Affirmative Action Debate*, pp. 183–189, 2002, Routledge. Reprinted by permission of Stephan and Abigail Thernstrom.

Derek Bok, once the dean of Harvard Law School, and William G. Bowen cannot grasp why a Stephen Carter might feel deflated and diminished by such treatment. Although they claim to be making the case for nuanced, holistic, highly individualized admissions decisions, in fact what they defend are crude judgments that reduce applicants to members of racial categories. From their perspective, society needs more black attorneys, and the elite law schools have to do their part. If energetic recruitment efforts do not yield enough minority applicants who would win admission strictly on the basis of their individual qualifications, schools must do their duty by accepting black and Latino applicants with weaker credentials. What's the problem? After all, everyone they admit is qualified. That many whites and Asians whom they reject are better qualified doesn't matter, because "society" already has enough white and Asian attorneys.

Bowen and Bok, of course, once headed two of the most distinguished universities in the United States—indeed, in the world. Bowen was president of Princeton University, and Bok was president of Harvard. The shining reputations of Princeton and Harvard derive primarily from the excellence of their faculties and their student bodies, and that excellence has been the result of a commitment to meritocratic selection procedures. They admit the very best students from their applicant pools, and they hire the best scholars they can find to teach them.

It was not always so. Before World War II, both Harvard and Princeton held Jewish applicants to a higher standard than gentiles, and kept the numbers of Jews in the student body severely limited, in order to leave ample room for alumni sons who were more notable for their social graces than for their intelligence. They also were extremely reluctant to hire Jews as faculty members.[1]

Bowen and Bok's effort to relativize the "meaning of merit" drains the concept of any clear meaning and echoes the arguments made by proponents of the Jewish quotas in the bad old days. Test scores and grades are but very limited measures of individual potential, they claim. Such objective measures of academic performance may not identify applicants who have "a deep love of learning" or "a capacity for high academic achievement," much less those who "will contribute most in later life to their professions and their communities," they say. Earlier Ivy League presidents would have added "character" to the list, but the notion of judging who will contribute most to "their professions and their communities" may amount to the same thing.

These are disturbingly subjective criteria, and it is well to recall that in the past they were applied in a manner that few would defend today. Isaac Levine from P.S. 164 in Brooklyn had a straight-A record and 1480 on the SATs, but Yale would have had too many Jews if it took him. Bowen and Bok tell us that "adding an extra carrot rather than one more potato" to the stew "may make excellent sense—and be eminently 'fair'—if there are already lots of potatoes in the pot." This metaphor is profoundly revealing—more revealing than its authors realize. Winthrop Brooks IV of Andover Academy might be the extra carrot that was needed. Despite his mediocre academic qualifications, he would likely "contribute" more to society when he joined his father's investment banking firm after graduation. Doubtless he had a better "character" as well, at least as character was rated by Yale admissions officers. Yale had enough students of Levine's "kind," and needed more of Brooks's kind. A supposedly nuanced judgment of competing individuals, in this instance, would have been made on the basis of gross ethnic and social class stereotypes.

Decisions like these amounted to naked discrimination against Jews, and were indefensible. And yet we wonder what Bowen and Bok would have to say about the matter. Their very long book about admissions to elite schools never mentions this unsavory history, although it seems extremely pertinent. It may seem difficult to deny that Jewish quotas were discriminatory, but that conclusion rests on the assumption that grades and test scores are a reasonable measure of the qualifications of an applicant to college— a reasonable gauge of his or her "merit." Once you relativize and racialize merit, as Bowen and Bok do, it is impossible to say that any unsuccessful candidate has been treated unfairly. "Sure, Levine was a good potato, but we had enough potatoes. We really needed more carrots in the pot."

Fortunately, academic merit as measured by high school grades and test scores matters far more to admissions officers at Harvard, Princeton, and other elite schools than Bowen and Bok would have us believe. Their stew metaphor implies that such institutions don't want too many students with exceptional academic qualifications—a stew with nothing but beef would not be very tasty. Presumably the carrots, potatoes, bay leaf, and thyme are people with weaker grades and lower SATs but other outstanding characteristics. However, a glance at any of the standard guides to colleges and universities will reveal that the average student admitted to such schools has SAT scores in the top 2 to 3 percent and ranks at or very close to the top of his or her high school class. Princeton cannot be accepting significant numbers of applicants whose grades and test scores are merely average or below average because it is convinced they nonetheless have a "deep love for learning," a "special rural perspective," or some other equally fuzzy attribute.

The authors' scorn for standardized tests even leads them to remark in a footnote that "Martin Luther King, Jr., now regarded as one of the great orators of this century, scored in the bottom half of all test-takers" on the verbal portion of the Graduate Record Examination. But of course no one defends SATs and GREs on the grounds that they identify people with Dr.

King's remarkable talents. These tests, however, do a good job in predicting academic performance, numerous studies have shown.

All of Bowen and Bok's rhetoric about how "merit" is a multifaceted, relative, many-splendored thing is designed to obscure a simple and regrettable fact. If students were admitted to the most selective colleges and universities strictly on the basis of their academic merit, the number of African Americans and Hispanics who would be successful in the competition would be very small.

Some figures from California illustrate the problem vividly. Admission to a campus of the University of California, the best state university system in the country, is guaranteed to state residents who rank in the top eighth of their high school graduating class. Grades are the primary criterion, but SAT scores are also considered in determining the list of students deemed to have the merit to make them "UC-eligible."

What is the racial mix among the UC-eligibles? The most recent data available are for 1999, and indicate that just 2.8 percent of African-American public high school seniors in the state had strong enough records to be guaranteed a place at the University of California. The proportion was only slightly higher—3.8 percent—for Latino students. This did not mean, though, that non-Hispanic whites had more than their proportional share of places in the top-eighth group. In fact, 12.4 percent of California's white 12th-graders ranked in the top 12.5 percent. The only group of overachievers was Asian Americans. An astonishing 31.5 percent met the requirements for admission. Asian-American students were 2.5 times more likely than their white classmates to qualify for admission to the University of California—a stunning achievement. At the two most prestigious and competitive schools in the UC system—Berkeley and UCLA—four out of ten students are Asian American. Remarkably, they outnumber whites on both campuses, even though there are four times as many whites as Asians in the population of California as a whole.

These huge racial disparities, it should be noted, cannot be blamed on the allegedly discriminatory nature of the SATs.[2] A 1997 study by the UC administration demolishes that common argument.[3] It found that if grades alone determined who is UC-eligible, the number of Hispanic students admitted would rise slightly—by 5 percent. The proportion of Asians would decline a bit—by 3 percent. The two groups most affected would be blacks and whites, but the effects would be precisely the opposite of what SAT critics maintain. The number of blacks admitted would *decline* by 18 percent if the SAT were eliminated from consideration, and the number of whites would *rise* by 17 percent. The racial mix of the entering class would have looked even less balanced racially than it actually was with SAT scores factored in.

Suppose that we wanted to make the student body of the University of California more representative of the population of the state. Proportional representation is the norm implicit in all proposals for engineering "diversity" by means of racial double standards in admissions. Bowen and Bok, we believe, are being disingenuous when they deny that they advocate proportional representation at elite schools. They may not insist upon going all the way to precise racial and ethnic proportionality, and indeed the pool of "qualified" black and Hispanic applicants, even by their expansive definition, is too small to attain proportionality. But the central theme of their long book is that without racial preferences, not enough non-Asian minorities would attend elite colleges, although it's not clear how they can conclude that a freshman class that is, say, 2 to 3 percent black does not have enough African Americans without some standard of what a sufficient share would be. And what could that standard be except the black share of the total population?

California could make the UC student body match the racial mix of the state's population by taking Bowen and Bok's relativistic conception of merit to its logical conclusion. It could simply declare that the top 12.5 percent of students *from each racial group* are qualified. If merit is relative to social circumstances, why not? That would quadruple black enrollment, triple Latino enrollment, and leave the white share of UC-eligibles completely unchanged.

The only losers would be Asian Americans, whose share would be cut by nearly two-thirds (dropping from 31.5 percent to 12.5 percent). The performance of an Asian-American high school student who hoped to attend the University of California would then be appraised not in comparison to all other students in the state but relative to that of other Asian Americans. People of Asian descent would be rejected even though their academic records were far stronger than those of whites, as well as blacks and Hispanics.[4] What principled objection could Bowen and Bok make to that? For them, after all, "fairness" in admissions does not mean that "grades and test scores must always be considered more important than other qualities and characteristics, so that no student with a B average can be accepted as long as students with As are being turned down."

Employing racial double standards in admissions, we have demonstrated in detail, elsewhere, does not have the benign effects Bowen and Bok attribute to them, and has many unintended negative consequences we lack the space to spell out here.[5] Suffice it to say that racial preferences reinforce the dreadful stereotype that blacks just aren't academically talented. And they involve the arbitrary assignment of individuals to racial and ethnic categories, and assume it is legitimate to offer them different opportunities depending upon the group to which they have been assigned. They state that race-neutral admissions are "unworthy of our country's ideals" and seem to believe that the sorting of American citizens along lines of race and ethnicity is what the framers of the Fourteenth Amendment had in mind. It is true that judging citizens by the color of their skin is indeed as American as apple pie. But the civil rights warriors of the 1950s and 1960s did not put their lives on the line to perpetuate such terrible habits of mind, we firmly believe, and their vision of a color-blind society was embodied in the Civil Rights Act of 1964.

In the concluding pages of their book, Bowen and Bok issue a warning. If forced to choose, today's educational leaders will see creating a certain racial mix on campus as more important than maintaining intellectual standards. Here we have a breathtakingly candid statement of the priorities of two of the most distinguished figures in higher education today—priorities that reflect those of the higher education establishment as a whole. Intellectual excellence should be sacrificed on the altar of diversity.

This repugnant trade-off would not be necessary, of course, if we concentrated our efforts on closing the yawning racial gap in educational performance among elementary and secondary school pupils. The massive database compiled by the National Assessment of Educational Progress reveals that the average African-American high school senior today reads at the same level as the average white or Asian in the eighth grade, and Hispanics do little better. Racial differentials are even sharper at the extremes of the distribution. Black and Latino high school graduates with academic records that would qualify them for admission to elite colleges and universities are in pathetically short supply, as the California evidence cited above makes clear.

As long as the average black high school senior reads at the eighth-grade level, efforts to engineer parity in the academy are doomed to failure. For a generation now, racial preferences in higher education have been a pernicious palliative that has deflected our attention from the real problem: the need for much better schooling in the pre-K–12 years. That desperate need is *the* civil rights issue of our time.

NOTES

1. The history of Jewish admissions quotas at Harvard, Yale, and Princeton is well told in Marcia Graham Synnott, *The Half-Opened Door: Discrimination and Admissions at Harvard, Yale, and Princeton* (Westport, CT: Greenwood Press, 1979). Synnott's account is too soft on Harvard, though, because key internal Harvard documents were not open to scholars when her research was being conducted. For the full story, based upon much newly available evidence, see Morton Keller and Phyllis Keller, *Making Harvard Modern: The Rise of America's University* (New York: Oxford University Press, 2001), which also includes disturbing evidence of Harvard's reluctance to appoint Jews to the faculty in the 1930s and 1940s.

2. See our critical appraisals of the most popular recent book attacking the SATs, Nicolas Lemann's *The Big Test* (1999): Stephan Thernstrom, "Status Anxiety," *National Review*, December 6, 1999, and Abigail Thernstrom, "Shooting the Messenger," *Times Literary Supplement*, June 9, 2000.

3. University of California, Office of the President, Student Academic Services, *University of California Follow-up Analyses of the 1996 CPEC Eligibility Study* (Berkeley, CA: 1997).

4. If this seems too fanciful, it should be noted that for many years the best public high school in San Francisco, Lowell High, operated a racial quota that worked exactly this way. An examination was used to sift out applicants, and Chinese-American students had to get a higher score than other Asians, with a lower cutoff score for whites and a still lower one for blacks and Hispanics. The San Francisco Unified School District was forced to abandon the system in 1999, after it was sued by Chinese parents complaining that the system deprived their children of the equal protection of the laws guaranteed them by the Fourteenth Amendment.

5. For a detailed and highly critical evaluation of Bowen and Bok's work, see Stephan Thernstrom and Abigail Thernstrom, "Reflections on *The Shape of the River*," *UCLA Law Review* 46, June 1999. A somewhat shorter version of this paper that includes newer evidence is "Racial Preferences in Higher Education: An Assessment of the Evidence," in *One America? Political Leadership, National Identity, and the Dilemmas of Diversity*, ed. Stanley A. Renshon (Washington, D.C.: Georgetown University Press, 2001).

STUDY QUESTIONS

1. What is "academic merit"?
2. Is it appropriate for a college or university to choose students in part on the basis of their athletic abilities, musical talents, or community service?
3. If a coeducational college has more female than male applicants, would the school be wrong to plan to admit a higher percentage of men than women to achieve balance by gender?
4. If a college seeks a national student body, would the school be wrong to give preference to students who come from previously unrepresented areas of the country?

V

PREFERENTIAL
FACULTY
APPOINTMENTS

Since its implementation in the early 1970s, affirmative action has been a divisive issue in the United States. While all agree that every effort should be made to eliminate bias from the process of appointing faculty members (a policy I call "procedural affirmative action"), opinion is sharply divided as to whether searches should favor women and members of certain minority groups (a policy I call "preferential affirmative action").

My essay attempts to clarify the issues involved in the complex dispute over preferential affirmative action. That policy has been defended on three grounds: (1) to offset past discrimination; (2) to counteract present unfairness; (3) to achieve future equality. The first is often referred to as "compensation," the second "a level playing field," and the third "diversity." My discussion touches on all three justifications but focuses on the third.

Laurence Thomas asks: "What good am I as a black professor?" He finds the role-model argument for affirmative action unsatisfactory, and does not view himself primarily as a mentor for black students. Rather, he considers his presence on the faculty to be a representation of the hope that the university will be an environment in which all can feel trust and gratitude. In his view, the oft-stated concern that women and minorities will flourish in academia has too often been only insincere talk that has not resulted in action.

9

Two Concepts of Affirmative Action

STEVEN M. CAHN

In March 1961, less than two months after assuming office, President John F. Kennedy issued Executive Order 10925, establishing the President's Committee on Equal Employment Opportunity. Its mission was to end discrimination in employment by the government and its contractors. The order required every federal contract to include the pledge that "The contractor will not discriminate against any employe[e] or applicant for employment because of race, creed, color, or national origin. The contractor will take affirmative action to ensure that applicants are employed, and that employe[e]s are treated during employment, without regard to their race, creed, color, or national origin."

Here, for the first time in the context of civil rights, the government called for "affirmative action." The term meant taking appropriate steps to eradicate the then widespread practices of racial, religious, and ethnic discrimination.[1] The goal, as the President stated, was "equal opportunity in employment." In other words, *procedural* affirmative action, as I shall call it, was instituted to ensure that applicants for positions would be judged without any consideration of their race, religion, or national origin. These criteria were declared irrelevant. Taking them into account was forbidden.

The Civil Rights Act of 1964 restated and broadened the application of this principle. Title VI declared that "No person in the United States

Originally published in *Academe* 1997:83; pp. 14–19. Reprinted by permission of the author.

shall, on the ground of race, color or national origin, be excluded from participation in, be denied the benefits of, or be subjected to discrimination under any program or activity receiving Federal financial assistance."

Before one year had passed, however, President Lyndon B. Johnson argued that fairness required more than a commitment to such procedural affirmative action. In his 1965 commencement address at Howard University, he said, "You do not take a person who for years has been hobbled by chains and liberate him, bring him up to the starting line of a race and then say, 'you're free to compete with all the others,' and still justly believe that you have been completely fair."

Several months later, President Johnson issued Executive Order 11246, stating that "It is the policy of the Government of the United States to provide equal opportunity in Federal employment for all qualified persons, to prohibit discrimination in employment because of race, creed, color or national origin, and to promote the full realization of equal employment opportunity through a positive. continuing program in each department and agency." Two years later the order was amended to prohibit discrimination on the basis of sex.

While the aim of President Johnson's order is stated in language similar to that of President Kennedy's, President Johnson's abolished the Committee on Equal Employment Opportunity, transferred its responsibilities to the Secretary of Labor, and authorized the Secretary to "adopt such rules and regulations and issue such orders as he deems necessary and appropriate to achieve the purposes thereof."

Acting on this mandate, the Department of Labor in December 1971, during the administration of President Richard M. Nixon, issued Revised Order No. 4, requiring all federal contractors to develop "an acceptable affirmative action program," including "an analysis of areas within which the contractor is deficient in the utilization of minority groups and women, and further, goals and timetables to which the contractor's good faith efforts must be directed to correct the deficiencies." Contractors were instructed to take the term "minority groups" to refer to "Negroes, American Indians, Orientals, and Spanish Surnamed Americans." (No guidance was given as to whether having only one parent, grandparent, or great-grandparent from a group would suffice to establish group membership.) The concept of "underutilization," according to the Revised Order, meant "having fewer minorities or women in a particular job classification than would reasonably be expected by their availability." "Goals" were not to be "rigid and inflexible quotas," but "targets reasonably attainable by means of applying every good faith effort to make all aspects of the entire affirmative action program work."[2]

Such preferential affirmative action, as I shall call it, requires that attention be paid to the same criteria of race, sex, and ethnicity that procedural affirmative action deems irrelevant. Is such use of these criteria justifiable in employment decisions?[3]

Return to President Johnson's claim that a person hobbled by discrimination cannot in fairness be expected to be competitive. How are we to determine which specific individuals are entitled to a compensatory advantage? To decide each case on its own merits would be possible, but this approach would undermine the argument for instituting preferential affirmative action on a group basis. For if some members of a group are able to compete, why not others? Thus defenders of preferential affirmative action maintain that the group, not the individual, is to be judged. If the group has suffered discrimination, then all its members are to be treated as hobbled runners.

Note, however, that while a hobbled runner, provided with a sufficient lead in a race, may cross the finish line first, giving that person an edge prevents the individual from being considered as fast a runner as others. An equally fast runner does not need an advantage to be competitive. This entire racing analogy thus encourages stereotypical thinking. For example, recall those men who played in baseball's Negro Leagues. That these athletes were barred from competing in the Major Leagues is the greatest stain on the history of the sport. While they suffered discrimination, these players were as proficient as their counterparts in the Major Leagues. They needed only to be judged by the same criteria as all others, and ensuring such equality of consideration is the essence of procedural affirmative action.

Granted, if individuals are unprepared or ill-equipped to compete, then they ought to be helped to try to achieve their goals. But such aid is appropriate for all who need it, not merely for members of particular racial, sexual, or ethnic groups.

Victims of discrimination deserve compensation. Former players in the Negro Leagues ought to receive special consideration in the arrangement of pension plans and any other benefits formerly denied these athletes due to unfair treatment. The case for such compensation, however, does not imply that present black players vying for jobs in the Major Leagues should be evaluated in any other way than their performance on the field. To assume their inability to compete is derogatory and erroneous.

Such considerations have led recent defenders of preferential affirmative action to rely less heavily on any argument that implies the attribution of noncompetitiveness to an entire population.[4] Instead, the emphasis has been placed on recognizing the benefits society is said to derive from encouraging expression of the varied experiences, outlooks, and values of members of different groups.

This approach makes a virtue of what has come to be called "diversity."[5] As a defense of preferential affirmative action, diversity has at least two advantages. First, those previously excluded are now included not as a favor to them but as a means of enriching all. Second, no one is viewed as hobbled; each competes on a par, although with varied strengths.

Note that diversity requires preferential hiring. Those who enhance diversity are to be preferred to those who do not. Those preferred, however, are not being chosen because of their deficiency; the larger group is deficient, lacking diversity.

What does it mean to say that a group lacks diversity? Or to put the question another way, could we decide, for example, which member of a ten-person group to eliminate in order to decrease most markedly its diversity?

So stated, the question is reminiscent of a provocative puzzle in *The Tyranny of Testing*, a 1962 book by the scientist Banesh Hoffman. In this attack on the importance placed on multiple-choice tests, he quotes the following letter to the editor of the *Times* of London:

> Sir—Among the "odd one out" type of questions which my son had to answer for a school entrance examination was: "Which is the odd one out among cricket, football, billiards, and hockey?" [In England "football" refers to the game Americans call "soccer," and "hockey" here refers to "field hockey."] The letter continued: I said billiards because it is the only one played indoors. A colleague says football because it is the only one in which the ball is not struck by an implement. A neighbour says cricket because in all the other games the object is to put the ball into a net. . . . Could any of your readers put me out of my misery by stating what is the correct answer . . . ?

A day later the *Times* printed the following two letters:

> Sir.—"Billiards" is the obvious answer . . . because it is the only one of the games listed which is not a team game.
>
> Sir.— . . . football is the odd one out because . . . it is played with an inflated ball as compared with the solid ball used in each of the other three.

Hoffman then continued his own discussion:

> When I had read these three letters it seemed to me that good cases had been made for football and billiards, and that the case for cricket was particularly clever . . . At first I thought this made hockey easily the worst of the four choices and, in effect, ruled it out. But then I realized that the very fact that hockey was the only one that could be

thus ruled out gave it so striking a quality of separateness as to make it an excellent answer after all—perhaps the best. Fortunately, for my peace of mind, it soon occurred to me that hockey is the only one of the four games that is played with a curved implement.

The following day the *Times* published yet another letter, this from a philosophically sophisticated thinker.

> Sir.—[The author of the original letter] . . . has put his finger on what has long been a matter of great amusement to me. Of the four— cricket, football, billiards, hockey—each is unique in a multitude of respects. For example, billiards is the only one played with more than one ball at once, the only one played on a green cloth and not on a field. . . . It seems to me that those who have been responsible for inventing this kind of brain teaser have been ignorant of the elementary philosophical fact that every thing is at once unique and a member of a wider class.

With this sound principle in mind, return to the problem of deciding which member of a ten-person group to eliminate in order to decrease most markedly its diversity. Unless the sort of diversity is specified, the question has no rational answer.

In searches for college and university faculty members, we know what sorts of diversity are typically of present concern: race, sex, and certain ethnicities. Why should these characteristics be given special regard?

Consider, for example, other nonacademic respects in which prospective faculty appointees can differ: age, religion, nationality, regional background, economic class, social stratum, military experience, bodily appearance, physical soundness, sexual orientation, marital status, ethical standards, political commitments, and cultural values. Why should we not seek diversity of these sorts?

To some extent schools do. Many colleges and universities indicate in advertisements for faculty positions that the schools seek veterans or persons with disabilities. The City University of New York requires all searches to give preference to individuals of Italian-American descent.

The crucial point is that the appeal to diversity never favors any particular candidate. Each one adds to some sort of diversity but not another. In a department of ten, one individual might be the only Black, another the only woman, another the only bachelor, another the only veteran, another the only one over fifty, another the only Catholic, another the only Republican, another the only Scandinavian, another the only socialist, and the tenth the only Southerner.

Suppose the suggestion is made that the sorts of diversity to be sought are those of groups that have suffered discrimination. This approach leads to another problem, clearly put by John Kekes:

> It is true that American blacks, Native Americans, Hispanics, and women have suffered injustice as a group. But so have homosexuals, epileptics, the urban and the rural poor, the physically ugly, those whose careers were ruined by McCarthyism, prostitutes, the obese, and so forth . . .
>
> There have been some attempts to deny that there is an analogy between these two classes of victims. It has been said that the first were unjustly discriminated against due to racial or sexual prejudice and that this is not true of the second. This is indeed so. But why should we accept the suggestion . . . that the only form of injustice relevant to preferential treatment is that which is due to racial or sexual prejudice? Injustice occurs in many forms, and those who value justice will surely object to all of them.[6]

Kekes's reasoning is cogent. In addition, another difficulty looms for the proposal to seek diversity only of groups that have suffered discrimination. For diversity is supposed to be valued not as compensation to the disadvantaged but as a means of enriching all.

Consider, for example, a department in which most of the faculty members are women. In certain fields, such as nursing and elementary education, such departments are common. If diversity by sex is of value, then such a department, when making its next appointment, should prefer a man. Yet men as a group have not been victims of discrimination. To achieve valued sorts of diversity, the question is not which groups have been discriminated against, but which valued groups are not represented. The question thus reappears as to which sorts of diversity are to be most highly valued. I know of no compelling answer.

Seeking to justify preferential affirmative action in terms of its contribution to diversity raises another difficulty. For preferential affirmative action is commonly defended as a temporary rather than a permanent measure.[7] Preferential affirmative action to achieve diversity, however, is not temporary.

Suppose it were. Then once an institution had appointed an appropriate number of members of a particular group, preferential affirmative action would no longer be in effect. Yet the institution may later find that it has too few members of that group. Because lack of valuable diversity is presumably no more acceptable at one time than another, preferential affirmative action would have to be reinstituted. Thereby it would in effect become a permanent policy.

Why do so many of its defenders wish it to be only transitional? They believe the policy was instituted in response to irrelevant criteria for appointment having mistakenly been treated as relevant. To adopt any policy that continues to treat essentially irrelevant criteria as relevant is to share the guilt of those who discriminated originally. Irrelevant criteria should be recognized as such and abandoned as soon as feasible.

Some defenders of preferential affirmative action argue, however, that an individual's race, sex, or ethnicity is germane to fulfilling the responsibilities of a faculty member. They believe, therefore, that preferential affirmative action should be a permanent feature of search processes, because it takes account of criteria that should be considered in every appointment.

At least three reasons have been offered to justify the claim that those of a particular race, sex, or ethnicity are well-suited to be faculty members: first, they would be especially effective teachers of any student who shares their race, sex, or ethnicity;[8] second, they would be particularly insightful researchers because of their experiencing the world from distinctive standpoints;[9] third, they would be role models, demonstrating that those of a particular race, sex, or ethnicity can be effective faculty members.[10]

Consider each of these claims in turn. As to the presumed teaching effectiveness of the individuals in question, no empirical study supports the claim.[11] But assume compelling evidence were presented. It would have no implications for individual cases. A particular person who does not share race, sex, or ethnicity with students might teach them superbly. An individual of the students' own race, sex, or ethnicity might be ineffective. Regardless of statistical correlations, what is crucial is that individuals be able to teach effectively all sorts of students, and seeking individuals who give evidence of satisfying this criterion is entirely consistent with procedural affirmative action. But knowing an individual's race, sex, or ethnicity does not reveal whether that person will be effective in the classroom.

Do members of a particular race, sex, or ethnicity share a distinctive intellectual perspective that enhances their scholarship? Celia Wolf-Devine has aptly described this claim as a form of "stereotyping" that is "demeaning." As she puts it, "A Hispanic who is a Republican is no less a Hispanic, and a woman who is not a feminist is no less a woman."[12] Furthermore, are Hispanic men and women supposed to have the same point of view in virtue of their common ethnicity, or are they supposed to have different points of view in virtue of their different genders?

If our standpoints are thought to be determined by our race, sex, and ethnicity, why not also by the numerous other significant respects in which people differ, such as age, religion, sexual orientation, and so on? Because each of us is unique, can anyone else share my point of view?

That my own experience is my own is a tautology that does not imply the keenness of my insight into my experience. The victim of a crime may as a result embrace an outlandish theory of racism. But neither who you are nor what you experience guarantees the truth of your theories.

To be an effective researcher calls for discernment, imagination, and perseverance. These attributes are not tied to one's race, sex, ethnicity, age, or religion. Black scholars, for example, may be more inclined to study Black literature than are non-Black scholars. But some non-Black literary critics are more interested in and more knowledgeable about Black literature than are some Black literary critics. Why make decisions based on fallible racial generalizations when judgments of individual merit are obtainable and more reliable?

Perhaps the answer lies in the claim that only those of a particular race, sex, or ethnicity can serve as role models, exemplifying to members of a particular group the possibility of their success. Again, no empirical study supports the claim, but it has often been taken as self-evident that, for instance, only a woman can be a role model for a woman, only a Black for a Black, and only a Catholic for a Catholic. In other words, the crucial feature of a person is supposed to be not what the person does but who the person is.

The logic of the situation, however, is not so clear. Consider, for example, a Black man who is a Catholic. Presumably he serves as a role model for Blacks, men, and Catholics. Does he serve as a role model for Black women, or can only a Black woman serve that purpose? Does he serve as a role model for all Catholics or only for those who are Black? Can I serve as a role model for anyone else, because no one else shares all my characteristics? Perhaps I can serve as a role model for everyone else, because everyone else belongs to at least one group to which I belong.

Putting aside these conundrums, the critical point is supposed to be that in a field in which discrimination has been rife, a successful individual who belongs to the discriminated group demonstrates that members of the group can succeed in that field. Obviously success is possible without a role model, for the first successful individual had none. But suppose persuasive evidence were offered that a role model, while not necessary, sometimes is helpful, not only to those who belong to the group in question but also to those prone to believe that no members of the group can perform effectively within the field. Role models would then both encourage members of a group that had suffered discrimination and discourage further discrimination against the group.

To serve these purposes, however, the person chosen would need to be viewed as having been selected by the same criteria as all others. If not, members of the group that has suffered discrimination as well as those prone to discriminate would be confirmed in their common view that members of the group never would have been chosen unless membership in the group had been taken into account. Those who suffered discrimination would conclude that it still exists, while those prone to discriminate would conclude that members of the group lack the necessary attributes to compete equally.

How can we ensure that a person chosen for a position has been selected by the same criteria as all others? Preferential affirmative action fails to serve the purpose, because by definition it differentiates among people on the basis of criteria other than performance. The approach that ensures merit selection is procedural affirmative action. It maximizes equal opportunity by demanding vigilance against every form of discrimination.

The policy of appointing others than the best qualified has not produced a harmonious society in which prejudice is transcended and all enjoy the benefits of self-esteem. Rather, the practice has bred doubts about the abilities of those chosen while generating resentment in those passed over.

Procedural affirmative action had barely begun before it was replaced by preferential affirmative action. The difficulties with the latter are now clear. Before deeming them necessary evils in the struggle to overcome pervasive prejudice, why not try scrupulous enforcement of procedural affirmative action? We might thereby most directly achieve that equitable society so ardently desired by every person of good will.

NOTES

1. A comprehensive history of one well-documented case of such discrimination is Dan A. Oren, *Joining the Club: A History of Jews and Yale* (New Haven and London: Yale University Press, 1985). Prior to the end of World War II, no Jew had ever been appointed to the rank of full professor in Yale College.

2. 41 C.F.R. 60-2.12. The Order provides no suggestion as to whether a "good faith effort" implies only showing preference among equally qualified candidates (the "tiebreaking" model), preferring a strong candidate to an even stronger one (the "plus factor" model), preferring a merely qualified candidate to a strongly qualified candidate (the "trumping" model), or cancelling a search unless a qualified candidate of the preferred sort is available (the "quota" model).

A significant source of misunderstanding about affirmative action results from both the government's failure to clarify which type of preference is called for by a "good faith effort" and the failure on the part of those conducting searches to inform applicants which type of preference is in use. Regarding the latter issue, see my "Colleges Should Be Explicit About Who Will Be Considered for Jobs," *The Chronicle of Higher Education*, XXXV (30), 1989, reprinted in *Affirmative Action and the University: A Philosophical Inquiry*, Steven M. Cahn (ed.), (Philadelphia: Temple University Press, 1993), pp. 3–4.

3. Whether their use is appropriate in a school's admission and scholarship decisions is a different issue, involving other considerations, and I shall not explore that subject in this article.

4. See, for example, Leslie Pickering Francis, "In Defense of Affirmative Action," in Cahn, op. cit., especially pp. 24–26. She raises concerns about unfairness to those individuals forced by circumstances not of their own making to bear all

the costs of compensation, as well as injustices to those who have been equally victimized but are not members of specified groups.

5. The term gained currency when Justice Lewis Powell, in his pivotal opinion in the Supreme Court's 1978 *Bakke* decision, found "the attainment of a diverse student body" to be a goal that might justify the use of race in student admissions. An incisive analysis of that decision is Carl Cohen, *Naked Racial Preference* (Lanham, MD: Madison Books, 1995), pp. 55–80.

6. Cahn, op. cit., p. 151.

7. Consider Michael Rosenfeld, *Affirmative Action and Justice: A Philosophical and Constitutional Inquiry* (New Haven and London: Yale University Press, 1991), p. 336: "Ironically, the sooner affirmative action is allowed to complete its mission, the sooner the need for it will altogether disappear."

8. See, for example, Francis, op. cit., p. 31.

9. See, for example, Richard Wasserstrom, "The University and the Case for Preferential Treatment," *American Philosophical Quarterly*, 13(4), 1976, pp. 165–70.

10. See, for example, Joel J. Kupperman, "Affirmative Action: Relevant Knowledge and Relevant Ignorance," in Cahn, op. cit., pp. 181–88.

11. Consider Judith Jarvis Thomson, "Preferential Hiring," *Philosophy and Public Affairs*, 2 (4), 1973, p. 368: "I do not think that as a student I learned any better, or any more, from the women who taught me than from the men, and I do not think that my own women students now learn any better or any more from me than they do from my male colleagues."

12. Cahn, op. cit., p. 230.

STUDY QUESTIONS

1. Does preferential affirmative action imply that on occasion a highly qualified candidate should be passed over in favor of one who is only qualified?

2. If a college or university decides that a position will be reserved for the members of a particular minority group, should the advertisement for that position contain this information?

3. Does the appeal to diversity favor any particular candidate?

4. Can procedural affirmative action be used effectively to address a situation in which an all-male department, while claiming to conduct fair searches, never appoints a woman?

10

What Good Am I?

LAURENCE THOMAS

What good am I as a black professor? The raging debate over affirmative action surely invites me to ask this searching question of myself, just as it must invite those belonging to other so-called suspect categories to ask it of themselves. If knowledge is color blind, why should it matter whether the face in front of the classroom is a European white, a Hispanic, an Asian, and so on? Why should it matter whether the person is female or male?

One of the most well-known arguments for affirmative action is the role-model argument. It is also the argument that I think is the least satisfactory—not because women and minorities do not need role models—everyone does—but because as the argument is often presented, it comes dangerously close to implying that about the only thing a black, for instance, can teach a white is how not to be a racist. Well, I think better of myself than that. And I hope that all women and minorities feel the same about themselves. . . .

But even if the role-model argument were acceptable in some version or the other, affirmative action would still seem unsavory, as the implicit assumption about those hired as affirmative action appointments is that they are less qualified than those who are not. For, so the argument goes, the practice would be unnecessary if, in the first place, affirmative action

Originally published in Steven M. Cahn, ed., *Affirmative Action and the University: A Philosophical Inquiry*, pp. 125–131, 1993, Temple University Press. Reprinted by permission of Temple University Press.

appointees were the most qualified for the position, since they would be hired by virtue of their merits. I call this the counterfactual argument from qualifications.

Now, while I do not want to say much about it, this argument has always struck me as extremely odd. In a morally perfect world, it is no doubt true that if women and minorities were the most qualified they would be hired by virtue of their merits. But this truth tells me nothing about how things are in this world. It does not show that biases built up over decades and centuries do not operate in the favor of, say, white males over nonwhite males. It is as if one argued against feeding the starving simply on the grounds that in a morally perfect world starvation would not exist. Perhaps it would not. But this is no argument against feeding the starving now.

It would be one thing if those who advance the counterfactual argument from qualifications addressed the issue of built-up biases that operate against women and minorities. Then I could perhaps suppose that they are arguing in good faith. But for them to ignore these built-up biases in the name of an ideal world is sheer hypocrisy. It is to confuse what the ideal should be with the steps that should be taken to get there. Sometimes the steps are very simple or, in any case, purely procedural: instead of A, do B; or perform a series of well-defined steps that guarantee the outcome. Not so with nonbiased hiring, however, since what is involved is a change in attitude and feelings—not even merely a change in belief. After all, it is possible to believe something quite sincerely and yet not have the emotional wherewithal to act in accordance with that belief. . . .

The philosophical debate over affirmative action has stalled . . . because so many who oppose it, and some who do not, are unwilling to acknowledge the fact that sincere belief in equality does not entail a corresponding change in attitude and feelings in day-to-day interactions with women and minorities. Specifically, sincere belief does not eradicate residual and, thus, unintentional sexist and racist attitudes.[1] So, joviality among minorities may be taken by whites as the absence of intellectual depth or sincerity on the part of those minorities, since such behavior is presumed to be uncommon among high-minded intellectual whites. Similarly, it is a liability for academic women to be too fashionable in their attire, since fashionably attired women are often taken by men as aiming to be seductive.

Lest there be any misunderstanding, nothing I have said entails that unqualified women and minorities should be hired. I take it to be obvious, though, that whether someone is the best qualified is often a judgment call. On the other hand, what I have as much as said is that there are built-up biases in the hiring process that disfavor women and minorities and need to be corrected. I think of it as rather on the order of correcting for unfavorable moral headwinds. It is possible to be committed to gender and racial equality and yet live a life in which residual, and thus unintentional, sexism and racism operate to varying degrees of explicitness.

I want to return now to the question with which I began this essay: What good am I as a black professor? I want to answer this question because, insofar as our aim is a just society, I think it is extremely important to see the way in which it does matter that the person in front of the class is not always a white male, notwithstanding the truth that knowledge, itself, is color blind.

Teaching is not just about transmitting knowledge. If it were, then students could simply read books and professors could simply pass out tapes or lecture notes. Like it or not, teachers are the object of intense emotions and feelings on the part of students solicitous of faculty approval and affirmation. Thus, teaching is very much about intellectual affirmation; and there can be no such affirmation of the student by the mentor in the absence of deep trust between them, be the setting elementary or graduate school. Without this trust, a mentor's praise will ring empty; constructive criticism will seem mean spirited; and advice will be poorly received, if sought after at all. A student needs to be confident that he can make a mistake before the professor without being regarded as stupid in the professor's eyes and that the professor is interested in seeing beyond his weaknesses to his strengths. Otherwise, the student's interactions with the professor will be plagued by uncertainty; and that uncertainty will fuel the self-doubts of the student.

Now, the position that I should like to defend, however, is not that only women can trust women, only minorities can trust minorities, and only whites can trust whites. That surely is not what we want. Still, it must be acknowledged, first of all, that racism and sexism have very often been a bar to such trust between mentor and student, when the professor has been a white male and the student has been either a woman or a member of a minority group. Of course, trust between mentor and student is not easy to come by in any case. This, though, is compatible with women and minorities having even greater problems if the professor is a white male.

Sometimes a woman professor will be necessary if a woman student is to feel the trust of a mentor that makes intellectual affirmation possible; sometimes a minority professor will be necessary for a minority student; indeed, sometimes a white professor will be necessary for a white student. (Suppose the white student is from a very sexist and racist part of the United States, and it takes a white professor to undue the student's biases.)

Significantly, though, in an academy where there is gender and racial diversity among the faculty, that diversity alone gives a woman or minority student the hope that intellectual affirmation is possible. This is so even if the student's mentor should turn out to be a white male. For part of what secures our conviction that we are living in a just society is not merely that we experience justice, but that we see justice around us. A diverse faculty serves precisely this end in terms of women and minority students believing that it is possible for them to have an intellectually affirming mentor relationship with a faculty member regardless of the faculty's gender or race.

Naturally, there are some women and minority students who will achieve no matter what the environment. Harriet Jacobs and Frederick Douglass were slaves who went on to accomplish more than many of us will who have never seen the chains of slavery. Neither, though, would have thought their success a reason to leave slavery intact. Likewise, the fact that there are some women and minorities who will prevail in spite of the obstacles is no reason to leave the status quo in place.

There is another part of the argument. Where there is intellectual affirmation, there is also gratitude. When a student finds that affirmation in a faculty member, a bond is formed, anchored in the student's gratitude, that can weather almost anything. Without such ties there could be no "ole boy" network—a factor that is not about racism, but a kind of social interaction running its emotional course. When women and minority faculty play an intellectually affirming role in the lives of white male students, such faculty undermine a nonracist and nonsexist pattern of emotional feelings that has unwittingly served the sexist and racist end of passing the intellectual mantle from white male to white male. For what we want, surely, is not just blacks passing the mantle to blacks, women to women, and white males to white males, but a world in which it is possible for all to see one another as proper recipients of the intellectual mantle. Nothing serves this end better than the gratitude between mentor and student that often enough ranges over differences between gender and race or both.

Ideally, my discussion of trust, intellectual affirmation, and gratitude should have been supplemented with a discussion of nonverbal behavior. For it seems to me that what has been ignored . . . is the way in which judgments are communicated not simply by what is said but by a vast array of nonverbal behavior. Again, a verbal and sincere commitment to equality, without the relevant change in emotions and feelings, will invariably leave nonverbal behavior intact. Mere voice intonation and flow of speech can be a dead giveaway that the listener does not expect much of substance to come from the speaker. Anyone who doubts this should just remind her- or himself that it is a commonplace to remark to someone over the phone that he sounds tired or "down" or distracted, where the basis for this judgment, obviously, can only be how the individual sounds. One can get the clear sense that one called at the wrong time just by the way in which the other person responds or gets involved in the conversation. So, ironically, there is a sense in which it can be easier to convince ourselves that we are committed to gender and racial equality than it is to convince a woman or a minority person; for the latter see and experience our nonverbal behavior in a way that we ourselves do not. Specifically, it so often happens that a woman or minority can see that a person's nonverbal behavior belies their verbal support of gender and racial equality in faculty hiring—an interruption here, or an all-too-quick dismissal of a remark there. And this is to say nothing of the ways in which the oppressor often seems to know better than the victim how the victim is affected by the oppression that permeates her or his life, an arrogance that is communicated in myriad ways. This in not the place, though, to address the topic of social justice and nonverbal behavior.[2]

Before moving on let me consider an objection to my view. No doubt some will balk at the very idea of women and minority faculty intellectually affirming white male students. But this is just so much nonsense on the part of those balking. For I have drawn attention to a most powerful force in the lives of all individuals, namely, trust and gratitude; and I have indicated that just as these feelings have unwittingly served racist and sexist ends, they can serve ends that are morally laudable. Furthermore, I have rejected the idea, often implicit in the role-model argument, that women and minority faculty are only good for their own kind. What is more, the position I have advocated is not one of subservience in the least, as I have spoken of an affirming role that underwrites an often unshakable debt of gratitude.

So, to return to the question with which I began this essay: I matter as a black professor and so do women and minority faculty generally, because collectively, if not in each individual case, we represent the hope, sometimes in a very personal way, that the university is an environment where the trust that gives rise to intellectual affirmation and the accompanying gratitude is possible for all, and between all peoples. Nothing short of the reality of diversity can permanently anchor this hope for ourselves and posterity. . . .

I do not advocate the representation of given viewpoints or the position that the ethnic and gender composition of faculty members should be proportional to their numbers in society. The former is absurd because it is a mistake to insist that points of view are either gender- or color-coded. The latter is absurd because it would actually entail getting rid of some faculty, since the percentage of Jews in the academy far exceeds their percentage in the population. If one day this should come to be true of blacks or Hispanics, they in turn would be fair game. . . .

[T]he continued absence of any diversity whatsoever draws attention to itself. My earlier remarks about nonverbal behavior taken in conjunction with my observations about trust, affirmation, and gratitude are especially apropos here. The complete absence of diversity tells departments more about themselves than no doubt they are prepared to acknowledge.

I would like to conclude with a concrete illustration of the way in which trust and gratitude can make a difference in the academy. As everyone knows, being cited affirmatively is an important indication of professional success. Now, who gets cited is not just a matter of what is true and good. On the contrary, students generally cite the works of their mentors and the work of others introduced to them by their mentors; and, on the other hand, mentors generally cite the work of those students of theirs for whom they have provided considerable intellectual affirmation. Sexism and racism have often been obstacles to faculty believing that women and minorities can he proper objects of full intellectual affirmation. It has also contributed to the absence of women and minority faculty which, in turn, has made it well-nigh impossible for white male students to feel an intellectual debt of gratitude to women and minority faculty. Their presence in the academy cannot help but bring about a change with regard to so simple a matter as patterns of citation, the professional ripple effect of which will he significant beyond many of our wildest dreams.

If social justice were just a matter of saying or writing the correct words, then equality would have long ago been a *fait accompli* in the academy. For I barely know anyone who is a faculty member who has not bemoaned the absence of minorities and women in the academy, albeit to varying degrees. So, I conclude with a very direct question: Is it really possible that so many faculty could be so concerned that women and minorities should flourish in the academy, and yet so few do? You will have to forgive me for not believing that it is. For as any good Kantian knows, one cannot consistently will an end without also willing the means to that end. Onora O'Neill writes, "Willing, after all, is not just a matter of wishing that something were the case, but involves committing oneself to doing something to bring that situation about when opportunity is there and recognized. Kant expressed this point by insisting that rationality requires that whoever wills some end wills the necessary means insofar as these are available."[3] If Kant is right, then much hand-wringing talk about social equality for women and minorities can only be judged insincere.

NOTES

1. For a most illuminating discussion along this line, see Adrian M. S. Piper's very important essay, "Higher-Order Discrimination," in Owen Flanagan and Amelie Oksenberg Rorty, eds., *Identity, Character, and Morality: Essays in Moral Psychology* (Cambridge, MA: MIT Press, 1990).

2. For an attempt, see my "Moral Deference," *Philosophical Forum* 24, no. 1–3 (1992–1993): pp. 233–50.

3. Onora O'Neill, *Constructions. of Reason: Explorations of Kant's Practical Philosophy* (Cambridge University Press, 1989), p. 90.

STUDY QUESTIONS

1. How persuasive is the role-model argument for preferential affirmative action?
2. Is it advantageous for a minority student to have a minority mentor?
3. Is the continuing small number of African-American faculty members evidence for Thomas's conclusion that "much hand-wringing talk about social equality . . . can only be judged insincere"?
4. Do Thomas's arguments in favor of professorial appointments for women and members of racial or ethnic minorities also imply the importance of adding to faculties individuals with a particular religious affiliation, political commitment, or sexual orientation?

VI

INSTITUTIONAL
NEUTRALITY

Colleges and universities are committed to the protection of academic freedom. One threat comes from those who seek to have a school adopt an official stance on issues unrelated to its educational mission. For how can free inquiry be preserved if certain opinions are declared false and others true? Whether a proof for the existence of God is sound or our government's foreign policy mistaken is an appropriate subject for discussion, not decree. In other words, schools themselves should remain neutral, taking no sides on controversial issues.

Robert Paul Wolff, however, maintains that institutional neutrality is a myth. In his view, not taking a position is equivalent to supporting the prevailing opinion. Robert L. Simon disagrees. He argues that just as the government preserves freedom of religion by not adopting any official religion, so the university preserves freedom of inquiry by not supporting any partisan stand.

11

Neutrality and Its Critics

ROBERT PAUL WOLFF

In the dialectic of charge, response, and confrontation which dominates the campus these days, one of the most familiar disputes revolves about the role of the university as supporter or opponent of government policy. Characteristically, the interchange proceeds something like this:

1. The university is engaged in a variety of extra-educational activities, such as contract research, the scheduling of job interviews, transmission of class standing to draft boards, and so forth. These activities accumulate haphazardly without deliberate university control and in the absence of a coherent policy.

2. Radical students and faculty focus attention upon some few of the extra-educational activities as evidences of the university's positive support for a controversial and evil government policy. Transmission of class standing to draft boards supports the Vietnam war. Acceptance of contract research on counterinsurgency supports the reactionary imperialism of the United States abroad. The university's real estate dealings discriminate against the poor and the Black in the surrounding community.

3. The university defends its activities on the grounds that it takes no position with regard to social or political issues. It leaves its faculty free to teach what it likes, and to do research as it chooses. It opens its doors to speakers of all persuasions and recruiters for virtually any enterprise

Originally published in Robert Paul Wolff, *The Ideal of the University*, pp. 69–76, 1969, Beacon Press. © 1969 by Robert Paul Wolff. Reprinted by permission of Beacon Press.

which is not illegal. Individuals within the university may engage in whatever political activities they like, but for the university as an institution to take an official political stand would be in violation of its fundamental principles of value neutrality and academic freedom.

4. The radicals reply that the university *is* endorsing positions and policies by its actions, but that it is endorsing the *wrong* positions and the *wrong* policies. What is needed is an about-face, so that the university will throw its considerable prestige and power into the fight against a reactionary establishment.

This debate, in all the many forms it takes from university to university, revolves about one of the oldest tenets of the liberal tradition—the myth of the value-neutral institution. Just as the state, in classical liberal economic theory, is expected to stand clear of the competitive battles waged between firm and firm, or capital and labor, merely maintaining the freedom and order of the market place of commodities, so the university is expected to stand clear of the intellectual battles waged between doctrine and doctrine, dogma and dogma, in the market place of ideas. Its sole function is to regulate the contest, ensuring a place in the debate to every position and every party. The university administration is charged with the responsibility of protecting those within the academy from the repeated assaults by outside critics, while at the same time guaranteeing that absolute freedom of debate reigns within. From this freedom in the market place of ideas, it is confidently believed, the greatest possible advance in truth and wisdom will flow.[1]

As a prescription for institutional behavior, the doctrine of value neutrality suffers from the worst disability which can afflict a norm: what it prescribes is not wrong; it is impossible. A large university in contemporary America simply cannot adopt a value-neutral stance, either externally or internally, no matter how hard it tries. This observation is scarcely original with me; indeed, I should have thought it was a commonplace of social analysis. Nevertheless, it is so often and so willfully forgotten that a few lines might profitably be spent demonstrating its truth.

Let us begin with the university's relation to society. A large university, in respect of its employees, faculty, students, land holding, endowment, and other material and human resources, is in many ways comparable to a large corporation. Columbia University, for example, is one of the largest property owners in the city of New York; the University of California must surely be one of the major employers in the state; and cities like Ann Arbor, Cambridge, and Princeton have somewhat the air of company towns. Now, one of the first truths enunciated in introductory ethics courses is that the failure to do something is as much an act as the doing of it. It is perfectly reasonable to hold a man responsible for *not* paying his taxes, for *not* exercising due care and caution in driving, for *not* helping a fellow man in need. In public life, when a man who has power refrains from using it, we all agree that he has *acted politically*. Omissions are frequently even more significant politically than commissions in American politics, for those in positions of decision usually rule by default rather than by consent.[2] Hence, acquiescence in governmental acts, under the guise of impartiality, actually strengthens the established forces and makes successful opposition all the harder.

For example, let us suppose that a university cooperates with the Selective Service System, motivated in part by a simple desire to be helpful to legitimate government agencies and interested students, and in part by the conviction that deliberate refusal to cooperate would constitute an institutional opposition to the draft which would violate the principle of political neutrality. Obviously, the university strengthens the draft system, positively by its cooperation and negatively by its failure to take the deliberate step of opposition which was open to it. To be sure, public refusal would have a greater political effect against, than quiet cooperation would have for, the government. Hence there must be better reasons for opposition than there are for cooperation. But the reasons need not be overwhelming or apocalyptic, and, in any event, the action, positive or negative, is a *political* act based on *political* considerations. No major institution can remain politically innocent in an open society.

When pressed with such obvious arguments, the administrators frequently retreat to the claim that they merely follow the law. Dow Chemical is permitted to recruit because it and its activities are legal. No moral or political judgment is superimposed on the accepted law of the land.

Now, in actual fact, this defense is false, for the CIA recruits freely on campuses even though it admits to repeatedly breaking domestic laws and violating international treaties. But even when true, the defense fails, for we live in a society which pursues policies by enacting laws. Hence, mere obedience to law is at the same time support for established policy. Suppose, to take a case which is presumably no longer possible, that a school in a state which legally forbids marriages between whites and blacks refuses to hire a white scholar on the grounds that he is married to a Black woman. It thereby lends its great institutional weight to the enforcement of an evil social policy, even though it does so merely by obeying the law. There is no difference between this hypothetical case and the case of defense research or cooperation with the draft, except of course that all good white liberal professors and administrators are opposed to the wicked segregation in the South, while many of the same people feel quite comfortable with America's foreign policy or with their own university's behavior in the surrounding neighborhood.

When we turn to the internal organization of the university, we find the same unavoidable evaluative bias. I have already rehearsed the radical complaint that American capitalism prepares young men for the rigors of the corporate world by the lockstep character of education. Whatever one thinks of this view, it is obvious that an institution imposes some set of values on its students merely by requiring that they maintain a passing grade average, attend classes regularly, take examinations on time, and leave after completing an appropriate assortment of courses. To be sure, the vehicle for the imposition of values is the *form* rather than the *content* of the educational process, but the effect is imposition nonetheless.[3]

An analogous bias is built into the free market place of ideas, which usually pretends to be neutral among competing dogmas and doctrines. By permitting all voices to be heard, the university systematically undermines all those doctrines which claim exclusive possession of the truth and seek therefore to silence opposed voices. By permitting a Catholic to preach his faith only so long as he allows others to preach theirs, one quite effectively repudiates precisely the central thesis of the Catholic Church. This fact is perfectly well understood in countries like Spain, where opposition to the censorship of the Church is a *political* act. It is also understood in Czechoslovakia, or Russia, or China. For some strange reason, American intellectuals cannot perceive that their own commitment to free debate is also a substantive political act, no more neutral than the prohibition of dissent in religiously or politically authoritarian countries.

Finally, every university expresses a number of positive value commitments through the character of its faculty, of its library, even through the buildings it chooses to build. Astronomy departments ignore astrology, psychiatry departments ignore dianetics, philosophy departments ignore dialectical materialism. Universities build laboratories for experimental research, thereby committing themselves to the importance of the scientific enterprise; libraries devote scarce resources to the accumulation of rare and ancient manuscripts; whole faculties are organized to teach and study social welfare, veterinary science, law, or business. Each of these institutional decisions embodies an evaluation which can easily become the focus of a political dispute.

The conclusion is obvious. No institution can remain politically neutral either in its interaction with society or in the conduct and organization of its internal affairs. To pretend otherwise is merely to throw up a smokescreen; it is a way of rationalizing the value commitments already made, by attempting to remove them from the area of legitimate debate. Students for a Democratic Society speak of the need to *politicize* the campus. Moderate professors and students oppose this *politicization*, which they protest would alter the character of the university for the worse. But the truth is that every campus is now politicized, necessarily and unavoidably. The radicals do not wish to inflict politics on a realm which once was happily apolitical. They only wish to force an awareness of the already political character of the university, as a first step toward changing the policies which the university embodies or pursues.

On the basis of this analysis, it might appear that the university should drop the mask of impartiality, openly acknowledge the political biases implied by its policies and educational practices, and confront the problem of deciding how its political orientation should be determined. That would, indeed, be the honest and consistent course to follow. To be sure, any system of majority rule or collegial decision would still leave members of a dissident minority unhappy at being associated with an institution whose avowed policies differed from their own; but that must inevitably be true in any case, and at least the policy would be openly and fairly arrived at.

However, the honest and consistent course is not always the best; and I am persuaded that in the United States, at the present time, such a course would have reactionary rather than progressive consequences. There are two reasons why radicals would he ill-advised to expose the incoherence and hypocrisy of the doctrine of institutional neutrality. In the first place, faculties and student bodies tend, by and large, to be conservative in their leanings; and once the university is forced to bring its policies out into the open, the majority is liable to move the direction of those policies even farther to the right. Students are always surprised to discover the melancholy facts of faculty-student conservatism. Since the liberals and radicals on the campus make most of the noise and grab most of the headlines, it is easy to be fooled into thinking that the campus is a hotbed of radical conviction barely contained by a manipulative and repressive administration. Inevitably, the day of disillusion arrives when a faculty vote or student referendum reveals the radicals to be in a distinct minority.

I confess that during the tumultuous events of Spring 1968 at Columbia, I permitted myself to hope that the forces of progress had acquired sufficient support to carry a meeting of the faculty. Each time we were convened, however, the pro-administration bloc defeated the challenges of the rebels by a two-thirds majority. Even in the faculty of Columbia College, a number of whose members had been beaten by the police during the two raids, there was not even a large minority for motions of censure or expressions of opposition to President Kirk's actions. In the end, we had our greatest effect through informal channels of discussion and pressure, where intensity of concern could in part compensate for lack of numbers.

It would be tactically unwise, therefore, to push to an open vote such matters as university acceptance of defense research or the policy of open recruiting. But this is hardly the greatest danger which the politicization of the university invites. Far worse is the ever-present threat of pressure, censorship, and witch-hunting by conservative forces in society at large. The universities at present are sanctuaries for social critics who would find it very hard to gain a living elsewhere in society. Who but a university these days would hire Herbert Marcuse, Eugene Genovese, or Barrington Moore, Jr.? Where else are anarchists, socialists, and followers of other unpopular persuasions accorded titles, honors, and the absolute security of academic tenure? Let the university once declare that it is a political actor, and its faculty will be investigated, its charter revoked, and its tax-exempt status forthwith removed. How majestic and unassailable is the university president who protects his dissident faculty with an appeal to the sanctity of academic freedom!

It is a bitter pill for the radicals to swallow, but the fact is that they benefit more than any other segment of the university community from the fiction of institutional neutrality. For the present, therefore, I would strongly urge both students and professors to hide behind the slogans "lehrfreiheit" and "lernfreiheit," and give up the attempt to politicize the campus. If this advice is too cautious to satisfy their revolutionary longings they may look on the universities as those protected base camps which, Mao Tse-tung tells us, are the foundation of a successful protracted guerrilla campaign.

NOTES

1. For a critical analysis of John Stuart Mill's famous defense of this thesis, see my *The Poverty of Liberalism* (Boston: Beacon Press, 1968), Chapter One.

2. I am referring here, of course, to the well-known theory of "veto groups." For a general defense of this anti-power-elite view of American politics, see *The Poverty of Liberalism*, Chapter Three.

3. Let me say that I *approve* by and large of the values thus imposed. I am personally very strict with regard to lateness of papers and the like. But I recognize that I must *justify* such requirements with an argument and not claim to be neutral on the issues involved.

STUDY QUESTIONS

1. Does a university express its support for a law by obeying it?
2. Does a university violate neutrality by requiring students to take examinations on time?
3. Does a university violate neutrality by not teaching astrology?
4. How does Wolff's claim that every campus is unavoidably politicized cohere with his conclusion that students and professors should give up the attempt to politicize the campus?

12

A Defense of the Neutral University

ROBERT L. SIMON

In times of major social controversy, should colleges and universities function as political agents on behalf of particular causes? Although this issue is often forgotten in times of political quiescence, it rises to the surface again during times of political conflict. Protests against the Vietnam War, as well as concern in the 1980s over divestment of university investments in corporations doing business in South Africa, have generated criticism of the view that universities should be politically neutral. Can academic institutions justifiably remain silent in the face of such events as genocide, the waging of unjust wars, systematic and pervasive racial discrimination, political oppression, and world hunger? On the other hand, if a university or college becomes a partisan political agent, can it fulfill other functions, including the academic ones that are its very reason for being? Are there moral reasons, based on academic functions, for the university to refrain from partisan political action?

Questions such as these have at least two important characteristics. First, they are normative in that they concern the principles or norms that *ought* to guide the behavior of institutions of higher learning in the political arena. Their focus is not what the behavior of such institutions is but what it should be. Second, they concern the behavior of colleges and universities as *institutions*, not the behavior of the individuals, such as faculty members and students, who may attend or be employed there.

Originally published in Steven M. Cahn, ed., *Morality, Responsibility, and the University: Studies in Academic Ethics*, pp. 243–259, 1990, Temple University Press. Reprinted by permission of Temple University Press.

Consider the claim that colleges and universities as institutions should be politically neutral. Before examining substantive arguments for and against it, it is important to realize that much of the controversy over the neutrality thesis is conceptual rather than moral. That is, what looks like heated moral disagreement over whether universities should be neutral will often, upon analysis, rest on divergent conceptions of the nature of neutrality itself. If different parties to an argument mean different things by neutrality, they may not be disagreeing about the same issue in the first place. It is important not to assume that the meaning of *neutrality* is clear or understood the same by all of us, in considering the issue with which I will begin: whether it is even possible for colleges and universities to be neutral.

I. Skepticism and the Concept of Neutrality

Many critics of the ideal of a politically neutral university would deny that the central issue at stake is whether colleges and universities should be politically neutral. On their view, since it makes sense to say universities ought to act a certain way only if they *can* act in that way, the fundamental issue is whether neutrality is even possible. In the view of many, it is not. Thus, Robert Paul Wolff argues in an acute critique of the university from the point of view of radicalism of the 1960s that

> As a prescription for institutional behavior, the doctrine of value neutrality suffers from the worst disability which can afflict a norm: what it prescribes is not wrong; it is impossible. A large university in contemporary America simply cannot adopt a value-neutral stance, either externally or internally, no matter how hard it tries.[1]

However, we need to be careful before accepting such a conclusion too quickly. Perhaps, as John Searle has suggested, skeptics about the very possibility of neutrality are like certain sorts of epistemological skeptics who question whether knowledge is possible. The kind of skeptic Searle has in mind simply defines knowledge in such a way that it can never be attained.[2] But of course, just because knowledge in the skeptic's sense is unattainable, it does not follow that knowledge in some other significant sense is unattainable as well. Similarly, perhaps the skeptic can show that neutrality, conceived in some particular way, is impossible. It does not follow, however, that neutrality conceived in some other way is necessarily impossible or worthless.

For example, one popular argument is that no university can be value-neutral, because the principle that the university *ought* to be value-neutral is itself a normative claim that expresses a value. A second argument points out that a university by its very nature is committed to values such as knowledge, truth, and rational discourse.

Such arguments do show that no university can be strictly value-free. They bring out the salutary point that the commitment to be neutral, like other value commitments, requires a rational defense. However, they undermine the ideal of the politically neutral university only if political neutrality and total value-freedom are equivalent. But as we will see, there are some significant senses of value-neutrality that are not equivalent to total value freedom. Hence, even if the university cannot (and should not) be value free, that is irrelevant to the evaluation of at least some significant versions of the neutrality thesis.

Other skeptics point out that the university's action (or inaction) must have political consequences. Therefore, they conclude that neutrality is impossible, for on their view, even the failure to take a stand on significant issues has causal implications. Therefore, no matter what the university does, it has political consequences. At the very least, the status quo is left unchanged. As Wolff argues in *The Ideal of the University*,

> Omissions are frequently even more significant politically than commissions in American politics, for those in positions of decision usually rule by default rather than by consent. Hence, acquiescence in governmental acts, under the guise of impartiality, actually strengthens the established forces and makes successful opposition all the harder.[3]

The skeptic makes a number of strong points here. Clearly, in at least some contexts, the failure to act can be of moral significance and require moral justification. Thus, if I learn that a killer will attempt to murder you at a particular place and time, and I can warn you at little cost to myself, my failure to do so is morally culpable.

However, from my moral responsibility for acts of omission as well as acts of commission, it does not follow that I automatically fail to be neutral. All that follows is that neutrality requires a defense, not that it is a myth.

This is an important point and is perhaps best illustrated by the constitutional prohibition in the United States against an establishment of religion. This clause requires at least that the government be neutral toward particular religions and is minimally satisfied if the government does nothing to favor one religion over another. Of course, the decision to be neutral in such a way requires a moral defense. It is not necessarily value-free. Nevertheless, the government is neutral toward particular religions.

The skeptic might protest that by not actively favoring a minority religion, the government is covertly preserving the status quo and so is not really neutral after all. But all the situation amounts to is that the government is leaving things as they otherwise would be. It is keeping its nose out of religion. That is just what proponents of governmental neutrality toward religion mean by governmental neutrality. So the skeptic's legitimate point that the decision to be neutral requires a moral justification does not establish that neutrality is a myth but only that neutrality itself is hardly uncontroversial or value-free.

Let us consider further the logic of "you are either with us or against us." The argument, when exposed to the light of day, seems to go as follows:

1. Failure to actually support me has the consequence of making my opponents' position better off than it would have been had you supported me.
2. Hence, your failure to support me has the consequence of making my opponents better off.
3. Hence, you have actually supported my opponents.
4. Clearly, you are not neutral but rather are my opponent as well.

One point worth considering is that premise 1 is not more plausible than position 1:

1'. Failure to support my opponents has the consequence of making my position better off than it would have been had you supported them.

By substituting 1' for 1 and then making the same inferences, one can with equal plausibility conclude that you have chosen my side rather than that of my opponents. It is of course true that failure to take a stand deprives one side of an issue of support. But the point is that it does so as well for the other side! That is exactly why it is neutral, not in the sense of being consequence-free but in the sense of being nonpartisan, of not interfering on behalf of any one religion.

The fallacy involved in the assertion that "you are either with me or against me" is that it can be said by *either side* to third parties. The implications are logically devastating. Both sides could regard the third party as an opponent (since if it is not with us it is against us) or, with equal plausibility, as an ally (since it is not for our opponent, it must be with us). Surely, any formula that implies such blatant contradictions must be rejected as logically incoherent.

However, if, in spite of this point, the skeptic still wants to stipulate that the failure to actively support one side aids the other, then it follows trivially (by definition) that *any* decision, including the decision not to make a decision, has political consequences and is not neutral. Let us call an act or policy that has no effect, from either action or inaction, on a political controversy consequentially neutral. Given the skeptic's assumptions, no agent can be consequentially neutral. However, even if we ignore the logical incoherence already pointed out, the skeptic's victory is a hollow one. Even if consequential neutrality is unattainable, many other kinds of neutrality may be quite feasible. Thus, even if the government fails to be consequentially neutral with respect to religion, it can be neutral in some other sense. For example, it can provide no active support for any particular religion over any other, and it may be important that it does not. Similarly, although it is doubtful if a university can avoid performing any act that would have political consequences—a conceptual impossibility once we define failure to aid one side as aiding the other—the university can still avoid becoming a partisan on many issues. It can also avoid acting with political motive or intent.

Accordingly, it is doubtful if the skeptical arguments I have considered show that neutrality is impossible. Moreover, even if they do show that some kinds of neutrality, such as absolute value-freedom or consequential neutrality, are impossible, they leave open whether other significant forms of neutrality are possible. Skeptical arguments do remind us that the decision to be neutral is itself a morally significant one for which the agent may be held morally responsible. Whether or not we ought to be neutral is itself an ethical issue. Be that as it may, the skeptic's premises that universities cannot be value-free, that the stance of neutrality itself is value-laden, and that inaction as well as action has political consequences, do not imply that all kinds of neutrality are conceptually incoherent or logically beyond our grasp.

II. Neutrality and Professorial Ethics

I recently came across an article on the teaching of ethics in which a philosophy professor declared that his goal as a teacher was to "save students from their parents."[4] I would have agreed with that statement when I started my teaching career, but as my children grew I started to have doubts. Now that my eldest son has just entered college, I'm sure it is false.

Be that as it may, the author's claim raises a number of important general issues. Should a professor in an ethics course attempt to get students to question their own values? Should the professor go further and aim at having the students reject a particular set of traditional norms? May such a professor permissibly aim at having students adopt the specific values deemed most acceptable by the instructor? Is there any sense in which the individual instructor in the college classroom should be neutral with respect to ethical or political values?

Let me begin by considering two admittedly extreme responses to this question. According to the first, which we can call the model of partisanship, the professor should try, using whatever means of persuasion will prove most effective, to get students to adopt the values the instructor thinks are most important.

Clearly, this model will have few if any adherents. It has little if anything to do with education but in effect views the professor as someone whose role it is to indoctrinate students. Students are not treated as persons in their own right but as things to be manipulated by whatever persuasive techniques work best. In effect, the veneer of education is employed to cloak what is really going on, namely, indoctrination of the less powerful by the more powerful. Indeed, using one's status as a professor to impose one's values on students through nonrational means is a form of harassment, ethically on par with sexual harassment, in which a person in a position of power uses it to coerce or to manipulate others.

If there are adherents of the extreme partisan view, they may retort that the alternative is nonexistent, since there really are no rules of rational inquiry that are ideologically neutral. According to this retort, even to adopt ground rules of inquiry is a political act that has covert ideological implications. Now, in a trivial sense, this reply is correct, if only because, as we have seen, rationality is itself a value. Moreover, the decision to adopt rational procedures may have as a consequence that certain political positions receive more support than others, since they appear more reasonable to rational investigators. It does not follow, however, that the rules fail to be neutral in a significant sense; they may have intellectual warrant or standing apart from the political preferences of those who hold them.

Thus, if the model of partisanship is to be defended in public discourse and not just imposed upon us by manipulative techniques or coercion, its adherents themselves must appeal to rules of rational inquiry. If no such rules had any warrant or justification, apart from the political preferences of those who employ them, the whole institution of public rational discourse and critical inquiry would be an illusion. Not only would the university itself be a fraud, but no partisan advocate of any position could show it to be more justified than any other. The very process of justification would be nothing more than a manifestation of the very political commitment to be justified. This is a very high price to be paid for the model of partisanship. Indeed, since the model implies that its advocates can give us no good reason for accepting it, since "good reasons" themselves are a fiction, we cannot both accept the model and conduct a rational inquiry into the nature of neutrality. Accordingly, the model of partisanship, at least in its extreme form, must be rejected by all those committed to the university as a center of rational inquiry and critical discussion.

This point does not necessarily presuppose that totally value-free or uncontroversial principles of inquiry and discussion can be justified. It does imply, rather, that the instructor is committed to employing some standards of inquiry and evaluation that are regarded as at least provisionally warranted, and not simply because their use supports the ideology or partisan value commitments of the user. Such warrant may be broadly pragmatic, and far from value-free, but it must constitute an independent test of the positions the user attempts to justify within inquiry itself. Thus, even the Rawlsian method of reflective equilibrium, which requires us to test our considered judgments of particular cases against our principles so as to promote overall systematic coherence in our moral conceptual scheme, allows the possibility that some of our most cherished beliefs may be undermined by the weight of overall systematic considerations with which they might clash.[5]

Consider now the second model of professorial ethics, which I can call the model of absolute neutrality. According to this model, the professor must be absolutely value-neutral in the classroom. The instructor's job, on this view, is just to present information, not to evaluate it. Where there is controversy in a discipline, different positions are to be explained, but the professor is not to take a stand on which is most plausible. While it might be permissible for the professor to take the position of an advocate of each important viewpoint as it is presented to the student, no special preference or weight is to be given for the viewpoint the professor favors. Thereby, respect is shown for the autonomy of students, since no one attempts to impose a position upon them, and instructors refrain from using their superior knowledge or the prestige of their position to influence students by non-rational means.

While the respect for individual autonomy underlying the model of absolute neutrality is admirable, it is far from clear that the model itself is even coherent. Surely an instructor *must* make at least some value judgments, for example, judgments about what material ought to be included in the course, what controversies are worth exploring, and what arguments are significant enough to explore in depth. Moreover, the instructor's commitment to respecting the autonomy of students is itself a fundamental moral value.

Accordingly, neither the model of neutrality nor that of partisanship is fully acceptable, at least in their extreme forms. Of course, the extreme versions of each model may be modified to escape the sort of objections I have considered. For example, an advocate of neutrality might attempt to distinguish between *professional* value judgments, such as judgments about the relative importance of various issues for the discipline, which cannot be avoided by the instructor, and personal *moral or political* value judgments, which can be avoided. An advocate of partisanship might acknowledge rational constraints on discourse but maintain that instructors should defend their moral and political convictions within the universe of critical discourse demarcated by such criteria of rationality.

Rather than pursue questions raised by various modifications of the different models, the important point for my purpose is that both kinds of modifications limit the *partisanship* of the instructor. Both presuppose that the instructor is a scholar first and a partisan second. More precisely, partisanship is governed by rules of scholarship and critical inquiry. Thus, on the revised model of neutrality, it is acknowledged that value judgments must be made, but they are to be based on the professional judgment of the scholar and presumably can be defended by appeal to commonly accepted professional standards. Similarly, advocates of a modified model of partisanship concede that advocacy must be limited by such canons of critical inquiry as respect for the evidence, rules of logical argumentation, openness to objection, and the like. Students are to be persuaded by rational discourse or not persuaded at all. Manipulation by persuasive but nonrational techniques is prohibited.

There is a sense, then, in which proponents of both models should concede that the professor is to be *neutral*. Proponents of both models should acknowledge that classroom discussion must take place within a framework of rules of critical inquiry. Adherence to those rules is neutral in the sense that adherence by itself does not dictate the substantive position that emerges. On the contrary, substantive positions that prove unsatisfactory within such a framework must either be revised or replaced when a more satisfactory competitor is available.

Let us call this kind of neutrality *critical neutrality* because it requires adherence to rules of critical inquiry that do not by themselves determine which substantive positions will prove most satisfactory within the realm of inquiry they govern. Such rules need not themselves be value-free or neutral in any other sense. They are neutral only in the sense that they constitute a court of appeal independent of the personal preferences of the investigators.

Adherence to critical neutrality does not require neutrality in any of the senses that the skeptic has found incoherent. In particular, it does not require value-freedom. Neither does it require consequential neutrality. On the contrary, adherence to canons of critical neutrality may have profound effects on students and on other professionals working in the discipline. Neither does it require that the teacher avoid advocacy of substantive positions. As long as advocacy is carried out within the critical framework, it may well be educationally desirable, so long as students are sufficiently mature and possess sufficient critical tools to be able to form reasonably independent judgments of their own.

Before turning to this last constraint, consider whether critical neutrality really is possible. If possible, is it desirable? Whether critical neutrality is possible depends upon whether rules of critical inquiry exist for various disciplines independently of internal substantive positions as specified. This is not the place to argue that such rules do exist. However, it certainly is possible that they do. More important, their existence seems to be a presupposition of critical inquiry itself. Indeed, it is hard to see how the skeptic could rationally maintain that there are no such rules without implicitly appealing to them in the course of the argument. Thus, at the very least, the burden of proof is on the skeptic why skepticism about critical neutrality is not itself incoherent, since it undermines the very framework within which justification takes place.

Assuming, then, that critical neutrality is possible, I can ask if it is also desirable. In fact, two sorts of arguments can be given for showing not only that critical neutrality is desirable but that adherence to the framework of critical neutrality is morally required for instructors in higher education.

The first is based on rights or entitlements generated by the autonomy of students and colleagues. As autonomous agents, such individuals are wronged if they are manipulated by the intentional presentation of misinformation or by persuasive use of nonrational emotive techniques designed to distort inquiry so as promote acceptance of the instructor's own views. In such a case, the offending instructor is subject to the same criticism as one who misuses professorial authority or prestige to secure sexual favors from students. In each case, power is being wrongly used to manipulate others to one's own advantage, thereby limiting the other's possibilities for autonomous choice.

Second, violation of critical neutrality is a violation of the canons of inquiry that govern the central educational function of the college or university. Respect for critical inquiry can be seen as intrinsically valuable, for an atmosphere where different points of view can be freely debated and examined best promotes free and informed choice by us all. Even if there are extreme cases in which it seems defensible to violate critical neutrality, general conformity surely is desirable. Moreover, given the moral weight of the reasons supporting conformity, only countervailing moral considerations of the weightiest kind could justify overriding the ethics of critical inquiry in specific cases.

We can conclude, then, that individual instructors should be committed neither to the extreme model of neutrality nor to the extreme model of partisanship. Rather, regardless of their other values or positions, they should be committed to a general policy of adherence to the ethics of critical inquiry. Because of the especially significant values underlying such an ethic, it can be outweighed only when even more significant considerations count in favor of making an exception.

III. NEUTRALITY AND THE UNIVERSITY

Although the university cannot be value-neutral in the sense of being totally value-free, my discussion so far suggests that there may be other senses of neutrality worth considering. In particular, it can be argued that just as the individual instructor is obligated to respect the rules and canons of rational inquiry in the classroom, so the university is morally required to maintain an institutional climate in which such rules govern discourse and inquiry. If so, it can be argued that the university as an institution must be neutral in a sense similar to the way an umpire in baseball must be neutral. Just as the umpire has an ethical obligation to be a neutral arbiter rather than a partisan of one team or another, the university also may have an ethical obligation not to become just another partisan with an interest in defeating opponents.

Perhaps, then, the kind of neutrality appropriate for colleges and universities may be *institutional critical neutrality*, namely, adherence to the values, rules, and principles of critical inquiry and discussion regardless of which substantive positions are thereby advanced.

Clearly, institutional critical neutrality is not an uncontroversial notion. To begin with, critics may argue that to support rules of rational discourse is itself to take a substantive position in opposition to opponents of rationality or adherents of faith over reason. But since proponents of institutional critical neutrality need not claim that the university can or should be value-neutral, the objection in this form need not bother them. Their point is not that neutrality requires total suspension of values. On the contrary, as we have seen, institutional critical neutrality is itself a value posture that requires an ethical defense. What such neutrality requires is not total value-freedom but rather adherence to and protection of those values and norms that are constituents of critical inquiry and promotion of conditions under which critical inquiry can flourish.

A more troublesome form of the objection is the denial that there is any neutral set of rules or norms constitutive of critical inquiry. Rather, critical inquiry itself is arguably an essentially contested concept, conceived of in different ways by proponents of different ideological positions.[6] Thus, the kind of norms of critical inquiry supported by a Marxist or a pragmatist may differ from those favored by an ethical emotivist, who relies on the epistemology of classical empiricism. Indeed, it is at least arguable that the values we hold influence the kind of norms of critical inquiry we think most warranted. Thus, a pragmatist might maintain that evaluation of scientific theories, and hence of what count as facts, properly takes into account value-laden judgments concerning the overall satisfactoriness of the theory and its rivals.[7] If so, there may be no favored conception of "the canons" of critical inquiry that is value-free.

While these points surely have force, it is far from clear that institutional critical neutrality requires the university to take a stand on such controversial epistemological questions. Rather, the commitment is to an institution within which such controversies can be pursued, where positions are defended by argument rather than force and debate is open to those qualified to participate in it. This commitment does not require the university to decide between, say, Quine and Popper, but only to ensure that the parties to the debate have a fair opportunity to present their arguments.

But aren't proponents of different ideological views all too likely to disagree over what counts as a fair opportunity to participate in debate? When debate is open or closed and what counts as defending a position by reason can be equally controversial. Neutral accounts of such notions, we may be told, are not to be found.

Important disputes can arise over the nature of free inquiry, but they arguably concern borderline cases. Arguably, there is a common core of principles that all constituents of a university community must accept, including the commitment to consider evidence, even evidence against one's own position, on its merits and the rejection of coercion as a means of silencing opposition. Without allegiance to these core elements of rational inquiry, no rational debate seems possible to begin with.

However, even if we ignore the case for core elements of rational inquiry, it doesn't necessarily follow that institutional critical neutrality is undermined. Even if the nature of critical inquiry is itself inherently controversial, it doesn't follow that the values at stake in debate among various conceptions of critical inquiry are political values, let alone the same political values at stake in currently controversial issues. Thus, canons of critical inquiry are still neutral in the sense that the position one takes in epistemological debate need not determine or be determined by one's partisan political stance. For example, parties who disagree on divestment can still agree that different sides should be heard in debate on each side of the issue. Similarly, commitment to divestment does not necessarily imply commitment to acceptance of the legitimacy of specific forms of protest against universities that do not divest. Thus, even if there are no inherently uncontroversial principles of critical inquiry, it still may be the case that for every dispute, there are some higher-order principles of inquiry accepted by all sides.[8]

But doesn't the university itself restrict debate in favor of already established positions? Aren't proponents of many "eccentric" epistemological positions excluded from the university community? Thus, there are no departments of astrology on campus, nor is creationism often defended, let alone given equal footing with evolutionary biology.

Clearly, not all epistemological positions or world views are represented in the university. But it does not follow that institutional critical neutrality is a fraud. To see why, consider again the constitutional requirement that prohibits the establishment of religion in America. As interpreted by the courts, the establishment clause does not require government hostility toward religion. Rather, it requires the separation of religion from public life and prohibits the active government support of one religion over others.

Now it would be absurd to argue that neutrality has been violated simply because some religions have no adherents. If commitment to particular religions is based on the decisions of the citizens themselves, rather than government intervention, neutrality is preserved. The point of neutrality is not to ensure that every religion has some supporters but rather to ensure that government policy does not officially sanction some religions and suppress others.

A related point can be made about institutional critical neutrality in the university. Just as individual citizens themselves have the right to make their own religious commitments, so scholars have the right (and obligation) to determine what views to explore and defend within their areas of professional competency. If such scholars, as a result of their inquiries, determine that some views are not worth examining, or are different in kind from those that can be examined within critical inquiry, then that decision does not violate the institution's neutrality. Rather, a major purpose served by institutional critical neutrality is to promote an atmosphere in which various hypotheses can be evaluated, whether they are metahypotheses about the rules for critical inquiry or first-order hypotheses within particular disciplines.

It is important to keep in mind here the distinction between limitations on debate *within* a field and limitations on metadebate *about* the limitations within a particular field. Thus, no respectable scientific department would offer courses in astrology, but debate on whether there is a justifiable difference between science and astrology might take place in a course on philosophy of science. Thus, I would suggest that limits on debate within the university, and on views that may be represented, are justified when (1) the limitations are supportable by appeal to the publicly accessible results of critical inquiry; (2) the limitations are proportional in force to the degree of support in their favor; and (3) the limitations are debatable in meta-inquiry about the discipline in question. These conditions allow inquirers to concentrate on areas of examination they consider significant, while containing checks against dogmatism and intolerance.

My discussion suggests that institutional critical neutrality is ultimately grounded on the values of personal autonomy and critical investigation. Such a justification of neutrality can now be examined more closely.

IV. Is the Neutral University Desirable?

Perhaps enough has been said to show that common skeptical arguments against the very possibility of a neutral university face serious problems. At the very least, the burden of proof is on the skeptic either to show how the objections can be avoided or to construct new skeptical arguments.

However, to say that neutrality is possible is one thing; to show that it also is morally defensible is another. Perhaps a beginning has been made in that direction by suggesting a connection between institutional critical neutrality and respect for the autonomy of individual members of the university community. The key idea here is that if the university becomes a political agent, individual members of the university community will be in a less favorable position to make decisions on the basis of the very kind of critical inquiry it is the university's first obligation to protect.

Although no knock-down proof of this thesis can be supplied here, perhaps the following considerations are sufficient to create a presumptive case in favor of the importance of institutional critical neutrality. As we will see, the argument for it is multifaceted. A variety of factors each lends some weight to the justification of neutrality. The argument gains force as the weight of the different factors is aggregated.

To begin with, when the university takes a partisan political stand in an area outside the sphere of values bound up with critical inquiry, it at least implicitly lends its authority, prestige, and power to a particular side. The university then becomes vulnerable to conflicts of interest between its duty to maintain the framework of political inquiry and its new political obligations. For example, if the university *qua* takes the position that aid to the Nicaraguan Contras is immoral and should not be supported, what policy implications follow for issuing invitations to speakers who support the Contras, appointing professors who are sympathetic to the Contras, donating funds to groups opposing the Contras, reacting to pro-Contra demonstrations, and the like? While it may be possible for the university to simply take a stand, yet take no other action, it is likely that if the stand is genuine, the very act of taking it may have negative implications for critical inquiry. Indeed, the same argument supporting the taking of a stand is also likely to support more direct and forceful action in favor of political goals as well.

Even if the university is still willing to appoint instructors who dissent from its political stands, to invite speakers representing a diversity of views, and so on, is it as likely that such people will be attracted to an institution where their views have been officially rejected, perhaps even designated as immoral, or at least placed in an initially subordinate position?

Even if some are attracted or remain, they have been labeled as dissenters from an official position and must argue under an imposed handicap that arises not from consideration or evaluation of evidence but from a political act by the institution that employs them. Loss of neutrality may result in the emergence of the partisan university, which stands for a set of political and ideological principles and is far too intellectually homogeneous as a result. The diversity so essential for critical inquiry would be absent or, at best, be at serious risk.

Moreover, once the university is identified in the broader society as a (perhaps powerful) political agent, it can expect to be on the receiving as well as the giving end of political battles. The privileges and immunities extended to it because of its nonpartisan character surely are likely to come under fire. Why should opponents of the university's political stance allow it tax exemptions because of its educational status when more and more of its resources and energies are devoted to support of political positions contrary to their own? Why not treat it like any other political opponent instead? Why not try to weaken it? And as still more of the university's resources are devoted to fighting off such attacks, greater conflict with the needs of and support for critical inquiry can be expected.

Most important, in the partisan university would each individual be as free as we would wish to pursue inquiry where it led, to dissent from prevailing views, to follow independent paths? If not, individuals themselves would have less of an opportunity to develop autonomously, and critical inquiry itself would be harmed. All of us would be impoverished in the same way we are impoverished whenever any view becomes orthodox not because of its merits as established in open inquiry but because it has been artificially protected from the challenges such inquiry generates.

But hasn't it already been conceded that at the individual level, the classroom instructor under certain conditions may argue for substantive positions without undermining the autonomy of students? Why doesn't a similar conclusion follow about the taking of substantive political stands by the university itself?

This objection would be decisive if the roles of the individual teacher and the college or university were logically parallel. However, consider whether the two are relevantly different. Classroom instructors are individuals whose primary professional obligation is to engage in inquiry and disseminate the results. The scholar's findings, in other words, should reflect judicious evaluation of evidence, and evaluation that can be criticized in appropriate professional and public forums. The university, however, were it to take overt political stands, is likely to do so not as a result of evaluation of evidence but because of compromise or consensus among its various factions. It follows, then, that the university's taking of a political stance is not a contribution to inquiry in the same way as is the taking of a substantive position by a trained scholar.

More important, the individual does not play the same institutional role as the university with respect to critical inquiry. The latter, but not the former, is the institutional protector of the values essential to critical inquiry. For the very institution designed to umpire the critical process also to become a player within the process raises the problems I have already discussed. Accordingly, it is at best far from clear whether my earlier analysis of the right and obligations of the individual instructor can be applied without modification to the institution as well. To assume the two are parallel is as dangerous as assuming that because individuals may adopt particular religious perspectives, the state may permissibly do so as well.

To summarize, for the university to become a partisan political agent would create inherent conflicts of interest between different kinds of goals. Thus, the prestige and power of the university would be placed on one side of various political debates; yet the university would also have the obligation to encourage independent thinking on these issues and not to load the dice in favor of particular positions in advance of inquiry. Not only would decisions favoring particular sides to political conflicts appear biased, they might actually be biased. The very institution charged with the responsibility of protecting the values of open, rational inquiry becomes committed to a second set of values, which, on occasion, may call for subverting open, rational inquiry or at least diverting substantial attention (and sometimes resources) from it. It would be as if the state were held to be the partisan of particular religious perspective and, at one and the same time, charged with protecting religious freedom and tolerance. Because the potential for conflict of interest is so great and the danger to religious liberty so serious, we require state neutrality toward religion. Is the case for university neutrality any different?

I do not mean to say that universities generally *are* neutral or that they generally *do* uphold the canons of critical inquiry. Rather, violations of neutrality may occur, but their existence does not refute the neutrality thesis. Violations of institutional critical neutrality are grounds for criticism in the name of neutrality, not reasons for rejecting neutrality itself.

My discussion suggests, then, that an important case can be made for institutional critical neutrality. That is, just as state neutrality toward religion is a significant protection for the freedom of individuals to make their own religious choices, so institutional critical neutrality provides similar protection for individuals to make their own choices within critical inquiry. The case parallels that for state neutrality toward religion. If neutrality in one area is justifiable, so too is a similar kind of neutrality in the other.

NOTES

1. Robert Paul Wolff, *The Ideal of the University* (Boston: Beacon Press, 1969), p. 70.

2. John Searle, *The Campus War: A Sympathetic Look at the University in Agony* (New York: World, 1971), pp. 199–200.

3. Wolff, *Ideal of the University*, p.71.

4. Richard Mohr, "Teaching as Politics," *Report from the Center for Philosophy and Public Policy* 6 (Summer 1986), 8.

5. John Rawls, *A Theory of Justice* (Cambridge: Harvard University Press, 1971), pp. 46–53. For appeal to "wide" reflective equilibrium in favor of a more radical form of egalitarianism than Rawls supports, see Kai Nielson, *Equality and Liberty* (Totowa, N.J.: Rowman and Allanheld, 1985), pp. 13–44.

6. Thus, there may be different conceptions of critical inquiry just as there can be different conceptions of justice, equality, or liberty.

7. However, even within pragmatism, "satisfactoriness" need not be construed to include political and moral value judgments. Rather, justification may depend on "systematic virtues", such as coherence and consistency, which need not be at issue in partisan political debates. See, for example, W. V. Quine and J. S. Ullian, *The Web of Belief* (New York: Random House, 1978), pp. 64–82, for an account of scientific justification in terms of the epistemic (but not necessarily political) virtues of systems of thought.

8. If not, it is unclear whether critical inquiry is even possible as a rational activity. That is, if there are no ground rules that different sides of a debate find acceptable, the debate has no rational resolution. If all or even most issues were like that, it is far from clear that an institution devoted to the pursuit of truth and rational inquiry would even be possible. Universities might still exist, but they would perform other functions, e.g., professional training. Accordingly, the belief that there are general ground rules of critical inquiry available for adjudication of particular disputes within disciplines is a presupposition of the institution of the university, as conceived in this paper.

STUDY QUESTIONS

1. Can you be nonpartisan on political issues?
2. What does Simon mean by "institutional critical neutrality"?
3. What limits, if any, should be placed on debate within a university?
4. Is a university ever justified in taking an official stand on a political issue?

VII

RESTRICTING RESEARCH

Another challenge to academic freedom is raised by the claim that in certain circumstances, merely undertaking research on a particular issue would be immoral. The best-known example of such controversial subject matter is the hypothesis that certain behavioral differences stem from matters of race or sex.

Philip Kitcher claims that in a specific set of societal conditions, which he explains in detail, we should refrain from undertaking research on such a hypothesis. Robert B. Talisse and Scott F. Aikin disagree, arguing that forgoing such inquiry would have a variety of unfortunate consequences, including leaving the field open to those who don't recognize such constraints and, instead, pursue studies that might yield misleading results. According to Talisse and Aikin, the most effective way to fight the spread of bias is not to refrain from inquiry but to expose error, an aim most effectively achieved by undertaking appropriate research.

13

Constraints on Free Inquiry

PHILIP KITCHER

Suppose we envisage scientific investigations as taking place within a society in which there are significant inequalities with respect to well-being. Members of a particular group within this society, a group I'll refer to as "the underprivileged," have lives that go substantially less well than is typical in the rest of the society. This relative assessment of the quality of their lives may turn on obvious economic disadvantages, lower life expectancy, or restricted access to coveted opportunities and positions. Moreover, the reduced average quality of life for the underprivileged is partially caused by the fact that, in the past, it was widely believed that those with characteristics prevalent within the group were naturally inferior or that such people were only fitted for a narrow range of opportunities and positions. Residual forms of this belief are still present, although the belief is repudiated in most public discourse.

Imagine further that some scientific investigations conducted within the society might be taken to support conclusions that bear on the officially discarded belief. Specifically, let the belief in question be, "People with a particular characteristic (call it C) are naturally less well-suited to a particular role (call it R)," and suppose that an area of science S might yield evidence for or against this view. The impact of pursuing S and uncovering the evidence is *politically asymmetrical*, in that both the following conditions obtain:

(a) If the evidence is taken to favor the hypothesis that those with C are naturally less well-suited to R, then there will be a change

Originally published in Philip Kitcher, *Science, Truth and Democracy*, pp. 96–103, 2001, Oxford University Press. Reprinted by permission of Oxford University Press.

in the general attitudes of members of the society toward those with C, constituting (at least) a partial reversion to the old state of belief; if the evidence is taken to favor the negation of this hypothesis, there will be no significant further eradication of the residues of the old belief.

(b) If the belief that those with C are naturally less well-suited to R again becomes widespread, then the quality of the lives of those with C—the underprivileged—will be further reduced, partly through the withdrawal of existing programs of social aid, partly through the public expression of the attitude that those with C are inferior to those who lack C; unless there is significant further eradication of the residues of the old belief, there will be no notable improvement in the lot of the underprivileged from pursuit of S.

Recognition of the political asymmetry lies behind the modest argument, outlined above [omitted here—S.M.C.], according to which standards of evidence must go up when the consequences of being wrong are more serious.

However, assume also that the society's pursuit of S will be *epistemically asymmetrical*, in that people will always take the belief to have more support than it deserves. More precisely:

(c) There will be significant differences between the probabilities assigned to the hypothesis that people with C are less well-suited to R and the probabilities that would be assigned by using the most reliable methods for assessing evidence; the probabilities assigned to the hypothesis by members of the society will typically exceed the probabilities that reliable methods would yield, and the probabilities assigned to the negation of the hypothesis will be correspondingly deflated.

Although there are already hints of danger for the underprivileged, troublesome consequences aren't inevitable. Evidentiary matters about the effects of having C might be clear-cut, favoring the egalitarian conclusion to a large enough extent to outweigh the bias towards the hypothesis.

Suppose, however, this isn't so. If the issues surrounding the impact of having C are confusing or complicated, and if the bias towards overestimating the support for an antiegalitarian answer is sufficiently strong, then the underprivileged are indeed threatened by the pursuit of S. Specifically, assume that

(d) With high probability, the evidence obtained from pursuit of S will be indecisive, in that the most reliable methods of assessing that evidence would assign a probability of roughly 0.5 to the hypothesis.

(e) The bias in favor of the hypothesis is so strong that most members of the society will take evidence that, when assessed by the most reliable methods, would yield a probability for the hypothesis of roughly 0.5 to confer a probability close to 1 on the hypothesis.

If all these conditions are met, there's a significant probability that the anti-egalitarian hypothesis will be taken to be extremely well supported, even though the evidence leaves the issue open, with consequent harm to the underprivileged. There is no chance of any genuine benefit for the underprivileged. From the perspective of the underprivileged, the expected utility of pursuing S is thus clearly negative. If we shouldn't engage in ventures that can be expected to decrease the well-being of those who are already worse off than other members of society, we should therefore refrain from engaging in S.

This argument is abstract and general. Its burden is that when a certain constellation of conditions is satisfied—the conditions (a)–(e)—the pertinent inquiries ought not to be pursued. I strongly suspect that there are cases in which the conditions obtain, and, indeed, that some of the disputes about human sociobiology and human behavioral genetics satisfy the conditions. If we were to take the underprivileged to be the set of women, the characteristics to consist of biological traits uncontroversially possessed by women and not by men, and the role R to be any of a number of prominent, and sought after, positions in American or European society, we could generate plausible instances. Even more obviously the assumptions appear to apply to members of various minority groups—African-Americans in the United States, West Indians in Britain, immigrants from North African and Near Eastern countries in European nations.

Consider, first, the political asymmetry. What would be the likely impact of widespread acceptance of inegalitarian conclusions—say that women, "by their nature," lack the competitive urge or the commitment to career to occupy challenging positions, or that minorities have genetic predispositions to lower intelligence? Surely the most predictable results would be the withdrawal of resources from any current efforts to try to equalize opportunity for filling R, and a diminution of self-respect and of motivation among the underprivileged. It is hardly cynical to believe that the supposedly scientific findings would inspire policymakers to "stop trying to do the impossible"—instead of "rubbing against the grain of human nature" they would save money now spent on wasteful public programs. Nor is it unreasonable to think that the psychological effects on members of the underprivileged would be damaging, either because they accede to the conclusion that they are less worthy than other members of society, or because they view this as a common perception of their status and thus develop a sense of alienation. At best, these deleterious consequences would be offset by an allocation of public funds to respond to what would now be regarded as the *real* needs and potential of the underprivileged—although it's not entirely obvious what programs of this type would do. Not only are the hypothetical gains extremely nebulous, but it's also far from clear that contemporary affluent societies have much political will for this type of expenditure.

Recent debates about inegalitarian claims support other aspects of the political asymmetry. When evidence is announced in favor of equality, the effect is only to offset whatever damage has been done by more flamboyant presentations of the case for inequality. Defenses of "natural inequalities" typically outsell the egalitarian competition. Furthermore, when rejoinders are published there is no groundswell of enthusiasm in favor of investing more resources in attempts to equalize social roles.

These remarks amount only to a prima facie case. A lot of detailed sociological work would be needed to show that (a) and (b) are satisfied in the scientific controversies about sex and race. Hence it would be reasonable for a defender of research into "the biological bases of social inequality" to protest the application of the argument *if that person were prepared to take on the burden of demonstrating that the consequences I have alleged do not ensue.* That is not, of course, how the defense usually goes, and, in what follows my chief aim will be to consider complaints that the general form of argument by appeal to political and epistemic asymmetries is invalid because it overlooks important aspects of inquiry.

With respect to the epistemic asymmetry it's possible to be more definite about the applicability of the argument, for here a wealth of historical studies hammers home the same moral. First, there is ample evidence of a bias in inegalitarian conclusions: patterns clearly discernible in the history of measuring those traits associated with cognitive performance, from the nineteenth century to the present, from the craniometers to the high priests of heritability, display one version of inegalitarianism (typically seen as preposterous by later generations) widely accepted until painstaking work exposes its lack of evidential support, followed by an interval of agnosticism until the next variation makes its appearance. Second, uncovering the flawed inferences underlying claims of a scientific basis for uncomfortable conclusions typically reveals just how complex are the issues with which investigators are trying to wrestle: analytical study of the methods of trying to show genetic differences in intelligence brings out what would be required to support responsible conclusions; examination of ventures in human sociobiology exposes how hard it would be to do it properly. Reliable knowledge about the topics is hard to come by. Combining this observation with the pattern that emerges from the history, the obvious explanation is that, in an epistemically cloudy situation, the probabilities assigned to the inegalitarian hypotheses are inflated, so that sincere investigators incorrectly believe themselves to have found a scientific basis for socially acceptable conclusions. So I think there's good evidence for the pertinent versions of (c), (d), and (e).

I turn now to some obvious criticisms. First comes the worry that the argument I've presented is myopic. Perhaps in focusing on a particular situation, we fail to understand the more general import of defending free inquiry. . . . So we might indict the argument for failing to recognize the disutility of closing down particular inquiries, a disutility that results from undermining a society-wide practice of fostering free discussion. Our choices ought to have been framed (so the accusation goes) in terms of a social context for scientific research that is thoroughly committed to a policy of free inquiry, and which occasionally encounters the unfortunate consequences my arguments expose, and a social context for research that hampers the freedom of inquiry, that avoids some local unfortunate consequences, but also suppresses valuable inquiries with appreciable losses in utility.

The obvious answer to this challenge is to deny that our choice is between these two contexts. The objection proposes to evade the argument by mimicking a familiar strategy: faced with the fact that breaking a promise might sometimes maximize expected utility, moral philosophers sometimes suggest that the *rule* of keeping promises promotes well-being and that breaking a promise on a particular occasion would undermine the rule. Unfortunately, the suggestion faces an obvious reply: why should we not adopt a practice of promise-keeping except in situations where it's clear that breaking a promise would maximize expected utility? In similar fashion, the scientific community might be committed to a practice of free inquiry except in situations in which it's clear that certain investigations will be socially disadvantageous (or disadvantageous for those who are underprivileged).

If it were genuinely difficult to distinguish situations in which pursuing some lines of inquiry could be expected to be socially damaging, there might be reason to think that a policy of admitting limits on inquiry would quickly decay to the detriment of society's intellectual health. We begin with good intentions to bar certain investigations but, in allowing the social consequences of an inquiry to determine its legitimacy, we enter a zone in which it's easy to lose our way, ultimately retreating from lines of research that would have proved valuable. Yet the arguments of the form we're considering plainly allow for definite instances, cases in which it's possible to judge that the expected utility of the pursuit of an inquiry is negative (or negative for those who are worst off), and we could block the alleged slide by adopting a policy of only abandoning inquiries when it's clear that the social consequences of pursuit are deleterious (free inquiry would be given the benefit of any doubt). The objection is right to remind us of the broader context in which decisions about the value of free inquiry should be made, but, so far at least, it seems possible to accommodate the point while allowing that some instantiations of the argument are cogent.

Consider a second objection, one that tries to subvert the argument by recalling the historical sources of the beliefs it employs. At any number of stages in the history of the sciences, people with values that were threatened by a particular line of investigation could have contended that the inquiry in question was likely to bring nothing but loss. Imagine committed Aristotelians campaigning against further efforts to determine the earth's motions, or devout Victorians objecting to "speculations" on the origins of species. Had the argument I've given been influential at earlier stages of inquiry, we would have forfeited enormous epistemic advantages. Precisely because we have liberated ourselves from the ideas of our predecessors, through allowing inquiry to undermine accepted beliefs, we are now in a position to make the kinds of evaluations on which the argument depends. Our values have themselves been shaped by the overthrow of previous systems of belief, systems that would have accepted the inequalities in contemporary society with equanimity. Consider, for example, the version of the argument that attacks research into racial differences in intelligence. The recognition that there would be costs if people classified as belonging to minority races were told that authoritative science had established their intellectual inferiority itself depends on a process through which people with particular superficial features and of particular descent were recognized fully as people, a process that depended on the possibility of free inquiry into unpopular topics.

Although this line of reasoning appears plausible, it rests on a number of controversial assumptions. The final step can be debated by questioning the role the sciences have actually played in fostering the acceptance of disadvantaged minorities. The chief defect of the objection lies, however, in the similarity it suggests between the heroic scientific liberators of the past and those who would investigate natural inequalities in the present. People who publish findings purporting to show that behavioral differences stem from matters of race or sex often portray themselves as opposing widely held views in the interest of truth. But do Galileo's would-be successors don his mantle legitimately?

Of course, what matters is *significant* truth, and there are serious issues about why the favored lines of inquiry should count as significant. At this stage, however, I want to focus on a different presupposition of the attempted defense. In understanding the epistemic asymmetry, we recognize a bias towards accepting inegalitarian conclusions because they resonate with attitudes publicly denied but nonetheless present in contemporary societies. Many champions of unpopular inquiries correctly believe their conclusions oppose doctrines affirmed by their colleagues (perhaps even by almost all of those working in the areas related to their discussions) and often upheld by the parts of the media with the strongest intellectual credentials. Their defenses typically fail to mention that there is a broad tendency to believe quite contrary things in private, that the views defended conform to inclinations that voters and public officials harbor and that may even be espoused by those who profess quite different views. In consequence, there's a deep disanalogy between contemporary investigators of racial difference (say) and the scientists of the past who defied the orthodoxies of their age.

Let's say that a belief is part of a *total* consensus just in case almost everyone in the pertinent society accepts it (or is prepared to defer to people who accept it), that a belief is part of an *official* consensus if it is publicly professed by everyone (or if people are at least prepared to defer publicly to people who publicly profess it), that it is part of an *academic* consensus if it is held by almost everyone within the academic community, and that it is part of a *lay* consensus if it is held by almost everyone outside the academic community. Galileo and Darwin opposed total consensus in their communities, and there were powerful biases *against* adopting their conclusions; thus the conditions for applying the argument I've reconstructed to them are not satisfied, and the social disutility of their inquiries can no longer be calculated in the same fashion. Contemporary investigators who claim important differences due to race or sex surely oppose an official academic consensus, and perhaps are at odds with both official consensus and academic consensus. It would be too strong to claim that there is a lay consensus on an inegalitarian conclusion inconsistent with the official academic consensus, but, outside the academy, there are sufficiently powerful inclinations to accept inegalitarian beliefs, held by sufficiently powerful people, to suggest that there will be an epistemic bias in favor of the inegalitarian conclusions, and that these conclusions are likely to be implemented in social policies. Furthermore, there may well be scientists whose embrace of egalitarian claims is sufficiently shallow that they too will be disposed to take indecisive evidence as demonstrating important differences.

Scientists quite understandably bridle at the thought that their research will have to conform to standards of "political correctness," so it's important to understand the exact nature of the argument. Recognizing that some types of research bear on struggles to achieve social justice, *and that there is a schizophrenic moral consciousness in which public "politically correct" attitudes coexist with inclinations to quite opposite beliefs*, we should see the impact of the research as affected by both a political asymmetry and an epistemic asymmetry. Instead of lumping together quite disparate examples from the history of science, it's important to focus on the special conditions the argument discerns in our contemporary predicament. The Millian arena, in which conflicting ideas battle for public approval on epistemically equal terms, and in which the bystanders are never hurt by the nature of the conflict, is a splendid ideal, but it would be quite naive to think that all pieces of controversial research are discussed in anything like this ideal arena.

The last objection I'll consider may be the most obvious. Perhaps all that the argument shows is the error of a consequentialist treatment of these questions—we go astray in thinking that decisions about the merits of inquiry can be judged by attending to the expected consequences. Of course, the main versions I've considered already incorporate the most prominent concerns about utilitarianism, in that they base judgments on the expected utility for the least fortunate (the underprivileged). Ironically, consequentialism is most sympathetic to inquiry into socially charged topics when we *ignore* the objections. If the response is to succeed, it must propose there's a moral basis for pursuing investigations independently of the impact on the underprivileged. One way to develop that idea is to suppose we have a duty to try to ascertain significant truths about nature. Can this duty override worries about the consequences for the unfortunate?

I think not. Far less controversial than any duty to seek the truth is the duty to care for those whose lives already go less well and to protect them against foreseeable occurrences that would further decrease their well-being. We should recognize a clash of duties whose relative importance must be assessed. To oppose the argument, one must believe that the duty to seek the truth is so strong that it is binding, even in situations that will adversely affect the underprivileged, that will offer little prospect for gaining knowledge, and that will afford considerable opportunity for error.

A different way of opposing the consequentialist framework would be to insist that the project of improving the well-being of the disadvantaged can't be allowed to interfere with rights to free inquiry. This libertarian response would abandon both the consequentialism of the argument and the attempt I've made to avoid typical foibles of consequentialism by focusing on the well-being of the least well-off. Any libertarian defense would thus have to claim that the distribution of rights doesn't matter, that if, through historical contingencies, subgroups of the population have been deprived of various rights we can't seek to remedy the situation by abridging the rights others enjoy, even if doing so would limit rights in small ways to enhance dramatically the ability of the disadvantaged to exercise rights others take for granted. It would also have to argue that the right to free inquiry is fundamental, that it overrides important rights of those who suffer from the pursuit of inquiries that reinforce incorrect stereotypes. I think it doubtful either of these challenges (let alone both) can be met, but, in any event, there is a simpler antilibertarian argument. Respecting rights comes at a price, and it's important that the price be distributed fairly. In situations where free inquiry would unfairly increase the burden on those who are already disadvantaged, there can be no right to free inquiry.

STUDY QUESTIONS

1. If someone asserts that certain behavioral differences stem from matters of race or sex, how can I provide reliable evidence to the contrary if conducting research on the matter is immoral?
2. In accordance with Kitcher's own principles, does ethics allow him to appeal to any research in support of his belief that no behavioral differences stem from matters of race or sex?
3. If undertaking research to test the truth of a particular hypothesis is wrong, is discussing the hypothesis in public or even in private also wrong?
4. If research on a particular hypothesis is immoral, why not withhold judgment on the truth of that hypothesis until testing it becomes moral?

14

On the Ethics of Inquiry

Robert B. Talisse
and Scott F. Aikin

I

The thesis that scientific inquiry must operate within moral constraints is familiar and unobjectionable in cases involving immoral treatment of experimental subjects, as in the infamous Tuskegee experiments. However, in *Science, Truth, and Democracy*[1] and related work,[2] Philip Kitcher envisions a more controversial set of constraints. Specifically, he argues that inquiry ought not to be pursued in cases where the *consequences* of its pursuit are likely to affect negatively the lives of individuals who comprise a socially underprivileged group. This constraint is controversial because it imposes moral obligations upon scientific inquirers that they do not have as moral agents generally.[3] That is, whereas the familiar prohibitions against the violation of the rights of experimental subjects amount to the enforcement of fundamental moral obligations in the laboratory and the denial that such obligations can be overridden for the sake of scientific discovery, Kitcher argues that scientists incur in virtue of their role as scientists a set of distinctive moral obligations with regard to individuals belonging to underprivileged groups. In this way, Kitcher is proposing an autonomous *ethics of inquiry* rather than arguing for the *extension* of familiar moral obligations to scientific inquiry.

Originally published as "Kitcher on the Ethics of Inquiry," Robert P. Talisse and Scott F. Aiken, *Journal of Social Philosophy* 1990:3; pp. 654–665. Reprinted by permission of Blackwell Publishing, Inc.

Much of Kitcher's argument is directed squarely at sociobiological and psychometric research concerning the native abilities of the sexes and races. Kitcher's "ambitious" conclusion against such inquiry is that "were we to recognize certain kinds of truths, the impact on some people would be to erode their sense of worth and make it difficult, even impossible, to frame a conception of their lives as valuable."[4] That is to say, the truth about some things will set no one free, and in such cases "free inquiry may be too dangerous to be tolerated."[5] His weaker conclusion is that given the political frame of these issues, we have no reason to embrace the Millian optimism that the truth will out. In fact, he claims, there is reason to believe such research, regardless of its conclusions, will most likely further entrench the standing prejudices.

The question of what kinds of moral considerations, if any, should constrain scientific practice is so difficult and complex that it cannot be properly addressed in a single essay. Accordingly, our objective in the present essay is modest: we shall argue that Kitcher's proposal is inadequate. Given that the issue of moral constraints on inquiry is especially pressing under contemporary social and political conditions, we hope that our critique of Kitcher will encourage further work not only among philosophers of science, but among ethicists and political philosophers as well.[6]

II

Kitcher begins with the observation that scientific investigation occurs within particular societies, and that most contemporary societies, if not all, are home to significant but remediable unjust inequalities with respect to the well-being of individuals. These inequalities range from economic disadvantage and lower-than-average life expectancy to restricted access to valuable opportunities and positions.[7] Following Kitcher, we shall call members of the group whose lives go considerably less well than justice allows *the underprivileged*, U for short. Kitcher asks us to suppose that a partial cause of the diminished quality of life for those in U is the belief, B, that those in U are naturally inferior to the rest of the population, and so are worthy of only a restricted range of educational and professional opportunities. Kitcher reasons that, since B generates injustice, a reduction in the number of persons who hold B, or in the degree of confidence with which persons hold B, is likely to increase justice in society. Kitcher asks us to suppose that until the recent past B was widely held, and so once exerted considerable influence on central political institutions and policies. Although B is now widely and officially repudiated, residual forms of it are manifest in the private attitudes and practices of various sectors of the population. We present these claims as follows:

1. There is an underprivileged class (U).
2. A partial cause for the lack of privilege for those in U is that the belief (B) that those in U are inferior was at a point in the recent past widely held.
3. Insofar as B is presently widely and officially repudiated, society has made moral progress; insofar as B is still present in residual forms, there is room for further progress.

Now, imagine that there is a set of researchers investigating whether B is true. Specifically, they are testing the hypothesis that "people with a particular characteristic (call it C) are naturally less well-suited for a particular role (call it R)."[8] The research program of an area of science S promises to yield evidence with regard to B. So:

4. Science S can yield evidence for or against B.

But, because of B's political implications, S operates under what Kitcher calls *political asymmetry*. That is, as a social and psychological fact, people are in general doxastically conservative—they seek to retain their current beliefs. So, with regard to evidence that *supports* their beliefs, they attend carefully to it and it strengthens their belief. Alternatively, they tend to ignore or dismiss countervailing evidence, hence such evidence has little doxastic impact. Thus, if S yields even modest evidence in favor of B, B will become more openly and widely held, the general attitude toward those with C will worsen, and injustice will increase.[9] However, if S yields even strong evidence for the negation of B, there will be minimal further eradication of B and thus no significant moral progress. So:

5. If S yields even modest evidence in favor of B, recently achieved moral progress will be partially undone.
6. If S yields even strong evidence contrary to B, no significant moral progress will follow.

Given the causal connection between B's being widespread and the suffering of those in U, it seems clear that if recently achieved moral progress with regard to U is undone, those with C will suffer. And if no additional progress is made in the form of further eradication of B from the population, then those with C are not helped, either. So:

7. If acceptance of B increases, the quality of life for those in U will be further reduced.
8. Without significant eradication of the residues of B, there will be no notable improvement in quality of life for those in U.

Kitcher notes a further psychological fact that complicates the matter, namely, that we often take ourselves to have more support for our beliefs than we in fact have. That is, in general, beliefs are subject to what Kitcher calls *epistemic asymmetry*.[10] With regard to B, this asymmetry yields the following result:

> 9. Those that hold B assign to it a higher probability of truth than reliable methods would warrant, and they will correspondingly deflate the probability of the truth of the negation of B.

Consequently, unless S yields evidence against B that is clear, powerful, and easily translated into terms that can be readily understood by the population at large, there will be no significant headway in eradicating B's residua. As the current results of most research in the biological and psychological sciences are cast in a precise and technical vocabulary that presumes a high degree of mathematical and other forms of sophistication, we may conclude that research in S cannot make significant progress in furthering justice with regard to U by furthering the eradication of B. So:

> 10. Research in S cannot make *significant* strides in eradicating B.

What follows, then, is:

> 11. Research in S cannot further social justice by effecting notable improvement of the lives of those in U.

Importantly, when the political and epistemic asymmetries are coupled with the moral consequences of B becoming more widely and strongly held, research in S places those in U in positive danger. Kitcher captures the conclusion as follows:

> If the issues surrounding the impact of having C are confusing or complicated, and if the bias towards overestimating the support for an anti-egalitarian answer is sufficiently strong, then the underprivileged are indeed threatened by the pursuit of S.[11]

Thus, if S yields *complex* or *indecisive* evidence concerning B, the existing bias in favor of B will yield a marked increase of public *support* for B. There is, then, "no change of any genuine benefit for the underprivileged. . . . [T]he expected utility of pursuing S is . . . clearly negative."[12] Inquiry in S regarding B, then, should not be pursued. So:

> 12. Research in S will lead to a worsening of the quality of life for those in U; thus research in S is morally unjustifiable, and should not be pursued.

These conditions obtain, Kitcher argues, in cases where those in U are women and those traits in C are those uncontroversially biological traits possessed only by women, and the R-roles are those of privilege and prominence. They also obtain where those in U are those in various minority groups in Western countries—African Americans in the United States, West Indians in the United Kingdom, and immigrants from Northern Africa and the Near East in most European nations.[13]

The consequence of Kitcher's argument, then, is that research concerning, for example, the Bell Curve thesis is immoral, *even if the proposed research promises to debunk it*. It is important to emphasize that the immorality consists not in the research's likely conclusions, or how experimental subjects are treated, or even the motives of those who pursue such investigations. Rather, such inquiry is immoral because under the above-mentioned political and epistemic conditions, it can be expected only to further existing injustice by placing the underprivileged in harm's way.

III

We trust that the foregoing sketch will suffice to show that Kitcher has developed a sophisticated view of the moral constraints to which scientific inquiry is subject under the political conditions that obtain in most contemporary developed societies. We would like to raise two general lines of criticism. The first targets the broadly consequentialist character of Kitcher's argument; the second aims more generally at the project of indexing the moral obligations of inquirers to the contingent demographic facts of particular societies.

We begin with the uncontroversial observation that consequentialist arguments must be based upon comparative judgments concerning not only the expected outcome of pursuing some action, but also that of other possible actions, including acts of omission. In light of this, it is odd that Kitcher does not consider the expected result of *not pursuing* inquiry concerning *B*. Leaving these consequences out of the analysis severely skews the considerations that Kitcher proffers. This is especially apparent once it is recognized that the moral requirement of refraining from *B*-related research amounts to the obligation to leave research on race to the racists and research on sex-related differences in ability to the sexists. This is due not only to the fact that the racists and sexists may be indifferent to moral argument concerning their views, but also to the fact that part of what it is to be a racist or sexist is to *deny* that inequities of opportunity and privilege for women or persons of color constitute injustice.[14] That is, according to the racist and sexist, the unequal status of women and persons of color that prevailed until the recent past is *morally proper*, and the extent to which beliefs like *B* are *receding* is the extent to which society is engaged in injustice.

To explain: To claim that persons in some demographic group are *underprivileged* is not simply to note the sociological fact of an unequal distribution of wealth, opportunity, and the like; rather, it is to judge that the inequality is *unjust*, that the persons in that group are *getting less than they deserve* by way of social goods or perhaps *more than they deserve* by way of social burdens. The judgment that some group or individual is *underprivileged* is therefore partly a judgment about *desert*. However, the question of what women and persons of color *deserve* is partly a question of *ability*. But this is *precisely* the question that the racists and sexists aim to investigate: they aim to show that social inequalities are generated by native differences in ability and thus are *not* unjust.[15] Accordingly, racist and sexist scientists can accept Kitcher's argument and yet pursue the kinds of inquiry Kitcher seeks to prohibit because they reject Kitcher's view regarding which groups are underprivileged.[16]

Thus, Kitcher's argument can persuade only those who are *not* racist or sexist to forego *B*-related research. Consequently, an outcome of Kitcher's view is that only racists and sexists will pursue race- and sex-related research. Yet surely *this* state of affairs would exacerbate existing epistemic and political asymmetries concerning *B*. That is, if only racists are doing the research, then presumably the majority of the reports on the research in *S* would be in support of *B*.[17] Given that *B* is subject to both political and epistemic asymmetries, we would find that whatever moral progress we have made would be undone with the same kind of reversion that Kitcher argued would come if *S* yielded support for *B* in *5*. If that is the case, then those in *U* are most certainly put in harm's way. So:

13. If research in *S* is taken to be morally unjustifiable, then only those who do not care for moral justification at all or those who reject the proposed determination of the membership of *U* will pursue *S*.

To simplify, let us call those who will persist in pursuing the research Kitcher seeks to restrict the *racists*. Hence, we infer:

14. If the racists are the only ones doing work in *S*, then most research in *S* will support *B*.
15. The remaining research in *S* will lead to lowered quality of life for those in *U*.

The thought here is that if left unchecked, racist and sexist science and pseudo-science threaten to undermine whatever moral progress that had been made in eliminating *B*. We can sustain and perhaps augment that level of moral achievement only if there are mainstream and level-headed answers to racist arguments and scientific research aimed at debunking supposed evidence for beliefs like *B*.[18]

Even granting Kitcher's central premises, once the expected consequences of refraining from the kinds of inquiry he deems immoral are countenanced, a strong case against Kitcher's constraints emerges. But consider a likely rejoinder. It could be argued that there is a further consequence of Kitcher's view that mitigates the above argument, namely, that public knowledge and policy will come to reflect the view that research in S is morally repugnant and politically beyond the pale. That is, Kitcher's view would generate a moral onus that hangs over those who persist with such research or use the conclusions of such research in public deliberation. Further, this onus is the reason why most researchers may begin to neglect the program and why its conclusions are disallowed from public deliberation. So, Kitcher's view, if widely adopted, can be expected to generate a public that is committed to the following:

16. Research in S is not to be countenanced, not because it fails to be indicative of what is true, but because it is morally reprehensible to pursue S's program or consider data from it.

But thoughts such as 16 lead to a kind of *epistemic backlash* where those who hold B or some residuum of it become suspicious that the popular conception of the matter is more an institutional requirement than a moral one, that the egalitarian party line is being taken as more important than the truth. Insofar as such *politically prudential* reasons are given for them to no longer proffer B as a public reason for policy, they will grow suspicious that the truth about B is being *legislated* instead of *inquired into*. The backlash consists in taking this as a case where ideology steps in to conceal uncomfortable truths.[19] The prejudices concerning B can be bolstered and buttressed by such requirements, because those who espouse and pursue research supporting B take themselves to be and present themselves as playing Galileo to a politically correct bishop of Padua. So:

17. If research in S is shunned in popular opinion, then the moral progress noted in 3 is jeopardized.

What follows, then, is:

18. If results from S are banned (or informally publicly debarred), then those in U are put at risk of lowered quality of life.

Kitcher concedes that this consequence of backlash looms for programs banned or even ones from whom funding is merely withdrawn. But he maintains that "these gloomy reflections do not touch the argument that the research under scrutiny is unjustified."[20] Yet it is unclear, now, given the expected consequences of *barring* B-related research, that *pursuing* it is so objectionable. The dilemma is that if S is pursued, then it is likely that either its results will refute B, but be too complicated for popular understanding, or else support B. If the former, it will not have any effect on changing the public attitude toward B (even though it refutes B), and if the latter, it will weigh public opinion heavily in B's favor. As a consequence, if

B-related research is pursued, then those in U will either have no improvement or be adversely affected. So pursuing B-related inquiry is unlikely to improve the lot of those in U and is very likely to worsen their standing. But, as we have argued, *refraining* from pursuing such research *guarantees* the reversion into previous injustice and thus *ensures* a worsening of the well-being of those in U. In refusing to do the requisite research or debunk the theories, the scientists forego the social process of public scrutiny and criticism that stands to eliminate biases behind injustice.[21] Although it is admittedly not without risks of the sort Kitcher has identified, pursuing S seems the better option. Thus, these "gloomy reflections" surely *do* touch Kitcher's argument. In fact, they overturn it.

Consequentialist arguments are notoriously adaptive. We suppose, then, that Kitcher might be able to meet the foregoing objections by adding additional stipulations that can accommodate our intuitions concerning the consequences of not pursuing B-related research. But even if we suppose that there could be a successful revision of this sort, there remains a more general difficulty with Kitcher's approach.

The difficulty we have in mind concerns the very project of indexing an ethics of inquiry to the political and epistemic conditions that prevail in a particular society. The problem is that whereas the epistemic and political asymmetries tend to respect national borders, the results of scientific research programs do not. Kitcher's argument that it is wrong to pursue B-related research in societies where the relevant asymmetries hold leaves open the possibility that research that is morally forbidden in one society could be allowed in another. Further, given the presumption that science policy should follow the moral requirement to further justice, it allows for the outcome that research that is morally forbidden in one society could be morally required in another. To see this, imagine a society whose major political institutions and practices are as yet directed by racist and sexist views, but is nonetheless *not* subject to the political and epistemic asymmetries Kitcher has specified. We might further suppose that the racism and sexism of this society is generated by the wide acceptance of empirical research that supports such views, and that members of this society hold their racist and sexist views *because* they believe that the best scientific evidence supports them. Under such conditions, it would be the case that scientific refutation of the racist and sexist theories is necessary for even the possibility of social improvement. Surely in such a society such research would be not merely permissible, it may be positively *required* by justice.

However, beliefs such as B are true or false regardless of which society or scientific community inquires into it, and the news regarding scientific research and the results of current experiments has a habit of crossing geographical, national, and political borders. The border-crossing tendency of science is on the whole a good thing—it makes for an efficient division of scientific labor, and thus produces the great benefits that come with sharing information and combining epistemic resources. It is this aspect of science that frustrates Kitcher's ethics of inquiry. Research regarding sex- and race-related differences that would be on Kitcher's argument immoral to pursue in, say, the United States could be morally permissible elsewhere; and the results of such research will surely reach interested parties in the United States. Accordingly, the negative effects of B-related research for U are not avoided by the moral constraints implied by Kitcher's argument, since those constraints are generated by relatively *local* considerations.

We can generalize the point in this way. Questions of social justice with regard to historically underprivileged social groups are by necessity indexed to particular societies. It is the business of states to enact what social justice demands. When it comes to science, however, the story is quite different. The moral result sought by Kitcher requires a *global* ethics of inquiry; however, his arguments derive from the historical and sociological facts of a specific society, and so generate constraints in inquiry that are *particular* to that society. In short, the strategy of appealing to local factors in order to achieve a global result cannot succeed.

IV

We have thus far developed two lines of argument against Kitcher's proposal. Both lines of argument have been directed at Kitcher's means rather than his ends; that is, we presumed the soundness of Kitcher's ends and tried to demonstrate the inadequacy of his proposal to achieve them. This presumption is not uncontroversial. Although we cannot in the present essay pursue fully such issues, we should like to close by raising two concerns regarding Kitcher's ends.

The project of developing an ethics of scientific inquiry is similar to the project of developing an ethics of individual action in that both require the identification of some discrete entity to serve as the object of moral evaluation. In the case of standard ethical theories, this entity is the *act*, the *intention* to act, or sometimes the *person*; in the case of an ethics of inquiry, it is the *research program*. To be sure, there is controversy among philosophers over what acts, intentions, and persons are. Yet such controversies do not normally obstruct ethical theorizing since there seems to be a sufficient degree of agreement at the commonsense level over when a person can be said to have acted or intended and when not. However, the case is not so clear when it comes to parsing scientific research programs. Consider, for example, an epidemiologist pursuing a new treatment for sickle-cell anemia. Is this scientist engaging in a race-related research program of the sort covered by Kitcher's argument? Or again, is a psychologist investigating patterns of cognitive development among boys for the purpose of developing new strategies for dealing with childhood behavioral disorders acting immorally?

This kind of question becomes especially thorny if we accept even a modest version of confirmation holism. Suppose that in the course of pursuing research related to the treatment of Attention Deficit Disorder, our psychologist unwittingly discovers some fact or principle that, when considered in the context of the findings of an otherwise unrelated and seemingly innocent research program in evolutionary biology, implicitly bears upon B. Does this render the psychologist's research immoral? Does it render the program in evolutionary biology immoral as well? Does a third scientist who makes explicit the connection between the two findings and their relevance to B act immorally?

Given the possibility of such cases, what conclusion are we to draw? The fact that research programs are not easily parsed into discrete categories such as "race-related" and "not race-related" complicates greatly the very project of developing an autonomous ethics of inquiry. More importantly, given even a modest confirmation holism, it seems that any research program, no matter how distant it may appear from issues of race and sex, may produce results that nonetheless bear significantly upon B. Furthermore, whether a given research program is likely to produce results that bear significantly on B in part depends upon what *other* researchers are working on and what the likely results of *their* research will be. The result, then, seems to be that, on Kitcher's view, *all* scientific research is potentially suspect and *all* researchers have the responsibility to consider the possible consequences of their inquiries vis-à-vis B. Such evaluations are extremely difficult to make with confidence under the best circumstances; moreover, if a more robust confirmation holism is true, they may be impossible.

Hence Kitcher's view does not simply amount to a moral prohibition on research that is overtly directed toward race- and sex-related differences in ability. It results rather in a requirement to subject *all* research to moral evaluation. Given the difficulty, if not impossibility, of calculating the likely consequences of some proposed research, this seems an unduly demanding moral burden.

Of course, to demonstrate that a proposed moral obligation is highly demanding is not to demonstrate that no such obligation exists. The demandingness of Kitcher's proposal occasions our second point of concern. Bernard Williams long ago raised a compelling criticism against consequentialism that focused upon the *kind of person* consequentialist theories require us to become. More specifically, Williams argued that consequentialist theories in general and utilitarianism in particular could not assign the proper moral weight to *long-term* moral commitments, what Williams called "projects."[22]

Kitcher's view invites the analogue of Williams' critique. Scientific research programs require *ex ante* commitments of personal, institutional, and financial resources. Contemporary research programs often involve the coordination over many years of several researchers working in different subfields and in different locations.[23] Long-term commitment is necessary for effective science. However, Kitcher's view requires scientists to subject their inquiries to perpetual moral evaluation based upon the likely consequences for particular social groups of seeing the research to its conclusion. As we have seen, the relevant consequences are partly determined by a range of contingent facts, including facts about what other researchers are doing and the degree to which the general public is subject to the kind of asymmetries Kitcher has identified.

These factors, including a population's epistemic attitudes, are prone to short-run fluctuation. It seems, then, that Kitcher's moral scientist, like Williams' utilitarian, will have to monitor these factors regularly (daily? monthly?) and adjust his activities accordingly. But this means that Kitcher's scientist cannot commit to a long-term research program, for research that may be permissible today could prove impermissible tomorrow. The consequence is that contemporary science, much of which proceeds by way of long-term research agendas, is hobbled. In this way, Kitcher's ethics of inquiry threatens to render contemporary science impracticable. This is clearly an unacceptable result, but it seems unavoidable if one adopts with Kitcher the aim of morally prohibiting research into particular questions for the sake of furthering specific social ends.

V

We noted early in this essay the importance of the issues Kitcher has addressed. It is reasonable to expect that the question of the nature of the moral constraints appropriate to scientific inquiry will become increasingly pressing in the coming years, as technology in the biosciences grows more powerful. We hope to have shown that further work is needed and to have opened a broader conversation among ethicists, political theorists, and philosophers of science.

NOTES

1. Philip Kitcher, *Science, Truth, and Democracy* (Oxford: Oxford University Press, 2001).

2. Philip Kitcher, "An Argument about Free Inquiry," *Nous* 31, no. 3 (1997): 279–306.

3. One could imagine a view according to which one is morally obligated at all times to act so as to not worsen the lot of underprivileged social groups. As far as

we know no one has proposed such a view, and we strongly suspect that any such a view would face insurmountable difficulties.

4. Kitcher, *Science, Truth, and Democracy*, 96.

5. Kitcher, "An Argument about Free Inquiry," 280.

6. The critical attention Kitcher has received for *Science, Truth, and Democracy* has come mainly from fellow philosophers of science, such as Brad Wray in "Science, Bias, and the Threat of Global Pessimism," *Philosophy of Science* 68, no. 3 (2001): 467–78 and Helen Longino in "Science and the Common Good: Thoughts on Kitcher's *Science, Truth, and Democracy*," *Philosophy of Science* 69, no. 4 (2001): 560–68. Contemporary work in ethics and political philosophy rarely engages directly the issues Kitcher has addressed. We think the lack of crossover work is unfortunate.

7. Kitcher, *Science, Truth, and Democracy*, 96; and Kitcher, "An Argument about Free Inquiry," 280–81.

8. Kitcher, *Science, Truth, and Democracy*, 97.

9. Ibid.; and Kitcher, "An Argument about Free Inquiry," 281.

10. Kitcher, *Science, Truth, and Democracy*, 97; and Kitcher, "An Argument about Free Inquiry," 282.

11. Kitcher, *Science, Truth, and Democracy*, 97.

12. Ibid., 98.

13. Ibid.

14. Many forms of racism and sexism are *morally blind* insofar as they are accompanied by a wholesale rejection of moral considerations relevant to race and sex. Such moral blindness is usually accompanied by an *epistemic blindness*, by which we mean a wholesale disregard for epistemic considerations with regard to beliefs about race and sex. Thus, the *blind* racists and sexists may be disregarded, since their blindness to the evidence means that they are not subject to the asymmetries Kitcher identifies. However, many prevalent forms of racism and sexism are *not blind* in this way; *sophisticated* racists and sexists are sensitive to moral and epistemic considerations, but hold that both support their views. Sophisticated racists hold that persons of color are decidedly *not* underprivileged, believing instead that they are *over-privileged* and that it is primarily white males that suffer in the form of unjust policies such as affirmative action. See the interviews in Carol Swain and Russ Nieli, eds., *Contemporary Voices of White Nationalism in America* (Cambridge: Cambridge University Press, 2002).

15. Michael Levin, *Why Race Matters* (Westport, CT: Praeger, 1997).

16. Many who pursue race- and sex-related research do so precisely because they see the social *status quo* as offering to undeserving groups special advantages, thereby underprivileging white males; see Levin's *Why Race Matters*. Christina Hoff Sommers argues in *The War Against Boys* (New York: Simon and Schuster, 2001) that existing inequalities in public education in America constitute injustice to boys and young men.

17. We take it that this is a plausible assumption for two reasons. First, on Kitcher's own notions of epistemic and political asymmetries with regard to *B*, those who hold it will be more likely to take *B* to be well-supported and take evidence running contrary to be misleading. Researchers holding *B*, then, will have such asymmetries at work when regarding their own data. Second, research in social psychology has shown that groups operating without serious intellectual confrontation with those who disagree tend to become more extreme and more

confident in their commitments. This research is canvassed in Cass Sunstein, *Why Societies Need Dissent* (Cambridge: Harvard University Press, 2003).

18. The claim 3 seems to be the central point of conflict for Kitcher's argument. The moral progress with regard to racism and sexism is in part posited on a set of results that have set the society on the right moral track. Presumably, the moral progress is partly the result of successful efforts to debunk racist and sexist theories. As a consequence, Kitcher's argument relies on the established progress of research in S for the conclusion that further research in S is morally retrograde. It seems odd that, at a certain point, the research that loosened the bonds for the underprivileged in society would suddenly be taken to tighten them. If the work in S has gotten the society to the point where B is widely repudiated, it would seem that the society needs more of the same. However, it may be noted that the racists, as a consequence of S's progress, may not have the requisite funding or institutional status to pursue their research, and this may mitigate the consequences. (Thanks to Kristen Intemann and one of our anonymous reviewers for this point.) However, it seems unreasonable, given the stipulated asymmetries, to expect that those funding research or conferring status are literate with regard to or convinced by the previous debunking research in S. In fact, given the asymmetries, it seems likely that there will be sources of funding and positions of status given *for the sake of rebutting* the debunking literature. If this is the case, things look considerably bleaker.

19. Kitcher, *Science, Truth, and Democracy*, 105.

20. Ibid., 106.

21. Brad Wray, in "Science, Bias, and the Threat of Global Pessimism," has argued on the basis of the requirement of challenging and utilizing bias in social scientific reasoning that the Millian ideal of free inquiry is attainable even when epistemic asymmetries are pervasive with respect to central issues. When members of a community forego the Millian ideal, then, they not only forego the chance to challenge bias, but they themselves appear biased in a way that undermines their claims to legitimacy.

22. Bernard Williams, "A Critique of Utilitarianism," in *Utilitarianism: For and Against*, ed. J. J. C. Smart and Bernard Williams (Cambridge: Cambridge University Press, 1963), 100f.

23. Peter Galison and Bruce Hevly, eds., *Big Science: The Growth of Large-Scale Research* (Stanford, CA: Stanford University Press, 1992).

STUDY QUESTIONS

1. Can research be immoral in one society but not in another?
2. If research on an issue is deemed immoral, how will public opinion on the matter be affected?
3. If developing evidence for the truth is immoral, how can that truth triumph over falsehood?
4. Would any potential issues in the biosciences be affected by this debate about the ethics of inquiry?

VIII

ADVANCING
KNOWLEDGE

Colleges and universities are committed to the advancement of knowledge, and to fulfill that mission they seek to appoint the strongest possible faculty members. The judgments made about the quality of applicants rest in part on their success in publishing peer-reviewed books and articles.

David Lewis wonders why, in deliberating about whom to appoint, members of a department do not consider whether the views of the various candidates are true. He concludes that we don't raise those concerns about others in exchange for their not raising them about us.

David Shatz explores how the workings of the peer review system may be incompatible with the academic community's usual commitment to encouraging the free exchange of ideas. He wonders how rejecting for publication most submitted articles coheres with encouraging the proliferation of ideas.

Both essays raise questions about aspects of academic life that at first appear unproblematic but upon more careful reflection lead to a variety of concerns about the ways in which academic colleagues relate to one another.

15

Academic Appointments

DAVID LEWIS

I

Universities exist for the sake of the advancement of knowledge: its transmission by teaching, its expansion by research. Most of those who make academic decisions on behalf of universities will take the advancement of knowledge as their predominant, ultimate aim.

Of course, some people in universities have different aims in mind. They may think the advancement of knowledge is meaningless, or square, or worthless, or unattainable, or just outweighed by some more urgent aim—the cultivation of entertaining new ideas regardless of truth, perhaps, or the civilizing of the future rulers, or the recruiting of a mighty army to smash the state. But let us imagine an especially lucky university, where nearly everyone pursues the ultimate aim of advancing knowledge and where the few dissenters pursue aims so diverse as to cancel one another out.

As a philosopher, I shall tell a story about the philosophy department of this lucky university. But the story applies more broadly. Not perhaps to the department of frenchified literary theory, where skepticism runs rampant and the pursuit of truth is reckoned passé. Not perhaps to the mathematics department, where they are in confident agreement about what's

Originally published in Steven M. Cahn, ed., *Morality, Responsibility, and the University*, pp. 231–242, 1990, Temple University Press. Reprinted by permission of Temple University Press. The ellipses are the author's. His use of masculine nouns and pronouns is not intended to be sex-specific.

true and how to tell, and they disagree only about what's fruitful and interesting. But in most departments, as in philosophy, (1) the advancement of knowledge is the agreed aim; but (2) there are prolonged disputes over what's true. Wherever both conditions are met, whether it's a matter of the extinction of dinosaurs or of superstrings or of legal realism, my story may be told.

One big academic decision is the decision whom to appoint to the faculty. In the lucky university we are imagining, this decision will be made by those who are already on the faculty in the discipline in question. When there is a vacancy in the department of philosophy, for instance, the members of that department will decide by vote who shall be offered the appointment. In making this decision, they will all be guided (or they will nearly all be predominantly guided) by the aim of advancing knowledge. They will make the offer to the candidate whose appointment would best serve that aim.

(Let me assume hard times: a buyers' market so bad that the disappointed candidates are unlikely to have an academic career elsewhere. Otherwise I might have to assume that the members of the appointing department aim not at the advancement of knowledge per se, but rather at the advancement of knowledge only insofar as it goes on at their own university.)

Note well that in discussing academic appointments, I am not discussing academic freedom. Nobody's academic freedom is violated if the job he wanted goes to someone else, provided he had no prior claim and provided the decision is made on proper grounds.

II

There are many disputed questions in philosophy—as in most disciplines—and each member of the appointing department will hold some opinions about which philosophical doctrines are true and which are false. The candidates for appointment likewise will hold, and will be known to hold, various opinions. Each member of the department can judge, by his own lights, to what extent any given candidate holds true doctrines, and to what extent he is in error.

Holding true doctrines, and not being in error, would seem *prima facie* to be an important qualification for a job of contributing to the advancement of knowledge by teaching and research. *Knowledge* means, in part, being right. It is redundant to talk of knowing the truth, it is a contradiction in terms to talk of knowing what isn't so. (Such talk cries out for scare-quotes: he "knows" it, that is he *thinks* he knows it.) What is not true cannot be known. Advancement of error cannot be advancement of knowledge.

ACADEMIC APPOINTMENTS · 173

Unless a teacher conceals his opinions altogether, or presents them in an especially unconvincing fashion (both faults in their own right), his students will to some extent come to share his opinions. But to the extent that the teacher imparts false doctrines, what the students gain cannot be knowledge. To the extent that a researcher is guided by false doctrines, he is liable to arrive at new and different false doctrines, since he will choose them partly to cohere with the doctrines he held before. To that extent, the fruits of his research cannot be new knowledge. So error makes one worse at doing the job of advancing knowledge. Being right is a big advantage.

So when the appointing department assesses the qualifications of the candidates, to choose the one who can contribute best to the advancement of knowledge, it would seem that they ought to give a great deal of weight to the doctrines the candidates hold true and hold false. They ought, *ceteris paribus*, to prefer the candidates who hold true rather than false doctrines. Of course this will be a difficult thing to do collectively, if the members of the department disagree with one another. But, as always, each should do the best he can by his own lights, voting in the way that best serves the advancement of knowledge according to his own opinions.

So, by and large and *ceteris paribus*, we would expect the materialists in the philosophy department to vote for the materialist candidate, the dualists to vote for the dualist, and so forth. Likewise elsewhere: we would expect the transformational grammarians to vote for the transformationalist, the Marxist historians to vote for the Marxist, the biologists who think that all evolution is adaptive to vote for the adaptationist. . . . I say this not out of cynicism. Rather, this seems to be how they *ought* to vote, and unabashedly, if they are sincere in their opinions and serious about doing the best they can, each by his own lights, to serve the advancement of knowledge. We can well understand how countervailing considerations might sometimes be judged to outweigh the advantage of being right, but it would be very strange if the advantage of being right were left out of the balance altogether.

Yet what do we see? I put it to you that an appointing department will typically behave as if the truth or falsehood of the candidate's doctrines are weightless, not a legitimate consideration at all. No speaker will ever argue that a candidate should rank high because he has the advantage of being right on many important questions, or low because he is sunk in all manner of error. No speaker will argue thus, not even if he thinks the great majority of his colleagues will agree with him about what is true and false on the matter in question. Most likely, there will be no mention of whether the candidate's doctrines are true or false. If there is mention, the speaker will make clear by hook or crook that what he says is a mere comment, not an argument for or against the candidate. (The signal might be a joking tone: don't say "false," say "goofy." Or it might be a reminder that one's opinion is only one's own, or it might be the placing of the comment within a speech to the opposite effect: "I hate his views myself, but still. . . .") There will be arguments galore that a candidate has academic virtues that conduce to getting things right or vices that conduce to error: "his work is undisciplined," "what he said was shallow and inane," but it will never be said that the virtues or vices have actually led to truth or error. (I wonder why traits conducive to truth and error should be relevant considerations if truth and error themselves are not?) Maybe someone will be accused of being influenced by the fact that he agrees or disagrees with the candidate's views, and all present will presuppose that this ought not to happen. It will seem for all the world, in short, as if the department were convinced that being right or wrong is an illegitimate consideration; but a consideration that tempts them and that they must guard against. It would be less shocking, I think, to hear a case made that some candidate should be preferred on grounds of race or sex, than to hear a case made that the department should appoint the candidate who holds the true philosophy.

(My evidence? Participation in the deliberations of two philosophy departments, in each case over a period long enough to permit a good deal of turnover of colleagues. But also, hundreds of letters written on behalf of candidates by referees hoping to be persuasive, and presumably guided by their expectations about which considerations a department will deem relevant and proper. To be sure, my experience does not come out of the lucky situation in which all concerned are wholeheartedly devoted to the advancement of knowledge. But it comes from something close enough that I think I may be permitted the extrapolation. Accordingly, I shall no longer bother to distinguish actual universities from the hypothetical lucky one.)

Suppose the question whether being right is an advantage came up in a different connection. Suppose we were considering the history of the advancement of knowledge about a certain subject. Then we would find it perfectly in order to explain the success of some researcher by noting that he had been on the right track, that he was right about a lot of things to begin with and therefore found it easy to get more and more things right afterward. And we would also find it easy to explain his head start, in turn, by the fact that he was the student of a teacher who also was right about a lot of things. In this connection, at least, we would have no trouble believing in the advantage of being right.

Or suppose a squad of detectives have investigated a murder, working independently, and different ones began by suspecting different suspects. If, after the fact, we know that Plum dunnit, then once we know that it was Poirot who suspected Plum from the start, we understand very well why Poirot's investigation progressed by leaps and bounds, while his rivals bogged down and got nowhere. Or if some bystander knows from the start who dunnit (as Plum does, for one) then once he finds out that it is Poirot who has the advantage of being right, he will expect Poirot to forge ahead. In fact, anyone who learns that Poirot alone is right about some aspect of the case (even if he does not know just what Poirot is right about) should expect Poirot to gain an advantage thereby in contributing to the advancement of knowledge.

If, instead of a criminal investigation, it were the history of some branch of science or of philosophy, the same should be true. (Unless it is history done from the standpoint of utter skepticism about the subject, in which case it could not claim to be history of the advancement of knowledge.) We know very well, outside the department meeting at any rate, that being right is one important factor that makes for success in advancing knowledge.

III

There are other factors, of course. We can list the costs of blindly going for the candidate who has the advantage of being right, and the possible benefits of preferring the candidate who is in error but has compensating virtues of ingenuity, rigor, originality, open-mindedness, clarity, curiosity, thoroughness, or just difference from the present members of the department. Up to a point, we can make the list *neutral*: equally acceptable to those on both sides of any of the disputed philosophical questions. First comes—

> **RISK OF ERROR.** *We might try for the candidate who has the advantage of being right, but we might be wrong ourselves and therefore choose the candidate who has the disadvantage of being wrong.*

Yes, we run a risk. But as Mill writes, "If we were never to act on our opinions, because those opinions may be wrong, we should leave all our interests uncared for, and all our duties unperformed. . . . There is no such thing as absolute certainty, but there is assurance sufficient for the purposes of human life. We may, and must, assume our opinion to be true for the guidance of our own conduct."[1]

But is it so, perhaps, that our philosophical opinions are not real opinions? Do we pay them lip service, but always give them credence so close to fifty-fifty that they can play no role in guiding decision? If that were so, and were expected to remain so indefinitely, then it is hard to see how philosophers could be aiming at the advancement of knowledge. For what isn't even believed cannot be known.

But I do think we might be guided by our philosophical opinions, even to the point of betting our lives. Consider our opinions about teletransportation, an imaginary process that works as follows: the scanner here will take apart one's brain and body, while recording the exact state of all one's cells. It will then transmit this information by radio. Traveling at the speed of light, the message will reach the replicator. This will then build, out of new matter, a brain and body exactly like the one that was scanned.[2] Some philosophical positions on personal identity imply that one survives teletransportation (unless it malfunctions). Others imply that teletransportation is certain death. Now imagine that a philosopher is caught on the seventeenth story of a burning building. He has some hope, but no certainty, of the ordinary sort of rescue. Then he is offered escape by teletransportation, provided he accepts the invitation right away.[3] At that point, I think his philosophical opinion may very well guide his decision. If he thinks what I do, he will accept teletransportation even if he reckons his chance of ordinary rescue to be quite high. If he thinks what many of my colleagues do, he will decline the offer even if he reckons his chance of ordinary rescue to be quite low. Either way, he stakes his very life on the truth of his philosophy. And yet if this philosopher does survive, only to find himself in a department meeting the next day, he will probably decline to stake the fortunes of the advancement of knowledge on the very same opinion.

However it may be with philosophy, consider the social scientists. A professor of economics, put in charge of the university budget in desperate times, may dare to stake the university's very survival—and *a fortiori* its contribution to the advancement of knowledge—on the truth of his disputed opinions about the causes of inflation. A professor of government who has been appointed to advise on national security may dare to stake the lives or liberty of millions on the truth of his disputed opinions about foreign affairs. If these same professors are not too busy to vote in their own departments, and if they must decide which candidates have the advantage of being right and which appointments best serve the advancement of knowledge, shall they then find their opinions too uncertain to play any role in guiding decisions?

When we bear in mind the risk of error, and so are less than certain of our own opinions, we might have reason to promote—

DIVISION OF LABOR. *The researcher who is not running with the crowd may do more to advance knowledge, if he does turn out to be right, just because he is not duplicating others' efforts. Even if we think it probable that he will fail because he lacks the advantage of being right, we can expect a more important success from him in case he does succeed. It may be worth backing the long shot in hopes of winning big.*[4]

Consider again that squad of detectives, and suppose you've just taken charge of the investigation. There are several suspects, and at the present stage of the investigation, there's good reason to suspect some more than others. What to do: assign your entire squad to concentrate on the leading suspect? That means giving each detective the maximum chance to benefit from the advantage of being right. But also it probably means diminishing marginal returns: some bits of investigating are apt to get done several times over. Divide your squad equally between the suspects, then, so as to minimize redundant effort? That makes sure that most of their work will go to waste. Compromise, say with five detectives assigned to the leading suspect, two to the runner-up, and one to all the rest? No solution is right a priori. It depends: on whether you're shorthanded, on how far the leading suspect leads the rest, on how good your detectives are at cooperating. . . . There may well be considerations that weigh heavily against the advantage of being right—but not necessarily.

Likewise, *mutatis mutandis*, if you are an only-moderately-convinced materialist choosing between two finalist job candidates. One would be the department's seventh materialist: probably right, you think, but also redundant. The other, would be only its second dualist: probably wrong, you think, but possibly right and not redundant. All things considered, the dualist may well be the better bet. But not necessarily—again, it depends.

Continuing our neutral list, we come to—

CHANGE. *He who is wrong today may be right tomorrow. If he is open to argument and not too proud to change his mind, his present errors may not persist. And he who is right today may afterward go wrong.*

That may happen, sure enough. There are philosophers whose position is in a state of permanent revolution. But it's rare. We would expect to find a strong correlation between positions held now and positions held twenty years later, therefore between having or lacking the advantage of being right now and having or lacking it then.

DIFFERENT QUESTIONS. *Someone who has been wrong about the questions he has so far addressed may yet, if he has the virtues conducive to being right, have the advantage of being right about different questions that he will take up later.*

There are two cases. One is that he may take up entirely unrelated questions and arrive at true views about them. The other is that he may be right about a host of subsidiary questions in the vicinity of the big question he is wrong about. An antirealist may be right about the flaw in the argument that was meant as the grand bombshell against realism; a champion of epiphenomenal qualia may be right about why one materialist theory of mind works better than another.[5] In general, a philosopher may be importantly right about what the menu of positions looks like, he may know all the advantages and drawbacks and moves and countermoves very well, even though he makes the wrong choice from that menu. Likewise an honest physicist might, on balance, favor the wrong explanation of superconductivity; and yet he might be the very one who best points out which problems his preferred hypothesis does not solve. And whenever the evidence is misleading, as sometimes it is, whoever is right about the balance of the evidence will be wrong about the truth of the matter, and vice versa.

> **DEAD DOGMA.** *The advocate of error will challenge those on the side of truth. He will keep them on their toes, compelling them to think of questions hitherto ignored, and causing them to improve their positions even more in order to answer his arguments.*

This may happen or it may not. It depends. Sometimes there is bedrock disagreement, and both sides go their separate ways. Sometimes our only answer to an argument—a fair answer, if unsatisfying—is that since it leads to a false conclusion, it must have some flaw we can't find.

> **THE SPECIMEN.** *The advocate of error may play a role somewhat like the native informant in the linguistics department, or the snake in formaldehyde in the biology department. Error can be better understood, and better rejected, when it is seen close up. Know your enemy.*

Not a respectful attitude toward a prospective colleague!—Still, there's truth to it.

IV

I am not satisfied. Yes, these considerations are cogent. Yes, they carry weight. But they do not, not even all together, carry *enough* weight to do the job. They might sometimes, or even often, outweigh the advantage of being right. But it is not credible that they always and overwhelmingly outweigh the advantage of being right; and that is what they would have to do before they could explain why we treat the advantage of being right as though it were weightless. It remains a mystery why, if someone aims to support the candidate who can contribute most to advancing knowledge, he should not even weigh the holding of true doctrine as one important qualification among others, but rather should dismiss it as an irrelevant or improper consideration.

Indeed, if it's specimens of diverse errors that someone wants, or challengers to dead dogma, or insurance against the risk of his own error, then he should not dismiss being right as irrelevant. Rather he should treat it as, to some extent, a *dis*advantage! This attitude to appointments is not altogether unknown, and not quite as disreputable as trying to pack a department with right-thinking colleagues would be. We hear of "zoo departments" that try to procure one specimen of each main school of thought. (Too bad for the candidate who's so original as to defy classification! And you might think it's a scruffy specimen who'd consent to live in a zoo.) Still, I think the more usual attitude is that the truth of a candidate's position is not a proper consideration one way or the other. Is that because we think the advantage of being right and the advantage of being wrong always cancel exactly?—No; they can't always cancel, because the listed advantages of being wrong will vary greatly depending on the initial composition of the department.

V

Why ignore the advantage of being right? The considerations just listed do not go far enough. But I think there is a better explanation. We ignore the advantage of being right because we comply with a tacit treaty to do so. It is reasonable for all of us to think that this treaty, and therefore our present compliance that sustains it, serves the advancement of knowledge. However we should not all think this for the same neutral reasons.[6]

First, take a simple two-sided case: the materialists versus the dualists. (Assume, what may be none too realistic, that all concerned think the errors of their opponents matter more than the errors of their misguided allies.) In my own opinion as a materialist, the best thing for the advancement of knowledge would be the universal acceptance of the true philosophy: materialism. Or near-universal, anyway; I can see some good in preserving a small dualist minority as insurance against the risk that we're wrong, or as challengers, or as specimens. Worst would be the universal, or near-universal, acceptance of dualist error. Second best would be a mixture, as at present. A treaty requiring us all to ignore the advantage of being right when we make appointments will raise the probability of that second-best outcome and lower the probability both of the best and of the worst. If the dualists are willing, we can have the treaty if we like. We cannot have what we might like better, which is a rule that only dualists shall ignore the advantage of being right (that is, of being what dualists take to be right). If the treaty is on offer, we can take it or leave it.

It may well seem to us materialists, on balance, that taking it is what serves materialism best, and therefore serves knowledge best. For if we decline the treaty, who knows what may happen in the long run? We cannot predict the fortunes of voting. Majorities in our department, and in the profession of philosophy at large, may shift in unpredictable ways. Even if we are on top here and now, some of us may move away, or change their minds, or decide that the advantage of being right is somehow outweighed in some particular case. And besides, we cannot predict the swing votes of those colleagues who suspend judgment between materialism and dualism.

Likewise, *mutatis mutandis*, according to the dualists' opinions. They too may fear the shifting fortunes of voting. So they may think it better for dualism, hence better for knowledge, to join us in making and sustaining the treaty. What they count as the main benefit of a treaty to ignore the advantage of being right is what we count as its main cost: it tends to prevent the triumph of materialism. And what they count as the main cost is what we count as the main benefit. But however much we disagree about which is the cost and which is the benefit, we may yet agree that the benefit exceeds the cost. It is not inevitable that they and we should both think this. (They will not think it if they think the triumph of dualism is just around the corner.) But if both sides do think it, as they reasonably might, that should come as no surprise. And if both sides are found complying with a tacit treaty, that is evidence that (in some inexplicit way) both sides do consider the treaty worthwhile. I suggest that this is exactly what we do find.

In the complex real world, we have not just one disputed question but many, dividing philosophers in crisscrossing ways. Should we therefore expect a big network of crisscrossing little treaties, each one binding the parties to ignore the advantage of being right on a certain specific question? That would be too complicated to be workable. It would be too hard to keep track of which positions are under the protection of which treaty and which are unprotected. Mistakes would be made; and since the treaties are sustained by the expectation of reciprocation, mistakes would tend to unravel the whole network. It would work better to have one big, many-sided treaty to ignore the advantage of being right across the board. True, that would protect schools of thought so weak that others have no need to make a treaty with them.[7] If that is the price we must pay for a workable, stable arrangement that prolongs stalemate, and protects true doctrine from the triumph of its opponents, we may find the price well worth paying. Alas, it stops us from doing all we can to keep error out of the university. But in return it helps stop error from keeping out truth.

I stipulated that at the lucky university, advancement of knowledge was the predominant aim. But if the treaty is sustained by a sense of fair play or by respect for customary propriety, are those not quite different aims? Yes, and maybe those different aims are there, but they are extra. The treaty does not require them. It can be sustained solely by its foreseen benefits for the advancement of knowledge. For we cannot gain its benefits once and for all, and then double-cross our partners. As we know all too well, the work of appointments is never done. There will always be a next time.

If we're serious about aiming for the advancement of knowledge, and if we sincerely believe that the advantage of being right matters to the advancement of knowledge, then why ignore it? Because if we, in the service of truth, decided to stop ignoring it, we know that others, in the service of error, also would stop ignoring it. We have exchanged our forbearance for theirs. If you think that a bad bargain, think well who might come out on top if we gave it up. Are you so sure that knowledge would be the winner?

NOTES

1. John Stuart Mill, *On Liberty* (Indianapolis: Bobbs-Merrill, 1959), pp. 23–24. These words are in the mouth of a hypothetical critic, but Mill does not dispute them.

2. Derek Parfit, *Reasons and Persons* (Oxford: Oxford University Press, 1984), p. 199. I have amended his description so as not to say that the scanned body is destroyed; for just as it may be held that the person survives teletransportation, so too it may be held that the brain and body survive. The same process, except with the scanning done remotely from the receiving end, is better known as "beaming up."

3. Do not grumble about a far-fetched example. The decision problem requires only that the philosopher *thinks* he is offered escape by teletransportation. It is far-fetched that teletransportation should be available. It is not farfetched that a philosopher should be bamboozled.

4. See Philip Kitcher, "The Division of Cognitive Labor," *Journal of Philosophy* 87 (1990), 5–22.

5. G. H. Merrill, "The Model-Theoretic Argument against Realism," *Philosophy of Science* 47 (1980), 69–81; and Frank Jackson, "A Note of Physicalism and Heat," *Australasian Journal of Philosophy* 58 (1980), 26–34.

6. Here I parallel the suggestion I offered in "Mill and Milquetoast," *Australasian Journal of Philosophy* 67 (1989), 152–71, concerning a utilitarian defense of toleration. Put society in place of the university; utility in place of advancement of knowledge; toleration of dangerous opinions in place of ignoring the advantage of being right. A Millian neutral list of the benefits of toleration does carry weight. But too little weight, sometimes, for those who most fear the grave disutility of dangerous opinions. If a utilitarian inquisitor thinks that exposure to heresy conduces to eternal damnation, he will find a Millian defense of toleration lightweight to the point of frivolity. But even he might think that a treaty of toleration serves utility on balance, if he sees it as preventing not only the eradication of heresy but also the possible triumph of heresy. Rather than chance the doubtful fortunes of war, he might think it better, for the cause of salvation and hence for the cause of utility, to give away both the hope of victory and the risk of defeat.

7. Maybe the treaty is limited to "respectable" schools of thought, as opposed to ratbag notions. Is this because a school of thought gains respectability when it gains numbers enough to be a threat, so that bringing it into the treaty is worthwhile protection? I think not. If I am not mistaken, hard-line paraconsistency— the thesis that there are true contradictions—is just now gaining respectability. But not because it has the numbers; the overwhelming majority of philosophers still think it certainly and necessarily false. To gain respectability, all it takes seems to

be a handful of coherent and otherwise respectable defenders. Or not quite that, even—rather, defenders who satisfy all standards of coherence save those that are part of the very question at issue (as consistency is at issue when paraconsistency is defended). Graham Priest, author of *In Contradiction* (Dordrecht: Nijhoff, 1987), probably could have made hard-line paraconsistency respectable even if he had been a minority of one.

STUDY QUESTIONS

1. What are the appropriate considerations in deciding whom to appoint to the faculty?
2. If the truth or falsity of a candidate's views is not referred to in departmental discussions of faculty appointments, can we presume that those views play no role in the appointment process?
3. Are faculties equally willing to appoint those who practice different methodologies as those who hold different doctrines?
4. Should a candidate's commitments on political issues be treated in the same way as the candidate's positions on scholarly matters?

16

Peer Review and
the Marketplace of Ideas

David Shatz

nyone who labors at academic scholarship knows how dependent
that enterprise is on a procedure known as "peer review." A scholar
submits a work to a journal, press, or conference committee, or
sends a proposal to a foundation; the submission is then evaluated by other
professionals who are experts in the area covered by the work. The judgment of these referees determines whether the work is published by the target journal or press, appears on the conference program, or is funded by
the desired institution. If rejected by peers at one venue, the work will have
to be floated elsewhere—and its ultimate fate may well be oblivion. . . .

LETTING MILLIONS OF FLOWERS BLOOM

Readers may think it obvious why peer review mechanisms exist: it is to
ensure that only quality work is brought before the scholarly community.[1]
However, this explanation needs clarification, expansion, and deepening.
For a case can be made that much rejected work would be of value.

In an issue of *Behavioral and Brain Sciences* devoted to peer review, one
contribution "not entirely facetiously" put forward a radical yet instructive
alternative to prevailing practice:

Originally published in David Shatz, *Peer Review: A Critical Inquiry*, pp. 1, 15–27, 31,
2004, Rowman & Littlefield. Reprinted by permission of Rowman & Littlefield and with
minor revisions by the author.

Let millions of flowers bloom. All one need to do to get published is to write an article, submit it for publication, and pay for its publication. In this way, all individuals, whether from recognized or unrecognized institutions, would be assured of having their words immortalized. Those articles that catch fire and are cited might come from beggars, thieves, princes, or future Nobel laureates. Let it all hang out: the garbage, mediocrity, and the crown jewels. One could argue that all people are "created equal," endowed with such inalienable rights as the pursuit of truth via totally unrestricted opportunities to publish what they wish.[2]

Essentially, the (partly facetious) proposal is to replace "closed peer review" with "open peer review." Open peer review is review by the scholarly community at large, instead of a few anonymous referees along with an editor or board. . . . [O]pen review could be implemented by means of electronic publishing—some have advocated this sincerely—and without authors necessarily paying for space as the passage (from 1982) suggests. Eventually, there could be one big journal for an entire field, or else journals within a field could be divided according to subject matter rather than standards. Of course scholars could compile and publish lists of works they recommend, but given the proposal anyone could publish such a list without it passing prepublication review.[3]

It is hard to say who would have the biggest nightmare were open review implemented: readers who have to trek through enormous amounts of junk before finding articles they find rewarding; serious scholars who have to live with the depressing knowledge that flat earth theories now can be said to enjoy "scholarly support"; or a public that finds the medical literature flooded with voodoo and quackery. Let us not forget, either, that editors and sponsoring universities would lose power and prestige even while their workload as judges would be eliminated. All in all, the proposal sounds not only radical but preposterous. And yet like many preposterous proposals, this one challenges us to clarify assumptions and objectives of prevailing custom. Policies that seem to us eternal and necessary in fact may have not always existed—and may well be expendable.[4] At the least it is worth asking whether a procedure less demanding than current peer review—even if less permissive than "letting millions of flowers bloom"—might be better than what we have.

Specifically, one may argue that closed peer review, with its emphasis on selectivity and limitation, conflicts with the pursuit of truth as conceived by liberalism. In his famed argument for free speech, John Stuart Mill asserted that the expression of multiple and diverging viewpoints is more likely to produce truth than would suppressing some viewpoints. Through the proliferation and collision of ideas, truth will emerge; and as for those individuals who already have the truth, they will hold it in a deeper, less dogmatic way by dint of having been challenged.[5] No doubt many philosophers would pay homage to Mill's argument and on that basis sing the virtues of a free exchange of ideas—an ideological marketplace.[6] Indeed, when the topic at hand is, say, diversity within university education, or free speech generally, the marketplace of ideas often takes center stage as a grounds for promoting diversity and free expression without prior review of contributions.[7] Yet prepublication peer review of articles and books *prima facie* runs contrary to Mill's argument. Universities and journals seem to differ sharply in their hospitality to proliferation.

There is also a problem of authority. If one or two of the peer referees do not like an author's ideas, arguments, orientation, methodology, organization, or even writing style, that will often ensure (pending whether revisions are invited) that the ideas will not appear in print where the author wants them and will not reach the hoped-for audience. Mill was concerned that even a majority might be wrong; should we not be all the more concerned, one may ask, that the few—that is, the referees, along with the editor who trusts them—might be mistaken? Why not let others participate in the judgment, putting more reactions in the marketplace? Many heads are better than one, two, or three. There can be vast disagreements among referees as to whether a particular work is of good quality. And even when the work is agreed to be of good—or poor—quality, this does not yet establish a true consensus. One referee may find it well reasoned save in point D, while another will say that point D is particularly telling. Given such discrepancies, why not throw the issue out to a wider net of evaluators—scholarly public opinion? Why not have the issues "settled in the intellectual agora of the whole community rather than by a few referees and an editor working in camera"?[8] Problems of referee competence and bias intensify this concern. Compounding the offense to liberalism, according to some, is the inherent conservativeness of peer review: new and imaginative ideas and methodologies are likely to meet with initial resistance and skepticism and ultimately be aborted.[9]

Referees should be representative of the wider community; they are its proxies. (There are interesting comparisons here to the jury system.) But the wider reception of an article often does not match two referees' recommendation. Replies often point out gaping holes and serious errors in published works. By the same token what if a rejected article contains crown jewels, as happened in the case of Nobel Prize work that was originally rejected? From this point of view, each idea belongs in the marketplace—of print—and the marketplace should be filled with responses to it.[10]

Yet hardly anyone, including liberals, accepts the marketplace objection to peer review. In fact, many academics express the opposite sentiment: that because universities demand that professors produce in quantity, too much gets submitted and too much published. Already in 1973, when the number of journals was significantly smaller than today, a study asserted that "in the view of a significant number of editors and press directors, the philosophy [of publish-or-perish] is in large measure responsible for the proliferation of second-rate material on topics that interest few."[11] Kenneth Eble flatly averred (1983) that "the bulk of what is submitted does not deserve publication anywhere."[12] W. V. O. Quine, one of the most eminent philosophers of the twentieth century, maintained that "quality control is spotty in the burgeoning philosophical press."[13] Drummond Rennie, editor of prominent medical journals, stated:

> There are scarcely any bars to eventual publication. There seems to be no study too fragmented, no hypothesis too trivial, no literature citation too biased or too egotistical, no design too warped, no methodology too bungled, no presentation of results too inaccurate, too obscure, and too contradictory, no analysis too self-serving, no argument too circular, no conclusions too trifling or too unjustified, and no grammar and syntax too offensive for a paper to end up in print.[14]

More recently it has been declared that in published articles in medical journals "poor methodology and reporting are widespread" and that "most medical studies are of low quality and of limited relevance to clinicians."[15] Significantly, one measure of quality in journals is rejection rate. The higher this rate—the more articles a journal refuses to publish—the more likely it is to be regarded as "top" and "prestigious." The best journals, it follows, are not those that proliferate ideas and maximize discussion; they are those that *limit* the public expression of submitted ideas to perhaps 5–10 percent in some fields. Physics journals have high acceptance rates, but here as elsewhere a higher rejection rate is a mark of quality.[16]

Can this attitude be defended on liberal principles? According to the Millian position, don't even rejected articles contain *some* interesting and convincing points, often by a rejecting referee's own admission? Don't most works advance the pursuit of truth to some small extent, if only by provoking opponents to sharpen their own positions? Many scholars evince keen interest in reading or hearing unpublished papers, whether in traditional or online form, and they find value even in works that do not win publication; that further feeds the argument for open review. Finally let us not ignore the salutary effects of speed, of getting points into a conversation right after the speaker makes hers, not two to three years later.

In short, the practice of peer review seems to sit uneasily with liberalism's commitment to the proliferation of ideas and to Mill's marketplace conception. It may be added that the publication process limits free expression even for authors whose work has been accepted. Published authors are sometimes not allowed to publish articles or books in the form that *they* think is best. To satisfy referees and editors, authors may have to delete things they think important, formulate points in a briefer form than they think is feasible (manuscripts often have to be shortened to be accepted), deal with objections they think divert and waste space, or add sections that in their opinion disrupt the flow of their argument. Editors may impose changes that authors do not like but cannot override. The final product in some sense is not the author's work. In this respect, too, the peer review process does not allow for completely free expression. While not raising new issues of principle, this point illustrates the extent to which peer review filters and limits the flow of ideas.[17]

If I am right that peer review and the marketplace conception do not sit well together, we face a choice between abandoning peer review and abandoning the marketplace conception. In my opinion it is the marketplace conception that has to go; peer review stays. In this chapter, however, I am interested primarily in establishing that a champion of the marketplace conception has no way to justify peer review with high rejection rates. Along the way we will encounter good reasons for peer review, reasons which I claim the liberal cannot allow.

Understanding the Marketplace Objection

The marketplace objection should not be misunderstood. Liberals typically invoke the marketplace of ideas as an argument against governmental censorship. The difficulty we are considering, however, is not that peer review subjects ideas to *censorship* and *suppression*. Not only is government nowhere in the picture, but a journal or press makes no effort to prevent an author from submitting rejected work elsewhere; for example, journals do not apprise other journals that a work has been rejected, nor do they pass on negative comments. Instead each journal and press begins a refereeing process anew.[18] Even in the extreme case, in which an article eventually is rejected by *every* available journal, the author can disseminate his or her ideas by snail-mailing or e-mailing the paper to colleagues, publishing the piece privately, or communicating via the Web. Thus the process of peer review is a far cry from suppressing or not tolerating ideas. As Alan Goldman points out in discussing free speech on campus, there is a huge difference between *censoring* an idea and *not subsidizing* it.[19] But the marketplace argument against peer review never put forward an equation between peer review and censorship. Rather, the objection was that even if rejection of manuscripts is not a form of censorship or suppression, "burying" a large proportion of them in unread and unprestigious journals or keeping them from circulation altogether frustrates the emergence of truth or at least its pursuit. For truth is best served when discussion and expression are maximized.

It will not do for a liberal defender of peer review to say that, absent suppression, a good article is likely to end up *somewhere* in the marketplace, so all good ideas get expressed eventually. Even apart from whether all good work *does* get published, problems confront this response. To begin with, articles in less prominent journals are multiply jeopardized: because readers will assume (often correctly) that these articles must have been rejected by more prestigious journals, the articles will be read less, cited less frequently, and stand a smaller chance of being communicated widely. Citation indexes, I would think, bear this out. The price of having a few extremely selective and demanding journals is that others are marginalized and in effect never enter the marketplace. Can a liberal justify this?[20] (Sometimes it is even argued that when some groups dominate the channels of communication, governments should step in to guarantee equal access to the marketplace![21])

The attitude of "they can try somewhere else" does not befit a liberal. If an article does contribute something to discussion, why shouldn't the liberal editor want it in *her* journal? If a liberal is willing to see a piece not appear, she must in consistency agree that there is *nothing* valuable in it, and that its being consigned to oblivion is no loss. But if that is her opinion, we are back to the original question: according to the marketplace conception, is it really plausible that *none* of the rejected pieces have *anything* to contribute?

To be sure, a liberal can acquiesce in the exclusion of a few categories of work, but these are limited. One such category is redundant material. If a viewpoint has already been expressed by others in a similar way and in a comparably accessible source, then perhaps it makes no contribution to the marketplace. We should bear in mind, though, that in many contexts—like the classroom and the public forum—expressions of ideas are not unwelcome to liberals just because they are familiar. On the contrary, the best way of settling competition in the market and arriving at truth is allowing one viewpoint to spread and to ultimately win the competition by dominating community opinion.

A second category that liberals can exclude is junk—articles defending the flat earth theory and voodoo. Some hold that Mill's arguments do not cover views that have had their day, lost the competition, and are taken seriously by almost no one.[22] Such weeding, presumably done by an editor in consultation with experts, would make open review sound less outrageous. On the other hand, as Joel Feinberg notes in connection with censorship, truly bizarre views do not even need to be screened since there is no risk in allowing them free circulation.[23]

Third, the utility of free speech is always subject to being outweighed by greater harms. In the applied sciences, for instance medicine, great harm would ensue to the public from eliminating peer review. However, in many areas of the humanities, there is no comparable harm in a relaxation of standards, in allowing scholars to publish papers weaker than those that currently appear.

We can leave it open how the liberal should rule on redundancy, junk, and the applied sciences. For the proposal for open review is but an extreme version of a point that can be stated more moderately and no doubt more plausibly: to wit, that a balance between proliferation and standards—not a top-heavy emphasis on standards—is called for on liberal principles.

RESPONSES TO THE
MARKETPLACE OBJECTION

The most natural justification of closed, demanding peer review would reject the marketplace conception: uninhibited dissemination of ideas is harmful, because the effect of proliferation is inundation, and inundation frustrates the pursuit of truth. Though few ideas are harmful enough to merit censorship, in an open review system the weeds will choke the flowers, leading to the demise of all standards.[24] Furthermore, those specialists who do refereeing can know, albeit not infallibly, the difference between the valuable and the worthless, a genuine contribution and wasted words; their judgment is on the whole worthy of credence.

However, anyone prepared to rescue peer review by thus rejecting Mill had better think through the consequences. I cannot embark here on a large-scale examination of these consequences, but free speech is one obvious area which would become limited. I also recognize that free speech can be defended by appeal to liberty rather than the marketplace;[25] and liberty, we have seen, is consistent with peer review, since peer review is not censorship. Still, because a marketplace model has been used to justify a wide range of institutions,[26] one should tread cautiously before rejecting it. For that reason, we should continue to consider whether a Millian framework can support peer review.

The liberal is surprisingly hard pressed to say why quality control is so important. Some of his responses are pragmatic, and I begin with those.

A. *Pragmatic Benefits not Related to Truth*

1. *Constraints on Editors*

Peer review is reconciled with Mill's marketplace [says the liberal] by reference to budgetary and manpower constraints. Journals have a limited amount of space only because of financial exigencies and limited staff. Otherwise they are fully committed to the marketplace.

I have already dealt with this argument by noting the possibility of journals moving to electronic publishing. But apart from that, if financial considerations are all-important, why aren't authors given the option of vanity publishing—paying for journal space when an article is not recommended by referees? It strains plausibility to claim that vanity publishing is bad only because an author's affluence should not be allowed to determine whether her article gets printed. Suppose that a top journal were given a huge donation, earmarked entirely to publish more articles in the interests of scholarly dialogue and the pursuit of truth. Would not many journals probably reject this loosening of standards?

2. *Free Enterprise*

Scholarly publications are goods offered to a certain consumer market. Limiting what the public receives is a common practice. Not every TV show, movie, play, op-ed piece, and letter to the editor reaches the public; television networks, movie studios, and newspaper publishers seek to attract consumers. Shoddy goods turn off potential patrons. So it is with scholarly journals: the more selective the journal, the more readers it will attract. Quality control is vital to maintaining the journal's "profits," which include the prestige that redounds to the sponsoring department and university. (Aesthetically attractive, browsable volumes are another reflection of this marketing objective.) A free market allows for the effects of reputation and the marginalizing or failure of inferior products. Peer review is the child of private enterprise.

However, liberals should not be satisfied with this explanation, even if it contains a kernel of empirical truth. In many other marketplace enterprises, there is only one value to be achieved—satisfaction—and satisfaction is defined by success in the market, that is, desirability to consumers. But in the case of the marketplace of *ideas*, the liberal believes, the value ultimately served by proliferation is truth. Sheer market success does not guarantee this independently defined value.[27] There is a possible divergence between market success and truth; and the present reply subordinates possible loss of truth and dialogue to consumerist goals. The consumerist argument seems crass coming from someone supposedly concerned with truth and dialogue.

One might add that the consumerist argument would justify too much, allowing journals to publish inferior material if that would titillate the readership or win benefactors.[28]

3. *Credentials-Building*

The existence of journals and scholarly presses with high standards for publication makes it easier to judge scholarly performance. If refereeing were eliminated, universities would lose these meaningful measures of scholarly performance.

But credentials can be established without prepublication refereeing; all that is required is postpublication review of a candidate's work and favorable citation by other scholars—as is required for tenure and promotion. With the increased volume of reactions in open review, committees will have plenty to go on (although there will also be more things to respond *to*, which may limit reaction to any particular piece).[29] Furthermore, if scholarship involves the proliferation of knowledge, that goal should not be subordinated to the need to generate a mechanism for fashioning credentials. As sociologist Gordon Fellman complains in another context: "Thus does the academy genuflect to the larger culture's defining the worth of products in terms of *what they can be exchanged for*, rather than their own intrinsic value."[30]

4. *Psychological Benefits*

Peer review creates pride and self-esteem for those whose work is accepted. When anyone can publish what he or she wants, publications mean less to authors.

But again, pride and self-esteem might be gained from reactions in open review. And what of the anger, depression, frustration, and demoralization that rejected authors feel in the closed review system?

A problem common to proposals 3 and 4 is that the liberal has defended peer review in a seemingly self-defeating way, by subordinating the quest for truth to values that for a liberal should be less important. Liberal defenders of peer review will do better to show how peer review promotes the pursuit of truth and dialogue than to show how, for example, it creates status. Non-liberals are not inhibited from appealing to such benefits of peer review as the building of credentials. For nonliberals, these consequences provide legitimate *additional* reasons for the practice.

We turn now to some other liberal responses.

B. *Clarifying the Marketplace Conception*

5. *Modifying What's Allowed in the Marketplace*

The liberal has been misunderstood. The proliferation of *views* per se does not advance the cause of truth. It is rather the proliferation of *well-argued views* that brings this result. Poorly argued views *should* be excluded from the marketplace.[31]

The problem with this suggestion is that what in a referee's opinion is poorly argued may not be poorly argued in the opinion of others. The author's opinion that X is a good argument for *p* will be shut out from the marketplace if referees disagree. According to liberals, the claim that X is a good argument for *p* itself belongs in the marketplace, and is to be evaluated by the wider community.

6. *The Proxy Theory*

Submitting a paper to a journal *already* places the author's ideas into the marketplace; the referees themselves are among the potential "buyers." If referees expose a problem with an argument, this already is a reaction from the marketplace, and the author must respond or else withdraw. Referees are *proxies* for the wider community of scholars. Since scholars find it immensely difficult to sort through all articles in their fields of interest, they prefer to have the good ones clearly labeled by other experts. Hence scholars tacitly consent to the refereeing system; it's like sending someone to the market to buy you some good fruit when you don't have the time or patience to do it yourself. You don't expect the proxy to pick exactly as you will; but it is not cost effective to do the choosing yourself. So you rely on the judgment of others.

Alas, the proxy idea does not explain why, on liberal principles, you would want so *few* articles as are *actually* published under closed peer review; maybe you would want to see ones a notch or two or three below that, in order to challenge your own views, look at matters from other angles, and promote dialogue. This is especially true when the proxy is not completely reliable. If your proxies have not always chosen wisely in the past, wouldn't you at least want the possibility of glancing at the other wares yourself? It would not make sense for the liberal to say, "Look, all I say is that the proliferation of views will lead to truth. I don't have to claim that I *personally* will benefit from hearing many views." For why *wouldn't* the liberal want to absorb many views, if truth and freedom from dogma are the liberal's aims? And wouldn't the attitude of liberals that they personally need not hear other approaches then justify their ignoring even views that are out there in the literature?

C. *Benefits of Peer Review Related to Truth*

We come finally to the idea that open review frustrates the emergence of truth while closed review nurtures it.

7. *The Effect of Inundation*

Letting "millions of flowers bloom" is bound to frustrate truth. Scholars could not sort through all the material available without an enormous wasting of time and energy. It takes too much time to read and evaluate a paper properly. That is why works have to be screened before appearing. Alvin Goldman speaks of the need for "product identification": "the capacity of a communication regime (a way of organizing communication) to ensure that interested readers locate and recognize intellectual products or documents that are evidentially appropriate to their products and inquiries."[32]

In my view, this argument, if cogent—which I believe it is—is not available to a liberal. The marketplace conception did not take into account the problem of inundation and product identification; that is why the notion that proliferation yields truth is *mistaken*. Thus, the inundation and product identification argument may not be consistent with liberalism.[33] If liberals maintain it is consistent, and that they do take inundation into account, then they need to reopen a range of free speech issues. They will, for instance, have to explain why the *government* cannot intervene to limit inundation. I am not saying that liberals have no answer here, only that they owe us one.

8. *Improvement in Quality*

A peer review system improves the quality of every published work. Knowing that there is intense competition for space motivates scholars to produce the best work of which they are capable. Absent a refereeing process, one would expect a drop in the quality of even the best papers. In addition, the refereeing process and the often protracted negotiations of points between authors and referees provide authors with valuable feedback, again bolstering quality. Scholars may even be under a professional obligation to submit their ideas for review in the interests of truth.[34] Some scholars will be arrogant enough to think that whatever they say is of quality; peer review forces them to answer to a higher standard, even if many of them do not incorporate referee criticisms when they submit an article to another journal.[35]

Let us first look at the claim that competition spurs quality. The problem with the liberal's use of this point is that even without prepublication peer review, many scholars will wish to produce their best in order to advance their reputations. (Sometimes, scholars back out of invited articles or even withdraw accepted manuscripts because they are dissatisfied with their own products.) Moreover, the liberal has to balance curtailment in quality with frustration of truth. Closed review excludes *so much* material that one has to question whether it strikes a happy balance. If not, the liberal will have difficulty defending closed review.

Regarding feedback: Rare even now is the scholar who does not circulate drafts to other specialists for comments. Since collegial commenting is reciprocally beneficial (people comment on each other's work), such comments are as a rule careful and helpful, possibly more helpful than referees' remarks. But even if comments from outside one's circle are more valuable than comments from acquaintances, we would not need peer review in its current form. Suppose we created a system by which (perhaps paid) referees would continue to provide feedback, but authors were free to do as they wished with that feedback; or a system in which everything would be published—including whatever referees' comments remain after author and referee exchange reactions. Such systems would also spur authors to produce quality, because how their work is received will determine their professional standing. Some authors will make bad decisions. But is it worth excluding so much just to prevent those bad decisions? It is the *exclusion* of too much work that makes peer review problematic on a marketplace conception, and the liberal has not justified that exclusion.

I have argued that the marketplace conception has no way to justify closed peer review with current rejection rates. A payoff of our discussion has been the emergence of several good reasons for adopting peer review. The practice of peer review as it actually exists is sustained by several convictions: that quality control by experts, rather than proliferation, is the avenue to truth; that proliferation leads to inundation, and inundation impedes truth; that scholars are consumers and want preapproved products; that a system of credentials is needed, and this requires refereeing. These considerations, I have suggested, are contrary to the marketplace conception. Hence our system of peer review implies a rejection of the marketplace conception, the very conception on which other features of academic life seem to depend.

NOTES

1. There is a second function often cited, and that is to improve the work on behalf of the author. However, it seems to me that this second function derives from the first: the reason for improving an article is to make it eventually presentable to the rest of the community.

2. Richard M. Perloff and Robert Perloff, "Improving Research on and Policies for Peer Review Practices," in *Peer Commentary on Peer Review*, ed. Stevan Harnad (Cambridge: Cambridge University Press, 1982), 48–49. Hans-Peter Dan-

iel, *Guardians of Science: Fairness and Reliability of Peer Review*, trans. William E. Russey (New York: Weinheim, 1993) refers to scientists who seriously advocate such a position.

3. I thank the late Robert Nozick for this last point.

4. *Proceedings of the Royal Society* and *Proceedings of the National Academy of Sciences* went without peer review for a while. See R. Roy and R. Ashburn, "The Perils of Peer Review," *Nature* 414 (2001): 393–94.

5. John Stuart Mill, *On Liberty*, chap. 2.

6. However, many would advocate free speech not because free speech results in truth and removal of dogma but because free speech protects liberty. On the difference between these arguments see, inter alia, C. Edwin Baker, *Human Liberty and Freedom of Speech* (New York: Oxford University Press, 1989). See also Martin P. Golding, *Free Speech on Campus* (Lanham, Md.: Rowman & Littlefield, 2000). The term "marketplace" is not John Stuart Mill's but rather Oliver Wendell Holmes's. See his dissenting opinion in *Abrams v. United States* 250 U. S. 616, 630 (1919).

7. Alvin Goldman distinguishes literal and metaphorical meanings of the "marketplace." See *Knowledge in a Social World* (New York: Oxford University Press, 1999), 192–217. In its literal meaning, the competitive market mechanism promotes the discovery of truth. In its metaphorical meaning, the marketplace of ideas is marketlike, in that debates are "wide open and robust," but this result is not necessarily achieved by the mechanism of the market. Government regulation might even be necessary to achieve the good result. I thank Martin Golding, the late Robert Nozick, and Ross Zucker for valuable discussion of the marketplace conception.

8. Robert K. Adair, "A Physics Editor Comments on Peters and Ceci's Peer-review Study," in *Peer Commentary on Peer Review*, ed. Harnad, 12. Adair is speaking only of controversial submissions, but I've taken the liberty of recruiting his formulation for my own purposes.

9. See, for example, Harnad, introduction to *Peer Commentary on Peer Review*, 1–2.

10. In a print environment, a published idea that is discredited remains available. In the context of the Internet, posted papers may be withdrawn once the marketplace quashes them.

11. W. Pell, "Facts of Scholarly Publishing," *PMLA* 88 (1973): 639–44.

12. Kenneth Eble, "Conflicts between Scholarship and Teaching," in *A Professor's Duties*, ed. Peter Markie (Lanham, Md.: Rowman & Littlefield, 1994), 216.

13. W. V. O. Quine, *Theories and Things* (Cambridge, Mass.: Harvard University Press, 1981), 192.

14. Drummond Rennie, "Guarding the Guardians," *JAMA* 256 (1986): 2391.

15. The first quote is from D. G. Altmann, "Poor-quality Medical Research: What Can Journals Do?" *JAMA* 287 (2002): 2765; the second is from K. Abbasi et al., "Four Futures for Scientific and Medical Publishing," *British Medical Journal* 325 (2002): 1472.

16. *The Guidebook for Publishing Philosophy*, ed. Eric Hoffman (Newark, Del.: American Philosophical Association), publishes data on acceptance rates by different journals. The journal *Ethics* publishes data each year on the fate of submissions. Certain physics journals accept nearly 80 percent of submissions, the prestigious ones 45 percent (my source, though, is from 1982: Robert K. Adair, "A Physics Editor Comments on Peters and Ceci's Peer-review Study," in *Peer Commentary on Peer Review*, ed. Harnad, 12). See also L. L. Hargens, "Variation in Journal Peer Review Systems: Possible Causes and Consequences," *JAMA* 263 (1990): 1348–52.

A 1971 study gives high acceptance rates for geology and linguistics as well; see Harriet Zuckerman and Robert K. Merton, "Patterns of Evaluation in Science: Institutionalization, Structure, and Function of the Referee System," *Minerva* 9 (1971): 77.

17. It seems unfair that readers might hold an author accountable for a change he or she did not want but was necessitated by another's judgment, regardless of whether the change was for the better or for the worse. Likewise it seems not right for an author to get credit for a well-written article when it is a skilled copy editor who has created that smooth flow in the prose. Those who evaluate candidates for tenure and promotion have only the hard, cold printed word to go by when they form their opinion.

18. That the earlier report is not solicited is odd if we try to build a consensus; the explanation seems to be that editors wish not to doom the rejected article. Gerald Dworkin, then editor of *Ethics*, inquires whether it is proper to retain as a referee for an article someone who has already refereed the article for another journal. See *Ethics* 103 (January 1993): 219–20.

19. See Alan Goldman, "Diversity within University Faculties," in *Morality, Responsibility, and the University*, ed. Cahn, 219–23.

20. Some have suggested that journals should allow multiple submissions—submission of an article to several journals at once—in order to make more journals competitive. For arguments both for and against this proposal, see D. V. Cicchetti, "The Reliability of Peer Review for Manuscript and Grant Submissions: A Cross-Disciplinary Investigation," *Behavioral and Brain Sciences* 14 (1991): 132; and Duncan Lindsey, *The Scientific Publication System in Social Science* (San Francisco: Jossey-Bass, 1978), 104–5.

21. See, for example, Baker, *Human Liberty and Freedom of Speech*, 5, 15; Golding, *Free Speech on Campus*, 20.

22. Something like this is suggested by Goldman, *Knowledge in a Social World*, 221.

23. Joel Feinberg, "Limits to the Free Expression of Opinion," in *Philosophy of Law*, ed. Joel Feinberg and Jules Coleman, 7th ed. (Belmont, Calif.: Wadsworth, 2004), 263.

24. This way of putting things was suggested by Margarita Levin.

25. See Baker, *Human Liberty and Freedom of Speech*.

26. Besides figuring in voluminous ethical and legal discussions of free speech (see, e.g., Baker, *Human Liberty and Freedom of Speech*, chap. 1), marketplace models have been used to defend democracy, free trade, and even pop culture. Common to these justifications is the notion that proliferation maximizes well-being.

27. I thank Michael Levin for clarifying this distinction and helping formulate this paragraph.

28. Interestingly, many journals would publish articles by famous philosophers because of who wrote them; the articles would not be published if written by someone else. One could argue that such articles are published out of a desire to give scholars (present and future) a more comprehensive view of this individual's thought, which is certainly a contribution to scholarship. But one might also view this practice as simply getting attention and earning status. On the whole I think the practice is defensible, but will not press that claim here.

29. The high acceptance rates in some fields (see note 16) suggest that a field can do evaluations of personnel even when acceptance rates are high.

30. Gordon Fellman, "On the Fetishism of Publications and the Secrets Thereof," *Academe* 81 (Jan.–Feb. 1995): 27. (Liberals might substitute the word

"instrumental" for "intrinsic," since ideas have value as contributions to a larger quest.) Describing scholarly publishing today, one observer writes: "Forget about advancing the intellect; for the academic, what scholarly publishing is for is to advance the intellectual." (Judith Shulevitz, "Keepers of the Tenure Track," *New York Times Book Review*, [October 28, 1995], 46.)

31. Alan Gewirth has advanced a similar argument in denying academic freedom to professors who ignore accepted criteria of academic argument. See his "Human Rights and Academic Freedom," in *Morality, Responsibility, and the University*, ed. Steven M. Cahn (Philadelphia: Temple University Press, 1990), 8–31.

32. Goldman, *Knowledge in a Social World*, 175.

33. Michael Levin pointed out to me that articles are often rejected not because referees think they contain false or redundant theses, but because they are so poorly "packaged" that they could not contribute to the pursuit of truth. This is a cogent point, but it points up a weakness in the marketplace conception akin to the failure to consider the effects of inundation. Liberals have not proposed to exclude views from the marketplace on the grounds that they are poorly expressed, let alone advocate prior screening for this defect.

34. See Theodore Benditt, "The Research Demands of Teaching in Modern Higher Education," in *Morality, Responsibility, and the University*, ed. Cahn, 93–108, esp. 105ff.; Markie, *A Professor's Duties*, 79–80. Benditt and Markie both ground this obligation in the teacher's responsibility to teach: if teachers are to present their own ideas to students, those ideas must first undergo testing. I find this particular argument problematic, but there may be other arguments for demanding that scholars submit to review.

35. For statistics on the failure of authors to revise in accordance with criticism when they submit to another journal, see S. Lock and J. Smith, "Peer Review at Work," *Scholarly Publishing* 17 (1986): 303–16; L. L. Hargens, "Variation in Journal Peer Review Systems: Possible Causes and Consequences," *JAMA* 263 (1990): 1348–52; A. Yankauer, "Peering at Peer Review," *CBE Views* 8 (1985): 7–10; S. C. Patterson and S. K. Smithers, "Monitoring Scholarly Journal Publication in Political Science: The Role of the APSR," *Political Science and Politics* 23 (1990): 647–56. J. V. Bradley, "Pernicious Publication Practices," *Bulletin of the Psychonomic Society* 18 (1981): 31–34, reports that 21 percent of respondents said they would be more careful if they knew it would not be refereed, 6 percent said they would be less careful, and the rest (73 percent) said they would be equally careful.

STUDY QUESTIONS

1. Does the pressure placed on professors to publish result in the proliferation of mediocre materials with limited interest and value?
2. If the editorial board of a scholarly journal is divided evenly between those who find a submitted article to be of high quality and those who find it not worth publishing, should the journal accept that article?
3. Should leading journals be encouraged to publish a higher percentage of articles they receive?
4. Does peer review promote the pursuit of truth?

IX

TELLING
THE TRUTH

An oft-cited example of immorality is telling lies. Yet in academic life situations frequently arise in which professors, while paying lip service to truth, may tell at most only part of it.

Paul Eisenberg considers a variety of such cases, including evaluating students, recommending courses, and writing letters of reference. In carrying out these responsibilities, professors often mislead in an attempt to avoid unpleasant situations.

George Sher considers in detail one such moral dilemma, that faced by a graduate professor asked to write a recommendation for a less than stellar student. Sher suggests how to compose a letter that avoids a candid assessment, while maintaining at least a tenuous connection to the truth.

17

The Truth, the Whole Truth,
and Nothing but the Truth

PAUL D. EISENBERG

Whatever may be true of them in other aspects of their lives, academics in their professional work and lives face some particularly knotty problems about truth telling. The difficulty is compounded by the many different areas of teaching and research, and even service work, in which such problems occur. In this essay I shall concentrate on some of the problems that arise in the areas of teaching and service; or rather, since the kinds of service work I have in mind may well be regarded as adjuncts to one's classroom teaching, I shall consider teaching and service together. Before turning my attention to these areas of one's academic life, where, it seems to me, problems about truth telling arise both more frequently and in a more troublesome form than is the case with research, I should like to say a few words, for comparison's sake, about truth telling in research.

There one encounters, for example, the kind of case, already much publicized, involving a researcher—usually young or untenured—who deliberately falsifies his data in order to obtain impressively new and interesting results, and thereby to gain tenure or to become a much stronger candidate for a major research grant. Perhaps we academics tend to think of this kind of falsification as quite new, and certainly in this "high-tech" age there are ways of falsifying data that *are* new. The basic problem is no doubt much

Originally published in Steven M. Cahn, ed., *Morality, Responsibility, and the University*, pp. 109–118, 1992, Temple University Press. Reprinted by permission of Temple University Press.

202 • TELLING THE TRUTH

older, however. Thus in *Gaudy Night*, first published in 1936, Dorothy Sayers makes much of the (fictional) case of a brilliant historian who deliberately suppresses evidence in order to make his own novel argument persuasive. Although that incident is fictional, its plausibility presupposes that Sayers and others in the academic world of her time knew of real incidents of that kind. And on the Continent in that same year, some German scholars were, presumably, quite deliberately suppressing information or otherwise falsifying their accounts in order to make themselves and their works attractive to, if not indeed usable by, the Nazis.[1] In this essay, however, I shall deal only with the present-day situation and, yet more particularly, with the situation now in nonsectarian American colleges and universities. Accordingly, there is, I like to think, no need to mention here the obverse case of someone who, like Descartes with *Le Monde*, has come upon an important scientific truth or, at any rate, has written a work in all sincerity that he nonetheless dares not publish because of the fear of reprisals from the church or the university itself. In small church-affiliated schools that problem may persist, however (just as it is not unlikely that even today a less daring counterpart to J. T. Scopes may be unwilling to advocate in the classroom or, perhaps, even to introduce into it a highly unpopular view that he accepts).

In the major colleges and universities, however, subtler pressures may—indeed do—exist that lead to suppressions of the truth, suppressions that, if not so blatant as those to which I have just referred, are nonetheless real. Sometimes, for example, a junior colleague may be unwilling to confess her interest in such and such a field or line of research—let us say, applied ethics or women's studies—because she knows her senior colleagues look with disfavor upon it. Or such a person fears to make, much less to publish, a rebuttal of a senior colleague's view lest her attempted cleverness cost her her job or, at least, lest it bring an end to the good will and support of the colleague in question. Senior scholars, however, sometimes face quite similar problems. I have heard of one distinguished researcher who, although he was prepared to acknowledge in private the force of a less well known scholar's objection to an aspect of his view, was unwilling to make the same acknowledgment in print or publicly to abandon the view that had made him famous.

Although such contemporary situations as I have just described do present the persons involved in them with difficult choices, it seems to me that "we" (that is, fellow academics) already know how at least most such cases should be resolved. From our (external) point of view, the ethical problems that such cases raise do not seem to be particularly difficult. Do we not think that in such cases the truth, the whole truth, should be told, and indeed nothing but the truth? For if one is "really" an intelligent person, one will (eventually) make one's way in the academic world even if one fails to get this or that important grant (there are always others), even if one loses (temporarily) the favor of this or that colleague (one has other colleagues; there are or will be other jobs), etc. At any rate, however sticky such problems may sometimes be in practice, they have typically one feature in common—one that, I think, tends to make them, as a class, less difficult cases for ethical theory than those that I am about to describe in the areas of teaching and service. That is, most of these problems confront "isolated" individuals who are tempted to do what (they themselves know) most of their colleagues in the academic world do not or would not do. It is because most of us do not deliberately falsify data, do not fail to make public acknowledgment of powerful objections to our (former) views, etc., that the behavior of those who do such things strikes us as so clearly reprehensible.

In other areas of academic life, things are not so clear-cut. Again, let me consider several examples:

1. One is teaching an introductory course in, for example, philosophy. One very much wants to tell one's students the truth about whatever topic one is discussing, but how much of the truth should be told? The whole story, one knows, is very complicated; and telling it would both confuse most of one's students and leave one with too little time for presentation and discussion of other topics that one had announced would be included (which would give the course as a whole proper balance, which one knew the students were more likely to be interested in, etc.). Incidentally, one may be concerned not to displease one's students for the further reason that their evaluations of the course will subsequently be considered in recommendations concerning one's annual salary increase or one's tenure or one's promotion; but here and in the subsequent cases, I wish to consider such a case in, so to speak, its pedagogical purity. Accordingly, then, how should one decide which portion of the truth to tell and which to leave untold? And should one tell one's students that one is simplifying (at the risk of appearing to condescend to them), or should one act as if there were no more to be said (at the risk of leading some of the students to think that indeed there is no more to be said)?

2. A particular undergraduate student, although apparently conscientious, has written a very poor paper or exam. In one's written comments on the assignment or in one's subsequent remarks to the student, should one tell him more or less bluntly what one thinks of the work? If one does not, the student may well think that the work is, after all, pretty good and, hence, that the very

low grade he has received on it is unwarranted. On the other hand, being candid with the student may hurt his feelings and, yet worse from a purely pedagogical point of view, one may thereby discourage the student and, hence, weaken his motivation to try harder in the future.

3. Indeed, will one dare to give such work the low grade one thinks it deserves? (Grading should here be thought of as "standing in" for a verbal assessment; so that, although the number or letter assigned cannot itself be deceitful, what it implies about the instructor's assessment of the work can be.) In addition to the considerations just mentioned under example 2, one knows also that other instructors—one's departmental colleagues among them—would not grade the work in question very low. Setting aside (if indeed one is able to do so) one's concern not to be regarded as a crank even by one's colleagues or to be unpopular with the students, one is still left to wonder whether one can justify, even to oneself, giving a very low grade to a student who chanced to take one's course but who might equally well have enrolled in another section of the course and received from the instructor in it a much higher grade. Is it not unfair to penalize the student, in effect, for taking one's own rather than some apparently quite similar course? Or perhaps one's departmental colleagues share one's standards but instructors in other departments do not. Should students be penalized for enrolling in elective courses in one's own department when they might equally well have taken something in another department?

4. A student relatively unfamiliar with the faculty of one's department asks one's advice about taking such and such courses with certain of one's departmental colleagues. However much one may admire those colleagues' research in certain areas or their teaching in certain courses, one has good reason to believe that this one among them has very little knowledge and, worse yet, is quite confused about a subject which he nonetheless confidently teaches to undergraduates, or that that one is doing more or less mechanically and for the nth time a course the lectures for which she carefully prepared a decade ago but about which she has thought very little in the interim. Should one tell the student what one really thinks? Or in a spirit of loyalty to one's friends and colleagues, should one enthusiastically recommend their courses (even as, one hopes, they will recommend one's courses to their present or past students)? At least, should one describe the courses in question somewhat more favorably than

one thinks they deserve? Or should one pretend to know nothing about those particular courses? Or should one deviously seek out reasons other than one's real ones for not recommending those particular courses—say, that the subject matter in such and such another course is more likely to interest the student or that the student will be able to take those courses (or ones very much like them) some other time but has meanwhile the special opportunity to study with such and such an illustrious visiting professor in the department or with such and such a distinguished pedagogue in this, the last year before her retirement?

5. The present case is, admittedly, a variant of example 2, but nonetheless, it may be thought worthy of mention in its own right. A senior who has majored in one's department but, so far, has not shown much talent or originality asks one's advice about whether she should think seriously about pursuing graduate studies in one's discipline. Should one tell the student exactly what one thinks? Or should one fall back on other reasons for being discouraging—for example, that jobs in that discipline are still very hard to get? Or should one think that a person ought not to be discouraged from at least trying to do what she most wants or what most interests her; that, after all, other departments are not so demanding as one's own; that sometimes students bloom late? And with such considerations in mind, should one proceed to recommend to the student various departments where one thinks she has a decent chance of being admitted and even of performing, if not at a distinguished, at least at a passable level?

6. A graduate student who has worked closely with one is now ready to look, for an academic position elsewhere and has asked one to write a letter of reference for her. She is very good but not indeed wonderfully talented and she still has a long way to go on her dissertation. She is really quite worthy of getting a good academic position, however. One knows that people from other schools and many in one's own department are prepared to write greatly inflated letters about *their* students. Should one, then, exaggerate somewhat about her ability, too, and, moreover, straightforwardly aver that she will have completed all work on her dissertation by the start of the next academic year (and thereby make her seem to be a no less attractive candidate than many others with whom she will be competing and who, one suspects, are no more talented or further along in their dissertations than is one's own student)? Or should one describe her and her situation exactly as one perceives them and thereby

206 • TELLING THE TRUTH

run the risk of making her appear a far less attractive candidate than she actually is?

It should be noted that in none of the six cases just described is one contemplating a choice between a clearly moral alternative and one that is merely self-seeking. In that respect also these cases differ from the ones I described previously. (Granted, one might be able to *redescribe* at least some of those earlier cases so that they were seen to involve a conflict between competing moral concerns.) Perhaps it is precisely because in these latter cases one is forced to choose between competing goods, neither of which is merely prudential or self-aggrandizing in character, that they are so problematic.

They are not, however, equally problematic. Thus really conscientious pedagogues may always feel a bit bad about presenting a deliberately sim-plified account, but they are likely to be able to find, or to have already found, a way of doing so which is more or less satisfactory to them; and similarly with several of the other cases presented. I do not mean to say, however, that in these cases there is a single right approach that will work equally well for all concerned teachers. In fact, it seems to me that these matters have to be decided by the individual instructor, and on a case-by-case basis. Thus, clearly, the extent of simplification required in an introductory account of Descartes's philosophy may well be less than that deemed appropriate in an account of Spinoza's philosophy, inasmuch as Descartes's philosophy is, in some more or less obvious sense, easier to understand than Spinoza's.[2] But whether one should decide to devote equal time to presentation of the two philosophies, or more to Spinoza's because it is indeed the more difficult, or less to it for that very reason—all this depends on the teaching style of the individual instructor and his purposes in a given course, in a given quarter or semester. I say "a given quarter or semester" to indicate that one may want or need to rethink these matters and, hence, to structure the contents of a course differently at different times in one's teaching career, in response to a variety of factors: for exam-ple, changes in one's own interests, perceived changes in students' interests, the availability of attractive new versions of certain texts.

In the matter of deciding how much to say about a given topic in one's classroom or what to say in one's comments on a student's paper or in advice that one gives a student about other courses or about pursuing a graduate degree in one's own field (and so on), one (very likely) has at least the relative advantage of *not* needing to consider what others are already doing. I mean to say that in these matters there is no already prevailing practice that one takes to be reprehensible or unsatisfactory, but which one cannot immediately change and which one must somehow take into account if one is to reach a morally acceptable conclusion about what one is to do. In contrast, what grade to give a student or how to describe a student in a letter of reference are examples of matters where one's conscientious decision must take into account prevailing practice—in other words, widespread grade inflation and inflation/exaggeration in claims made about prospective young academics.

Traditional ethical theories have *nothing* (helpful) to say about the former sort of cases; what is called for is casuistry (in the best sense of that term) and individual judgment. Traditional ethical theories do have something to say about cases of the latter kind, but such theories do not speak to us with one voice. On the one hand, Kant tells us that the knowledge of what other people generally do *in fact*, if it is not morally acceptable, should carry no weight whatsoever with the individual moral agent as she sets about deciding how to behave. In contrast, classical utilitarianism invites—indeed, requires—us to consider what others are already doing as we set about our own ethical decision making; for a situation of a type in which most other people are already behaving in a certain way (albeit a way that is ethically shabby or reprehensible) is one in which one's own decision/action will very probably have consequences significantly different from the consequences of one's decision/action when either there is no relevant prevailing practice or the prevailing practice is not ethically reprehensible. Thus a Kantian in Nazi Germany, for example, would tell the truth, whatever the cost to oneself and one's family; an (act-)utilitarian in the same situation might very well reach an opposite decision, since the contribution that the consequences of one's truth telling would make to the well-being of those concerned might well be less than the cost of a lie that helped to preserve the lives and the liberty of oneself and one's family.

My present concerns relate to situations that are "merely academic" and, hence, likely to be much less dire than those to which I have just alluded. Granted, one could, easily enough, somewhat increase the moral intensity of the cases with which I am concerned. For example, it might be true that if I give such and such a student a low grade in my course, that student will not get into medical school, whereas a student who in other relevant respects is equal to mine and who indeed has performed in approximately the same way but in another section of the course, where the grader is quite generous, stands a much better chance of being admitted. Or because I write a wholly truthful account, my student fails to get a job in academe, whereas another student whose career I have followed and whom I know to be on the whole less able than my protégé gets various people to write quite glowing letters and, on their basis, is offered a good position. But whenever one gives a low final grade to a student or writes a candid assessment in a situation where others are not proceeding similarly, *something* is likely to be hanging in the balance. At the very least, it seems that an injustice of some sort has been done the students who get only the grade or the assessment that they "deserve" when others who have performed no better and perhaps have performed even less well get a higher grade or a much stronger recommendation. Is it proper, then, for me, the instructor, to consider only the matter of fidelity to my own standards (which I have examined and reexamined and which I find to be quite acceptable) and thereby to be *true to myself*; or should I not, rather, have an even greater concern for my students, a concern that will sometimes lead me to put my devotion to justice and well-being for them before my devotion to the truth itself and truth to myself?

It is clear that different but equally conscientious instructors have answered and continue to answer that question differently. As I come to reflect upon it once again, I find myself reaching the same conclusion as I have done previously; now I should like to share it with you, though (I can imagine) you may well disagree with it. I am inclined to think that one should regularly reexamine the acceptability of one's standards but that while one does find them acceptable, one should use them and only them in reaching one's decisions about the grades to assign to one's students and the strength of the recommendations to write on their behalf. I think so for several reasons. First, one usually cannot be sure that anything else affecting the student's long-term well-being really does hang on this grade or that letter, whereas one can be sure when one gives the student an inflated grade or recommendation that the truth (as one sees it) has not been respected and that one has therefore been untrue to oneself.

Second, it is not clear, on balance, that one's student, if graded/assessed honestly, is then being treated unjustly (vis-à-vis comparable students who have happened upon more "generous" instructors). I mean to be speaking here not of instructors who in all honesty have adopted standards less demanding than one's own (we shall never reach consensus in such matters, and that is a fact of the world which all of us must recognize); I am referring to those others who one knows or has good reason to believe have standards very much like one's own but who have "given in" to the pressure of widespread academic inflation. The matter of (in)justice here is itself very complicated. Granted, there is something amiss when my student gets, let us say, B– for the same level of work to which you give an A but which, you admit to me privately, is "really" worth only the lower grade. My student is at a disadvantage in an obvious respect. In a less obvious respect, however, so too is yours. For your student is not getting from you one thing that she or he deserves—namely, your honest evaluation of her or his work. Not to give students what they deserve is to do them an injustice!

Moreover, it seems to me that in our role as academics—more particularly, as teachers—we serve our students as role models, whether or not we wish to. We in academe have the opportunity—or is it not indeed the duty?—to be, and to present ourselves as being, disinterested servants of truth (as we see it). Or rather, since, like Nietzsche, I think that, strictly speaking, there are and can be no disinterested human actions, let me say, instead, that we have the opportunity, if not the duty, to be and to present ourselves as being interested in discovering and conveying the truth. Why set such a high value on truth and truth telling? The question is age-old and very important. There is a sense, however, in which no (serious) academic should be asking that question, for if the academic life is or ought to be concerned with any one thing preeminently, surely that thing is truth (in its many manifestations and guises).

Finally, just as one is, willy-nilly, a model for one's students, so is one also for one's fellow academics. Thus, for example, if some of them see me writing in a manifestly honest way about my student, they may not only appreciate my honesty with them but may come to think that they ought to write no less honestly themselves. If, however, I am afraid that my merely truthful letter will be taken to be a weak recommendation (either because the exaggerations or partial truths in others' letters have not been recognized for what they are or because it has been presumed, in view of the widespread practice, that my statement, for all of its qualifications, is itself inflated), I can take the trouble to comment in the letter, or in a covering letter (a sort of "metaletter"!), on the significance of my letter-writing style. I can also join with other like-minded academics in urging our various professional organizations to produce official statements condemning various types of academic dishonesty.

There may be other measures I can adopt as well. What I must recognize, however, is that such problems as I have raised in this essay do not have easy answers; that despite my academic's desire to reach a decision quickly so that I can get on with other aspects of my academic life (in particular, my research), they deserve careful attention; and—by no means least of all—that I do not need to meditate on these questions in solipsistic splendor but can and should discuss them with interested colleagues, of whom there will always be many.

NOTES

1. Cf., for example, Walter Kaufmann's discussion of this matter in his chapter "The Master Race," in his by now classic study *Nietzsche: Philosopher, Psychologist, Antichrist*, 4th ed. (Princeton: Princeton University Press, 1974).

2. The question of why one philosophy is easier to grasp than another is an interesting one to consider in detail. Is it a matter of the vocabulary and typical sentence structure, the extent of agreement with various prephilosophical intuitions, the extent of the antecedent absorption of the philosophy in the general culture, or some combination of these and yet other factors? This, however, is not the place to engage in detailed investigation of that question; our business lies elsewhere.

STUDY QUESTIONS

1. Under what circumstances, if any, should a professor mislead a student?
2. Would grading be made fairer if transcripts included not only a student's course grade but also the average grade of all students in the course?
3. Is it ethical to share with a new faculty colleague details about the deliberations that led to that colleague's appointment?
4. When, if ever, should a professor refuse to share with colleagues personal information relating to the professor's students or advisees?

18

The Letter Writer's Dilemma

George Sher

Mr. Adam Pendicks has asked me to write in support of his application to your institution, and I am obliged to do so. Adam is a sixth-year graduate student in philosophy here at Ragland University, where he has compiled a satisfactory though undistinguished record. Overall, I would place him in the third quartile of the students in our program.

Adam is currently writing a dissertation under my supervision on a variation of a possible objection to a potential difficulty with a defense of the killing/letting-die distinction that two philosophers, Benson Hedges and the late Arve Suissinnen, once deployed, the former in the middle 1960's and the latter in the early 80's. Although the Suissinnen-Hedges line has not achieved wide currency—no one, to my knowledge, has actually said anything about it—a careful refutation of the variant of the possible objection to the potential difficulty that Adam discusses would nevertheless be an incremental addition to our understanding of the topic. Although Adam has now completed drafts of five of his seven chapters, the dissertation won't be in any shape to defend by this coming September, and I'm not sure about the following September either. There is, however, a probability greater than zero that some of it will eventually be published.

Originally published in Robert B. Talisse and Maureen Eckert, eds., *A Teacher's Life: Essays for Steven M. Cahn*, pp. 107–111, 2009, Lexington Books. Reprinted by permission of Rowman & Littlefield and with minor changes by the author.

Adam is sometimes helpful in discussions. I rarely have to explain things to him more than twice, and when he manages to avoid irrelevancy, his points can be helpful targets for others. I think of him more as a student than a colleague.

Adam's social skills, like those of many in our profession, leave something to be desired. He is, however, a well-meaning person whose inappropriate laughter and other gaffes are rarely held against him. For the most part, he fulfills his duties adequately. Any department that hires him will gain a faculty member who will meet with his classes. I recommend him with all the enthusiasm his candidacy deserves.

The department in which I teach has just been conducting a job search, so I have just finished reading about 150 sets of letters of recommendation, not one of which is anything like this letter for Adam Pendicks. Over the years, I have read many other letters, and have written many myself, and not one of them was anything like this letter either. Yet many graduate students do of course rank in the third quartile—a full quarter do—and not a few are socially maladroit, derivative in their thinking, and/or at best indifferently dependable. Since most faculty members are at least decent people, and since a good number are admirable human beings, their routine willingness to omit some facts and to stretch others beyond the breaking point can hardly be attributed to a simple lack of veracity. Its source, rather, is a tension, often severe, between two different and equally legitimate moral demands, one the duty to tell the truth the other the obligation to do one's best to get jobs for one's students. The basic difficulty is that it is logically impossible both to tell the full truth and to write a letter that will get a student a job that he would not get if the full truth were told.

Although this is hardly a tragic choice, I do think it is a genuine moral dilemma. I think, that is, that those who must write on behalf of their students are sometimes in a position in which anything they do will be at least somewhat wrong. When a faculty member's being in this position is not due to any prior wrongdoing or negligence on his part, it is a case of bad moral luck.

There are of course some who believe neither in moral dilemmas nor in moral luck. To these optimistic souls, keeping your nose clean means never having to say you're sorry. Applied to the case at hand, what their position comes to is either that (1) anyone who now must either violate his duty of veracity or fail to fulfill his obligation to a student must previously have created the problem by doing something he shouldn't, or that (2) our obligations to our students never require that we distort the truth or omit important facts, or that (3) we owe our students plenty of distorting and omitting, but doing these things in letters of recommendation is not wrong. To bring out the full scope of the letter-writer's plight, and also to score some general points against the optimistic dilemma-denier, I now want to argue against each claim.

Consider first the proposal that whenever everything a recommender can do would be wrong, he must have put himself in this position through some previous moral lapse. This proposal concedes that letters of recommendations may confront us with genuine dilemmas, but denies that these are ever unavoidable. But where, exactly, has Adam's advisor gone wrong?

There are a number of possible places, some farther in the past than others. Early on, the advisor may have fallen short by entering a profession that generates obligations that regularly conflict with the duty of veracity. More recently, he may have erred by accepting employment at an institution whose students are not strong enough to win every competition on their merits. Still more recently, he may have gone wrong by agreeing to supervise a weak student or by subsequently agreeing to write on that student's behalf. But none of this is at all plausible. Locating the wrong act at the point where the advisor entered academic life is silly because the academy is at least no more morally tainted than any other institution and is probably less tainted than most. Criticizing him for joining an institution that enrolls students whose prospects will be harmed by truthful letters is unreasonable both because every graduate program has such students and because jobs at the places with the fewest such students are beyond the reach of most job-seekers. Identifying his moral lapse with his agreement to take on a weak student is objectionable both because we often cannot tell how our advisees will pan out and because anyone who avoids weak students to keep his hands clean merely shifts the moral burden to his colleagues. And, finally, to say that the advisor should not have agreed to write on behalf of his weak student is merely to relocate the dilemma; for anyone who takes on an advisee has already undertaken a de facto commitment to write on that student's behalf.

Given all this, those who claim that letters of recommendation never confront us with moral dilemmas may retreat to their second option. They may argue not that any apparent dilemmas can be traced to earlier moral lapses, but rather that we are never obligated to distort or omit important truths to further our students' prospects for employment. But how, exactly, is this last claim to be defended in its turn? The argument can hardly be that we can't be obligated to distort the truth because distorting the truth is wrong, since whether distorting the truth in this context is wrong is just what is at issue. Moreover, although it sounds good to say that Adam's advisor did the right thing by telling the full truth, it doesn't sound quite as good to say that he did the right thing by writing a letter that he knew full well would doom Adam's chances for employment. This last claim would certainly be hard for Adam to swallow ("with supporters like that . . ."), and given that none of us actually writes such letters despite the students' near universal willingness to waive access, the rest of us evidently find it hard to swallow too. There is, to be sure, the occasional maverick who prefaces his recommendations with the disclaimer that unlike his weak and compromised colleagues, he intends to write only the plain and unvarnished truth and hopes his students will not be harmed by his stubborn integrity. However, remarkably, the students on behalf of whom such letters are written turn out to be just as uniformly superior as all the others.

Given all this, those who deny that letters of recommendation confront us with dilemmas may find it advisable to retreat once more. Instead of maintaining either that anyone who has only wrong options has only himself to blame or that our obligations to our students never require that we distort or omit important truths, he may take the position that we often *are* required to distort or omit but that doing so in letters of recommendation is not wrong. Of all the strategies for denying that recommendations confront us with genuine dilemmas, this is the one that seems the most promising. One obvious thing that can be said for it is that even when the currency is very inflated, some letters remain clearly stronger than others, and so real distinctions can still be made. A different but related point is that the need to convey real information has led to the development of a kind of code which any veteran letter-reader can decipher. Taken together, these facts suggest that instead of distorting or omitting important truths, hyperbolic letters may convey accurate information non-literally. Because there's nothing wrong with expressing oneself non-literally as long as the message is clear, we may after all seem capable of fulfilling all our obligations without violating our duty to be honest.

But I don't think we can get off the hook quite this easily; for precisely because we know that our inflated letters will automatically be downgraded, we also know that keeping our students competitive means inflating our letters further to withstand the inevitable downgrading. If "he is among the finest minds of his generation" will be translated as "he is competitive with some of the better students at very good institutions," then we cannot set him apart from the competition without touting his virtues in even more effusive terms ("the very finest mind," "many a generation"). Instead of having to abuse the truth in plain language, we now have to abuse it in recommendationese, but nothing else has changed. As I have said, the basic problem is that it is logically impossible both to tell the full truth and to write a letter that will get a student a job that he would not get if the full truth were told.

So what's a professor to do? In a word, what we all do: compromise. To serve both masters, we must make concessions to each. To do what we can for our weaker students, we can try to write letters that will not disqualify them outright and that may be overlooked if their other letters come in stronger, while to preserve at least a tenuous connection to the truth, we can avoid saying things that are flatly false while playing up every scrap of positive information that is even marginally relevant. Like democracy, it's the worst way of doing things except for all the others.

Over the years, I have witnessed many impressive efforts to airbrush students whose prospects would be damaged by a candid assessment, and in the spirit of professional solidarity, I want to share some of what I've learned. To keep a weak student in the game, a letter-writer can do any or all of the following. First, he can discuss at great length the interest and importance of the problem to which his student is proposing an uninteresting and unimportant answer. Second, he can magnify the student's accomplishments by defining his specialty narrowly enough to guarantee that he will be one of the best at it. Third, he can finesse the all-important question of how this student stacks up against others by comparing him to weaker past students of whom few readers will have heard. Fourth, he can make the student sound good by saying positive things that somehow sound like they're job-related but really aren't. Finally, he can bring his letter to a satisfying conclusion by ending with a resounding but meaningless expression of support. When these techniques are used together, and when they're backed by strategic omissions as required, they are virtually certain to locate any letter squarely in the no-man's land between truth and falsity.

Let me end with an example. I began with a letter that gave Adam Pendicks no chance of being hired. Here, by contrast is one that gives him a fighting chance.

Mr. Adam Pendicks has asked me to write in support of his application to your institution, and I am delighted to do so. Adam is a sixth-year graduate student in philosophy here at Ragland University, where he is working on the later stages of a dissertation on the moral importance of the act/omission distinction. This distinction occupies a strategic position in both theoretical and applied ethics. Within the theoretical realm, the distinction raises fascinating questions about the scope and nature of moral responsibility, and disagreements about its importance can be seen to underlie many of the disputes between consequentialists and their opponents. On a more applied level, some version of the distinction informs many common beliefs about end-of-life decisions, famine relief, and other topics of pressing practical importance. Given all this, it is obviously crucial to gain a clearer understanding of the distinction, and that is precisely what Mr. Pendicks's project is intended to yield. He is already one of the world's two leading experts on the line of inquiry that he is pursuing, and he will in due time be recognized as the single leading expert.

To convey a sense of the regard in which Adam is held here, it may be helpful to compare him to some of our other recent graduates. As far as I can judge, the consensus in our department is that Adam is somewhat better than Waxie Links, formerly of the Friendship Institute and now at Fulham A&M, that he's probably also better than Bibi Freund, who recently received a tenure-track appointment at Land O' Lakes University, but that he ranks just a touch below Lance Puller of Snake State. Adam is an enthusiastic contributor to the life of our close-knit community whose infectious laugh will be greatly missed when he leaves. I am pleased to recommend him warmly.

Isn't that better?

STUDY QUESTIONS

1. If a professor sends a letter of recommendation that omits important information, has the professor acted ethically?
2. If Sher's revised letter leads the members of a department to appoint the candidate he recommends, but those members subsequently are disappointed with the candidate's performance, should they blame themselves entirely or, instead, should they hold Sher partly responsible?
3. Would it be inappropriate for a professor to include in a letter of recommendation the following truthful remark: "This candidate is not among the best students I have taught, nor among the worst"?
4. Would it be useless for a professor to send an honest reference letter that began: "This is a candid recommendation. As such, it necessarily contains criticism as well as praise. Please read it in the spirit in which it is written"?

X

INTERCOLLEGIATE ATHLETICS

Most universities, and to a somewhat lesser extent most colleges, place a high premium on producing winning athletic teams. Of course, each time one team wins another loses. Thus while all schools can simultaneously achieve academic success, only a limited number of institutions can attain athletic success at any time.

Why does it matter how often a particular school is victorious in athletic competitions? What does a school's sports records have to do with the eminence of its faculty or the quality of education its students receive?

Myles Brand argues that athletics are part of the central mission of the university. He believes that the development of physical skills, like the development of mental skills, has a legitimate place in academic life. Robert L. Simon notes Brand's failure to make clear which specific skills should be regarded as within the proper domain of a university or college education. In Simon's view, however, when properly conducted, academic studies and intercollegiate athletics can be mutually reinforcing.

19

The Role and Value of Intercollegiate Athletics in Universities

MYLES BRAND

America began its fascination with college sports in the middle of the 19th century. First it was primarily its version of football, and then all sports took root in institutions of higher education. By the latter half of the 20th century, the general public often knew some of its universities not as centers of learning but as hosts for big-time sports. The interests of the broadcast media have made these sporting events even more popular and accessible in the past few decades.

This relationship between sports and higher education is not without its detractors. The list of criticisms is long, from the exploitation of student-athletes to overpaid coaches, from the unfairness of limited opportunities for women students and minority coaches to performance-enhancing drug use. The central criticism is that sports on campus distort the mission of institutions of higher learning.[1]

My view is that many of these criticisms are false or exaggerated, and where they are warranted, strong reform efforts are underway that will, for the most part, rectify the problems. College sport is far from perfect, but it is a popular cultural artifact that serves well both the university community and the students who participate.

In this article, my focus will be limited. I will not attempt to defend intercollegiate athletics from all its critics for all its alleged shortcomings.

Reprinted by permission from *Journal of Philosophy of Sport*, 2006:33(1); pp. 9–20. © 2006 International Association for the Philosophy of Sport. The words in brackets are the editor's.

Rather, my target is to defeat some of the objections of one crucial constituency, namely the faculty and other members of the academy. In particular, I will argue for the following thesis: The role and importance of intercollegiate athletics are undervalued by the academy.

Intercollegiate athletics has the potential to contribute far more to the academic enterprise than it does currently. The contributions of intercollegiate athletics have failed to be realized because of misconceptions of college sports and preconceptions in the academy. Removal of these impediments provides an opportunity for sports on campus to better support the academic mission of universities and colleges.

Most of my defense of this thesis will focus on refuting [attacks on] it. I will also outline, very briefly, a constructive prospective of the value of sports in higher education.

THE STANDARD VIEW

The Standard View conceives of intercollegiate athletics as an extracurricular activity. It resembles participation in student government and protesting against the university administration. It has more educational value than fraternity parties but less than the chess club.

According to the Standard View, college sports may have some redeeming developmental value for students, but they are not part of the educational experience. Intercollegiate athletics can be eliminated from the campus without in any way diminishing the educational mission of the institution. Some critics go beyond the Standard View to claim that intercollegiate athletics detracts from the institution's ability to educate, and it is a strong negative force on campus.

College sports are merely "beer and circuses," as one author puts it, designed to entertain and distract attention from universities' failures (11). The Standard View, though not necessarily this stronger version, is widely held by faculty members, academic administrators, and many external constituents not closely allied with the university. It is not widely held by students, alumni, local community members, and national fans or by many governing-board members. The Standard View tends to pervade the nonstudent campus culture, mostly because of faculty influence.

The main problem with the Standard View is that it misrepresents college sports and the experiences of student-athletes. As a result, it creates problems for the functioning of an athletics department, and it inhibits the positive, constructive values of intercollegiate athletics from influencing campus life and the education of undergraduates. The Standard View is the leading contributor to the undervaluation of college sports.

Let me begin the argument with a seemingly small point. When the educational experience of student-athletes is compared with those studying the performing arts such as music, dance, and theater, as well as the studio arts, it is difficult to find substantive differences. Consider, in particular, music students at universities with major music programs. These students must be accomplished before admission. They have to audition, and the best of them receive scholarships. Those with exceptional talent are often admitted even if their purely academic credentials, demonstrated by their grade-point averages and SAT scores, are below the range of normally admitted students.

Many of the music students admitted to the best music departments and schools have ambitions for professional careers. Once admitted, they practice innumerable hours on their own and as members of the university's symphony orchestras, vocal and choral groups, and jazz ensembles. They perform with these groups on weekends and evenings during the semester, and, on occasion, they miss class to perform at off-campus locations. These performances often involve paid admission. In nearly every case, both performance and practice are intense, highly competitive for lead roles, time demanding, and year-round. Participation is similar to working a full-time job.

There are musical prodigies who bypass college and perform as soloists with international orchestras. Some who do enroll leave college early to follow career opportunities. Highly successful professional musicians, with or without college degrees, are well compensated and receive a great deal of public adulation.

Of course, the vast majority of music students never have a significant music career. Even in the best university music departments, the proportion of students that become international stars is infinitesimal. Some music graduates teach music; most, however, enter careers that are, at best, indirectly related to their music education. Nonetheless, these individuals benefited from their college education, not only in music but also because of the learning achieved in general-education coursework and because of broadly based intellectual and personal growth.

The similarities of the experience of music students and student-athletes should be apparent. Student-athletes must be accomplished in their sport before enrollment, especially at the National Collegiate Athletic Association (NCAA) Division I institutions, and they must "audition" through game performances and camps.[2] Like musicians, the best are sought by universities and receive scholarships. Some talented prospects are admitted even if their grade-point averages and SAT scores are below the range of the student body. Student-athletes practice on their own and as members of teams, they play on weekends or evenings during the semester, and they travel to off-campus sites. Their games provide entertainment to the college community, and tickets normally must be purchased.

There are rare athletics prodigies, but most attend college. Very few of those who play in college become professionals in their sports. In Division I men's basketball, for example, less than one half of 1% of Division I scholarship players each year have an opportunity to play in the professional National Basketball Association (NBA), and the large majority of those have short careers. Some teach their craft after graduation—that is to say become coaches—but most pursue other careers, only some of which are related to college sports.

Like student-musicians, student-athletes receive public praise for the exercise of their abilities. In both cases, their successes—and failures—reflect on their home institutions. Both groups tend to form strong bonds with their mentors—their coaches or master teachers—as well as other students in the program. Student-musicians tend to major in music, though not always. Student-athletes undertake a broad array of majors, with business and the social sciences being the predominant ones, although sometimes their majors reflect their interests in athletics, such as kinesiology and broadcasting.[3]

These similarities point to a convergence of educational experiences between student-athletes and others engaged in certain preprofessional courses of study. Given this convergence, it might be expected that the student-athlete experience and that of students in the performing arts would have similar academic standing, but that is not the case.

In general, music students receive academic credit for learning their instruments, practicing, and playing in the school symphony. In general, student-athletes do not receive academic credit for instruction by coaches, nor do they receive academic credit for team practice or play. Many institutions give credit to members of the general student body to take classes in sports, say golf or tennis instruction. When physical education was required, as it tends not to be now, credit was awarded to nonathletes. But again, at NCAA Division I institutions, students do not receive credit for intercollegiate athletic participation.

What are the reasons for this apparent disparity in academic standing between student-athletes and student-musicians? There appear to be two primary ones. The first is the claim that credit is awarded only when the activity has content and the class (or its equivalent) is taught by a qualified instructor. This reason for the difference between student-musicians and student-athletes is not tenable, however.

How are we to specify content in this instance? In the case of physics, psychology, and philosophy courses, for example, the content is relatively clear. It is the systematic knowledge that is organized and conveyed by the instructor and textbooks and learned by the students. This is factual knowledge, knowledge "that." For example, physics students are expected to know that the speed of light is a constant, and philosophy students are expected to know that Western philosophy began with the ancient Greeks.

Music performance students are expected to gain knowledge "that" in some of their classes, such as music theory, but, by and large, performance students gain knowledge "how." That is, they learn how to do certain things, for example, how to play Bach's Brandenburg concertos. Learning how to do something is to gain a skill or to exercise an acquired skill in specific circumstances (8).

Student-athletes, too, must learn factual knowledge. They must know the rules of the game and about nutrition and exercise. But the most important learning undertaken by student-athletes is to come to know "how." Individual and team practices provide opportunities for student-athletes to learn skills and to apply those skills in specific situations.

Content includes knowing "how," as well as knowing "that," both facts and skills. Content need not be restricted to propositional representation. Other kinds of mental representation including skill schemata and imagery also qualify as content. Nonpropositional representation is critical to action (3: part IV, ch. 7 and 8).

Thus, student-athletes and performance students each learn content in the same way. Some content is acquired in cognate courses, and that tends to be factual knowledge. The primary content, however, in both cases is knowledge how, and that is acquired in individual or group settings with a master teacher or coach. It is this knowledge how that enables them to perform in the concert hall or on the playing field.

Another account of the educational value of athletics participation is often offered. This account, compatible with the one given here but different, focuses on student-athletes learning cognitive skills (10: pp. 154 ff; pp. 160–161). In mastering their game, student-athletes gain skill in critical thinking and problem solving. These cognitive skills transfer to learning in the sciences, humanities, and other areas. Being successful on the field of play requires observation, weighing alternatives, assessing probabilities, and hypothesizing solutions. Of course there are other ways to learn to think critically and solve problems, but athletics participation stimulates and encourages the learning of these skills.

This account focuses on learned cognitive skills, whereas the perspective I am stressing is based on learned physical skills. Cognitive-skill learning is, for the most part, gaining knowledge that; physical-skill learning is, for the most part, gaining knowledge how. No doubt, both occur through athletics participation, and both contribute to a student's education, but the main part is that, although athletics participation may well generate learning that is assimilable to the intellectual model of a university education, there is another type of learning that occurs in athletics participation that focuses on physical-skill development and that is a legitimate and worthy part of a university education.

The remaining part of this defense of the Standard View is that there is a difference between learning by student-athletes and performance students because of the differences in qualifications of the instructors. Here, too, the claim does not stand up to scrutiny. At fine universities and colleges across this nation, we expect a large majority of the instruction of undergraduates to be undertaken by those with terminal degrees or the equivalent in their fields. We do permit those in training—graduate students—to render instruction, but only under the supervision of senior teachers.

In the case of physics, psychology, and philosophy, among other disciplines, the terminal degree is the PhD. That is the appropriate degree when the primary, often exclusive, learning is factual knowledge. In the case of skill-based disciplines, however, such as the performing and studio arts, the PhD is not ordinarily the terminal degree. In these cases, it is usually the MFA, though that, too, might not be required. Rather, in these disciplines, the underlying requirement is that there is a track record of excellence, verified by peers, of teaching the skills appropriate to the activity. Peer judgment in the cases of skill instruction plays at least as important a role in asserting qualifications, and likely more so, than it does in factual knowledge instruction.

In athletic coaching, and to a large degree in the performing and studio arts, there is an apprenticeship system for instructors. Of course, minimal academic credentials are required, usually at least the baccalaureate degree, but after that, one learns from masters. Coaches begin as assistants and, through involvement with successful coaches, emerge, if they are talented, as head coaches. Similar routes to leadership in their fields are followed by performing and studio master teachers. Often, though certainly not always, coaches and master teachers themselves have or had high skill levels in their areas of expertise.

Those who teach in the performing and studio arts tend to be on the tenure track. That often held for coaches in the past, but Division I coaches are not now on the tenure track, except for a few elders who retain their faculty positions. There are some institutions in Divisions II and III that continue the practice of putting coaches on the tenure track, especially when they teach classes to the general student body.

Thus, the first purported reason for the disparity in academic standing between athletics and performance students—namely, differences in instructional content and teacher qualifications—is not defensible.

The second reason for the disparity between athletics and performance disciplines cuts to the heart of the matter. It focuses directly on the role and value of intercollegiate athletics in universities. This reason is that there are unsubstantiated cultural preconceptions within the academy about intercollegiate athletics.

Not all faculty members and academic administrators are antiathletics. There are many faculty members who are fans and many who work toward the success and proper conduct of intercollegiate athletics, for example, through service as NCAA faculty representatives and on campus-based committees. Nonetheless, on the whole, there is an underlying and growing disconnect with intercollegiate athletics within the campus-based academic community. Academic fraud; academically underperforming student-athletes; growing athletics department budgets; large compensation packages for some coaches; student-athletes, coaches, and even presidents misbehaving; and many other issues fuel this discontent.

Some faculty members are helping to resolve these issues in intercollegiate athletics that lead to discomfort, especially the academic issues. Recently, for example, the Coalition on Intercollegiate Athletics, which consists of Division I faculty-governance leaders, has been a strong advocate for integrity in intercollegiate athletics (4). Aside from these efforts to understand and reform intercollegiate athletics, however, there is serious and growing discontent among faculty members. The underlying reason is that, for the most part, faculty members hold intellectual powers in higher esteem then they do bodily abilities. Put provocatively, the American academy is prejudiced against the body.

Most faculty members are engaged in disciplines that are intellectual. Universities generally are involved in research and scholarship involving factual knowledge. This approach was inherited from the 19th-century German universities, which in many respects are the forerunners of the American research university. But there is also a long-term trend, which is distinctively American, that attempts to democratize higher education and emphasize the practical. This perspective led to the Morrill Act of 1862, by which universities were founded through a federal grant of land in order to teach agriculture and the mechanical arts (engineering). Nonetheless, despite this practical, skill-oriented history of American higher education, the intellectual, cognitive approach prevails. In it, emphasis on bodily skills is inappropriate; indeed, it subverts the true aim of the university. A focus on bodily skills leads to a vocational or purely professional view of education, and that, it is held, is antithetical to the mission of an institution of higher learning. Ballet counts; hip-hop does not. The core of the university is the study and advancement of the liberal arts.

Music and dance performance, though not purely intellectual, are treated as exceptions because they fall into the category of art. Actually, that is not entirely correct. It depends on what kind of music or dance. Classical music qualifies; rock and roll does not. The art form must relate to high culture. Rock and roll can be studied in a disinterested, intellectual way, and there are college courses on the history and sociology of rock and roll, but playing in a rock band does not ordinarily warrant college credit toward graduation.

In sum, the prejudice against the body, and with it professional studies that emphasize physical skill, is deeply rooted in the American academy. It was not until the middle of the 20th century that music, even classical music, rose to departmental status in many universities. This bias against the body and toward cognitive and intellectual capacity is the driving force of the disdain by many faculty members for college sports and the acceptance of the Standard View.

FINANCING INTERCOLLEGIATE ATHLETICS ON THE STANDARD VIEW

The Standard View of intercollegiate athletics has far-reaching consequences. It affects the way Division I institutions budget for intercollegiate athletics. Because athletics is merely an extracurricular activity, according to the Standard View, the athletics department is to be treated like an auxiliary, similar to residence halls and parking, and not like an academic unit. Therefore, general-fund resources should not be used to support athletic departments. Rather, in Division I, athletics departments should be self-supporting or, better, return revenue to the institution for central academic purposes.

Universities are budgeted through a system of cross-subsidization. Graduate programs are subsidized by undergraduate programs. Some undergraduate programs, such as service courses in English and the social sciences, subsidize other undergraduate programs. One of the most costly programs in the university is music; one of the best revenue producers is Psychology 101. Auxiliary units such as residence halls and technology-transfer operations do not have academic value by themselves and they are not to be subsidized, if at all possible.

Because athletics is conceptualized in the Standard View as an auxiliary, as something without academic value, it should not be entitled to a university budgetary subsidy if at all possible. Athletics should earn its own way. This perspective has been codified as part of the NCAA Division I philosophy statement: "[A member of Division I] strives to finance its athletics program insofar as possible from revenues generated by the program itself" (5).

Divisions II and III institutions do not, and cannot, expect their athletics departments to be self-sufficient. The reason is that they lack the ticket and broadcast-media proceeds and donor contributions to produce substantial revenue. In those divisions, intercollegiate athletics is a subsidized activity, but in the high profile, high-cost athletics programs of Division I, the expectation is for self-sufficiency.

Faculty members and academic administrators like this principle. There is enormous competition for resources in a university; in fact, the contemporary university can almost be defined by saying that the good ideas of the faculty always outstrip the available resources. Faculty members tend to strongly prefer to invest university resources in academic programs and not subsidize athletics or other auxiliaries. Indeed, in this time of limited resources, there is increasing pressure to not subsidize athletics, or at least minimize the subsidy by, for example, increasing student athletic fees.

Many athletics administrators, especially athletic directors, also like this principle. Although they certainly want additional resources that come from institutional subsidy, this principle justifies a degree of autonomy within the university not achieved by most academic units. Athletic directors are expected to find ways to generate resources through ticket sales, media contracts, entrepreneurial activity, and fundraising. They are permitted, with considerable autonomy, to undertake these activities.

In Division I, especially for institutions with the most successful athletics programs, revenue can be increased, even dramatically so, through broadcast-media contracts. For example, in men's and women's basketball, the NCAA conducts postseason tournaments. Long-term agreements for the men's postseason basketball tournament provide a payout of more than $6 billion over the 11-year length of the contracts.[4]

Given the principle that intercollegiate athletics is to be self-supporting, presidents and athletic directors have also sought to make improvements and investments in their athletics programs in order to be highly competitive. Competitive success, they reason, will increase their revenue streams. One example of investments for enhancing competitiveness is new or renovated facilities. Football stadiums are enlarged, and luxury boxes are added to increase ticket revenue and to satisfy donors and supporters. As the perceived value of winning teams increases, the market for the best coaches does, too. The competition for these coaches is such that they command seven-figure compensation packages. The recent escalation of the costs of competitive Division I athletics programs has been labeled the "arms race."

There is competition in other parts of the university, as well. English departments compete to hire the most accomplished faculty members, which then drives up personnel budgets. Biology departments compete not merely on the basis of salaries but also on laboratory facilities and scientific instrumentation. Investments are made in residence halls and recreation centers to attract more and better students. In these cases, however, the university, through its normal budgetary process, makes priority decisions about which units to support.

Because according to the Standard View athletics departments are not taken to be central, or even part of the academic mission of the institution, the tendency is to not make budgetary decisions within the overall institutional context. The autonomy of the athletics department at some institutions enables the department to make its case directly to the president or even, in some cases, to the university's governing board.

But recent studies conducted under the auspices of the NCAA cast serious doubt on the claim that continued increases in expenditures results in improved competitiveness or in an enhanced ability to satisfy the principle of self-support (6). These studies are predicated on the best databases ever assembled. They show, for example, that for every dollar invested in football or men's basketball in Division I, the institution can expect a dollar back. That is, the rate of return is 0%. These studies also show that there is no correlation between winning teams and funds for operational expenditures. Overall, the studies do not support the rationale often given for increased expenditures on athletes.

Of the 117 Division I-A athletics programs, the highest level engaged in football, over one third claim that they cover their expenses or are producing excess revenue on an annual basis. This claim is presently difficult to evaluate because there is no uniform means of accounting for athletics expenditures. For example, some do not fully count facility costs such as bonded indebtedness and physical-plant maintenance; some do not fully account for academic support for student-athletes, such as advising and tutors; and others fail to include student fees in institutional support. Based on the economic studies, it may be more reasonable to believe that fewer than two dozen Division I-A schools, perhaps as few as one dozen when everything is taken into account, actually meet the principle of self-support. The 100 or so Division I-A institutions and the remaining 900 other schools with NCAA athletics programs all subsidize them.

Is that bad? It is only if one is committed to the Standard View that athletics lies outside the central mission of the university. If the Standard View is relinquished, and with it the principle of self-support, then subsidizing athletics becomes acceptable in Division I, as it is in the other divisions. Athletics departments, like every other unit in the university, should and will continue to seek ways to increase revenue, but the felt need to ratchet up investment in the hope of improving revenues should diminish. Athletics-department budgetary decisions can, and should, flow through the normal university budget process, once it is clear that subsidization is an acceptable reality of life. The stigma of subsidies for athletics is removed when the Standard View is foregone.

THE INTEGRATED VIEW

The Standard View should be replaced by a more balanced view about athletics that integrates it into the mission of the university. Call this the Integrated View. The primary and defining feature of the Integrated View is that athletic programs are made part of the educational mission of the university. Although they are not part of the liberal-arts core, they play the same type of role as music and art and, perhaps, business and journalism.

The Integrated View is based on a different perspective of the role of physical-skill education than that of the Standard View. The Integrated View disposes of the bias against physical-skill development. The Attic Greeks had a good perspective. They believed that the mental and the physical should both be part of a sound education. Even someone as committed to the superiority of the mental as Plato held that physical accomplishment was necessary for successful citizenship. The central idea here is that of harmony. The harmony, the unity, of mind and body is crucial to a happy life (7: Book II 376E, Book III 412B, Book VII 521C–541B).[5]

The idea of harmony between mind and body in education comports well with the underlying philosophy of education in this country. America is the only country in the world that includes athletics extensively in its educational system. In Europe, sports are played mostly outside the university. Independent club sports, many of which involve payment to the athletes, substitute for intercollegiate athletics. Some Asian countries are reconsidering the separation of sports and education. Mainland China is reviewing its educational system, and there is some prospect that they will emulate the American system and incorporate athletics directly into it.

By focusing on the harmony between mind and body in education, athletics takes on a more central role. That role is not unlike the role of music in education, once again following the ancient Greeks. Some students specialize in music, but not many. Nonetheless, music is to be appreciated and enjoyed by all. It is considered a valuable part of the curriculum and the campus environment. Similarly, a minority of students are focused on intercollegiate athletics—from less than 2% of the general student body at large Division I institutions to 30% or more at some highly selective Division III liberal-arts colleges. Nonetheless, athletics and student-athletes should find a central role in university life. Athletics should be a valuable part of the educational environment.

The Integrated View raises a provocative issue. If athletic participation is relevantly similar to music performance with respect to content—namely, in knowledge of skills—as well as instructor qualifications, then if academic credit is provided for music students, should it not also be provided for student-athletes? There are some obvious limitations in providing credit to student-athletes. We should not offer majors in basketball or other sports. But it appears reasonable to provide a small number of credits, one time only, provided that the course has been approved through the normal process by appropriate faculty committees and it has an attendance requirement. There is the potential for abuse and academic fraud but, with faculty oversight, not more so than with some other courses in the university. In any case, the idea of offering credit for students participating in intercollegiate athletics is worthy of consideration, once the Integrated View is established at an institution.

Intercollegiate athletics, at its best, demonstrates positive values. These values include striving for excellence, perseverance, resilience, hard work, respect for others, sportsmanship and civility, and losing—and winning—with grace. Consider for a moment reactions to losing. Most undergraduate students, especially freshmen, have difficulty with failure, but student-athletes, who are accustomed to competition and the failures that accompany it, become good at overcoming adversity. If they lose a big game on Saturday afternoon, they are on the field the next Monday working doubly hard. Many students would do well to embrace this value of resilience and coping with failure early in their college careers.

In general, it would be good if the positive values exhibited by student-athletes were learned and adopted by the general student body. A college education is not only an exercise in gaining factual and skill-based knowledge; it is an opportunity to develop a value system, a set of enduring goals, and a perspective on life. In large part, college is about becoming a productive citizen and a mature person. This developmental aspect of a college education is especially pertinent to traditional-age students who have a residential experience. The positive, constructive values of student-athletes, gained through their experiences in intercollegiate athletics, are apt models.

Given that certain types of physical-skill development have roles to play in an institution of higher education and that intercollegiate athletics is one such type of skill development, intercollegiate athletics should be treated similarly to music education and education in other areas that involve skill development. For example, departments of intercollegiate athletics and schools of music should be relevantly similar in terms of the university's organizational chart.

Athletic directors should have a role similar to those of deans of major units such as medicine and arts and sciences. It would be good if there were a direct reporting relationship between the athletic director and the president (although it can be helpful for a vice president or other high-level administrator to work with the athletic director on local operational issues). The athletic director should serve in the president's cabinet or similar body. Doing so enables the athletic director to gain knowledge of and contribute to the strategic priorities of the institution, as well as providing an opportunity for university leadership to be informed about the issues facing the athletics department and to assist the department in fulfilling its institutional role.

The advantage of mainstreaming the athletic department into the mission and structure of the university is that it reflects the balanced approach to education that includes both cognitive and physical capacity. It also has the advantage of removing the impetus for the bias against intercollegiate athletics underlying the Standard View. Mainstreaming, undertaken successfully, should yield a better appreciation for the athletics enterprise by faculty members. One expected result is that there will be an increased willingness among faculty to accept, if necessary, cross-subsidization of athletics, at least to the extent that there is acceptance for cross-subsidizing music and art. By placing athletics in the mainstream of the university, its value to the education of undergraduates becomes more apparent.

Students' education may include both intellectual- and physical-skill elements. Although an emphasis on the intellectual certainly has had salutary effects, a university education should not be limited in that skill development is necessarily excluded. The structure of the university, in turn, should reflect this integrated approach. On the defensive side, failure to place adequate operational controls on intercollegiate athletics is a recipe for deep problems, including public exposure by the media. On the constructive side, mainstreaming intercollegiate athletics into the campus structure is likely to yield value for the institution in terms of broadly based developmental educational opportunities.

CONCLUSIONS

The rationale for the Standard View is weak. It discredits intercollegiate athletics, ignoring its educational value and relegating it to mere extracurricular activity. The underlying rationale for it is that a university education should be dedicated entirely to the mind. By contrast, I have been arguing that there is a legitimate place in the university for physical-skill development. Not everyone, of course, should concentrate on skill development, as do music, drama, dance majors, and student-athletes, but a university should accommodate those who, in addition to learning factual knowledge, gain certain physical abilities.

In a university in which this integrated approach is undertaken, the constructive values associated with intercollegiate athletics, even for those who do not themselves participate, can influence the campus culture. The values of hard work, striving for excellence, respect for others, sportsmanship and civility, team play, persistence, and resilience that underlie the ideal of sport should be brought into the developmental aspects of a college education affecting all students. The Integrated View of college sports, as opposed to the Standard View, not only puts intercollegiate athletics in its proper perspective but also has positive effects for the campus community.

The role of intercollegiate athletics in universities has been undervalued. The problems surrounding intercollegiate athletics, often sensationalized, should be kept in perspective. The constructive values represented by the sports ideal can positively influence students and enable them to become productive citizens. Intercollegiate athletics can, and should be, a positive part of undergraduate education and campus culture.

NOTES

1. The best statement of the contemporary problems of college sports, which is based on sound social-science research, is reference 9. The follow-up volume is reference 1. This latter book focuses on highly selective private schools and also makes specific recommendations to resolve the issues. For a summary of some of the criticism, see reference 10, especially chapter 7. See also reference 2.

2. The NCAA divides colleges and universities into three divisions reflecting athletic scholarship (grants-in-aid) support, the level of competition, and differences in philosophy. For example, Division III, unlike Divisions I and II, does not offer athletic scholarships. Division I, in turn, is subdivided in football, and only in football, into Divisions I-A, I-AA, and I-AAA. Division I-AAA does not field football teams. Division 1-A, which consists of 117 schools, plays at the highest competitive level and receives the lion's share of fan and media attention. Overall, there are approximately 360,000 current student-athletes in the NCAA competing at more than 1,000 colleges and universities. See www.ncaa.org for details of structure and membership.

3. See reference 9 for the majors and postcollege careers of student-athletes.

4. The NCAA national office uses less than 5% of the funds from media contracts to conduct its operations and redistributes the remaining 95% of the proceeds to member colleges and universities and to student-athletes.

5. See also reference 10: pp. 156ff. Simon quotes A. Bartlett Giamatti, former president of Yale University and commissioner of Major League Baseball: "The Greeks saw physical training and games as a form of knowledge, meant to toughen the body in order to temper the soul, activities pure in themselves, immediate, obedient to the rules so that winning would be sweeter still" (10: p. 157).

REFERENCES

1. Bowen, W.G., and Levin, S.A. *Reclaiming the Game: College Sports and Educational Values.* Princeton, NJ: Princeton University Press, 2003.

2. Brand, M. "Academics First: Reforming Intercollegiate Athletics." Address delivered to the National Press Club, January 23, 2001. *Vital Speeches of the Day.* 67(12), April 2001, 367–371.

3. Brand, M. *Intending and Acting: Toward a Naturalized Action Theory.* Boston: The Massachusetts Institute of Technology, Bradford Press, 1984.

4. Coalition on Intercollegiate Athletics Web site: www.math.umd.edu/~jmc/COIA.

5. *NCAA Division I Manual,* Article 20.

6. Orszag, J., and Orszag, P. "The Empirical Effects of Collegiate Athletics: An Interim Report," "The Physical Capital Stock Used in College Athletics," and "Division II Intercollegiate Athletics: An Empirical and Case Study Analysis." Available at www.ncaa.org.

7. *Plato.* Trans. F.M. Cornford. *The Republic of Plato.* New York and London: Oxford University Press, 1951.

8. Ryle, G. "Knowing How and Knowing That." In *The Concept of Mind.* London and New York: Hutchinson's University Library, 1949.

9. Shulman, J.L., and Bowen, W.G. *The Game of Life: College Sports and Educational Values.* Princeton, NJ: Princeton University Press, 2001.

10. Simon, R.L. "Do Intercollegiate Athletics Belong on Campus?" In *Fair Play: Sports, Values, and Society.* Boulder, CO: Westview Press, 1991.

11. Sperber, M.A. *Beer and Circus: How Big-Time College Sports Is Crippling Undergraduate Education.* New York: Henry Holt and Co, 2000.

STUDY QUESTIONS

1. Are student-athletes comparable to students who specialize in the performing and studio arts?
2. Do you agree with Brand's claim that "the American academy is prejudiced against the body"?
3. Do athletics lie outside the central mission of the university?
4. If Brand is correct that students should receive some academic credit for participating in intercollegiate athletics, why not institute majors in basketball or other sports?

20

Intercollegiate Athletics and Educational Values: A Case for Compatibility

Robert L. Simon

College sports, particularly as played by teams from athletically elite Division I institutions of the NCAA, have come under increasing critical scrutiny. Various scandals, involving recruiting violations, misbehavior by athletes including alleged criminal activities, and significant academic fraud, have attracted much public attention but as critics have noted, the problems of intercollegiate athletics go deeper. Of particular concern are lack of academic involvement by some, perhaps many, elite athletes, the recruiting of athletic stars many of whom may have little if any interest in or aptitude for higher education, and consequent low graduation rates in some highly visible sports, primarily men's basketball and football, at some athletically elite institutions. Critics maintain that the problems go well beyond highly publicized scandals; rather the extensive amount of time intercollegiate athletics teams devote to travel, competition, and practice, which in many elite sports involves commitments for virtually the entire year, in effect assigns priority to athletics over academics. On this view, intercollegiate athletics are in conflict with and often undermine the academic mission of the university.

Originally published in Robert B. Talisse and Maureen Eckert, eds., *A Teacher's Life: Essays for Steven M. Cahn*, pp. 113–124, 139–140, 2009, Lexington Books. Reprinted by permission of Rowman & Littlefield.

However, criticism has not been restricted to institutions with major athletic programs. For example, the Ivy League in Division I and the nation's most selective liberal arts colleges, such as those that play in the New England Small College Athletic Association (NESCAC), have long been thought to be shining examples of the value of intercollegiate athletics at their best. Such schools do not award athletic scholarships, have high standards for admitting recruited athletes, and aim at integrating athletics and academics within their institutions. However, recent studies, such as the widely cited *The Game of Life*, have argued that intercollegiate athletics even at these kinds of institutions is harmful to the academic enterprise.[1] This is because, according to the book, athletes make up a significant proportion of the student body of such schools, between 30 and 40 percent of the student body, yet do not perform nearly as well as other students in the classroom, thus dragging down the academic atmosphere at the entire institution.

Such critical views have attracted considerable support from many college and university faculty. These men and women quite naturally see the academic purposes of their institutions as of the highest priority and are alarmed by the manner in which intercollegiate athletics seems to undermine those purposes and even threaten the academic integrity of their programs.

In this paper, I explore the extent to which their views are warranted and offer an assessment of the claim that intercollegiate athletics as currently constituted is inconsistent with the academic mission of the university. In particular, I argue that . . . its role in promoting critical inquiry and civic values can also apply to some forms of intercollegiate athletics.

Of course, the label of intercollegiate athletics covers a diverse set of practices and institutions, ranging from athletically elite large state universities through different layers of Division I, which, with the exception of the Ivy League, normally involves award of athletic scholarships, to the more regional but nevertheless often intense competition at Division III, where no athletic scholarships are awarded and significant attempts are made to integrate academic and athletic goals. Any attempt to draw general conclusions about intercollegiate athletics must be sensitive to such differences, since conclusions about one sphere of competition may be inapplicable to others that differ significantly from it.

THREE THESES: IRRELEVANCY, INCOMPATIBILITY, MUTUAL SUPPORT

To sharpen our discussion, let us consider three claims that might be made about the relation of athletics to academics within institutions of higher learning. According to the first thesis, athletics simply are irrelevant to the main mission of the university that is conceived of as intellectual, not physical. On this view, athletics are at best a tolerable but sometimes distracting extracurricular activity but with no real connection to the function of colleges and universities. While the implications of such a view sometimes are unclear, it might be thought to lead to the following argument. Since athletics are not vital to the educational mission of the university, which always should take priority over other activities, athletics should not be assigned the importance they presently have, particularly at athletically elite Division I institutions. Rather, they should be assigned a recreational role, perhaps best pursued at the level of intramurals or loosely organized student clubs.

According to a second view, expressed by the more robust Incompatibility Thesis, intercollegiate athletics undermines or is incompatible with the academic mission of colleges and universities. Although some may assert this thesis as a conceptual truth, it is best understood as making an at least partially empirical claim: namely that in the context of actual higher education in America, intercollegiate athletics operates so as to undermine or conflict with major academic goals that colleges and universities should be pursuing. For example, the practice of recruiting athletes may be held to interfere with the educational goal of recruiting the most academically qualified student body.

A third thesis, that I will call the Mutual Support or Reinforcement Thesis, often is defended by representatives of athletic departments but also by some educators and philosophers of sport. It states that rather than undermining academics, intercollegiate athletics *properly conducted* actually can reinforce the academic mission of colleges and universities and even contribute more directly than the critics acknowledge to the support of academic values.[2]

The third thesis may be understood in a variety of ways. For example, it might be understood as claiming that important values presupposed by or expressed in athletic competition are identical to or sufficiently similar to those presupposed by or expressed in academic inquiry, so key values in each sphere of activity are the same or similar. It also might be understood as at least partially causal in asserting that when properly conducted, appreciation of the values central to athletic success can encourage adherence to those values in academic pursuits. It might also have an epistemic version; that illustration of certain values in athletic contests can reveal them or make them known and appreciated by wider audiences. Finally, it might function critically, as when violation of key athletic or parallel academic values are grounds for criticism; for example, when students or student-athletes are not sufficiently dedicated to achievement or honest with themselves about their weakness. So although this position can be developed in a variety of ways, and might apply differently at different levels of intercollegiate competition, it expresses an important alternative to the irrelevancy and incompatibility hypotheses.

In what follows, I will make a start toward evaluating these three approaches by considering three specific responses to the Incompatibility Thesis. Evaluation of these responses will give us some idea how to evaluate the dispute between adherents of the Incompatibility Thesis and supporters of Mutual Support or Reinforcement.

Three Responses to the Incompatibility Thesis

Provision of Entertainment as a Public Service

Many critics of intercollegiate athletics start with the surely acceptable premise that a primary mission of the university is academic and intellectual and then jump to the conclusions that the *only* major or fundamental missions of the university are academic and intellectual. This inferential jump is questionable, however. Surely, the academic and intellectual mission of the university might sometimes be compromised in the interests of student safety, for example, as when a controversial speech is postponed to prevent widespread violence, or when budget allocations are assigned to preserve the beauty of the campus rather than to strengthen an academic department, or when schools devoted to purely professional training receive support from the institution that might have gone to the humanities, arts, or sciences. These examples, while debatable, suggest that the nature of the fundamental mission(s) or function(s) of the university is ethically controversial.

If the mission of the university is conceived more broadly than purely academic and intellectual, why wouldn't it plausibly be extended to cover the provision of public service, including the provision of entertainment to the student body and wider community that intercollegiate athletics can provide? According to proponents of this view, it is clear that the university provides entertainment for the community in a variety of areas including theatre, music and other performing arts such as dance, as well as through programming on college sponsored radio and television stations. Intercollegiate athletics is simply another way in which academic institutions provide this good to their students and staff and to the population at large.

Indeed, proponents of this view argue, the university may have a duty to do so. Thus, Peter French . . . points out that the mission statements of many universities, especially large state institutions, include explicit mention of service to the community, often including reference to serving the economic and cultural needs of the population. Similarly, some mission

238 • INTERCOLLEGIATE ATHLETICS

statements of athletic departments, sanctioned by their universities, specifically include entertainment among the functions of their programs. Developing this line of thought, French maintains that:

> The honest and potentially successful defense of intercollegiate athletics, especially including the elite sports, is that they are the way, or at least one way and probably the most visible and successful way, the university responds to its public service obligations in the area of public entertainment. In fact, they likely touch the lives of more members of the public in a positive and effective way than any other service the university may extend in that direction.[3]

Accordingly, once we abandon the assumption that the only fundamental mission of the university should be purely academic, encompassing teaching and scholarship in recognized academic disciplines, the sponsorship of intercollegiate athletics can be defended as fulfilling other legitimate functions of the university. As French puts it, "the tension in the university, particularly within the faculty, that sets the academic and the athletic sides of the campus at odds is caused by a general failure to appreciate the multiple missions of a contemporary university and on the part of the academic faculty typically to think that only their function is the 'real' mission of the institution."[4]

How should such a position be evaluated? First, even if correct, this position applies with the most force to highly visible sports, such as men's football and basketball and perhaps women's basketball, at large athletically elite universities, particularly state institutions. It has less force at a small liberal arts college that emphasizes the excellence of its undergraduate education. I believe intercollegiate athletics does have an important function at small liberal arts colleges, but the case for such a conclusion may have less to do with provision of entertainment to the wider community than with other factors. So even if French's argument does have force, that force is greatest when applied to high profile sports at athletically elite levels of the NCAA and loses strength (although probably not to the vanishing point) when applied to different sorts of institutions or to lower profile sports.

A second criticism is that even if the university does have an obligation to provide entertainment, the kind of entertainment provided by athletics differs in kind from other kinds the university legitimately provides, such as concerts and art exhibits. Programs in the arts, as French recognizes, arguably have a much more direct link to the academic programs of colleges and universities than intercollegiate athletics. These can be defended as extensions of academics while, at least according to the critics, athletics cannot.

Is this second criticism decisive? I think not, for two reasons. First, as we have seen, the issue of what activities of the university are fundamental is itself an ethically contested issue. To assume that only entertainment closely linked to academic programs is legitimate is to beg the question about what functions universities should fulfill. More important, however, the objection begs the question in a more basic way. If the presumed divide between athletics and academics is nowhere near as deep as the critics assume and if there is or can be a significant degree of coherence and mutual support between the two, then intercollegiate athletics does not differ from university sponsored entertainment in other areas, such as the arts, to the degree critics assume. I will explore this point more fully in later sections of this paper.

That leads to the third criticism of the entertainment defense; namely, that athletics involves abuses of academic ethics that other activities of the university, including artistic performances, normally do not. If this means that some scandals have plagued high profile athletic programs at elite Division I schools, including cases of academic fraud, it clearly is true. Low graduation rates, particularly of minority athletes, at some institutions clearly are unacceptable. Moreover, if admissions standards for athletes differ so drastically from those of other students that a significant number of athletes are unprepared for college level work and as a result their academic course load is so diluted as to be educationally vacuous, then the charge of abuse is warranted.

However, such abuses occur mainly in high profile sports at some institutions and are not a reason for regarding all forms of intercollegiate athletics, even at the Division I level, as involving abuses of academic values. Moreover, the NCAA has taken some significant steps to raise graduation rates and insure that athletes are taking a core of serious academic courses. For example, Division I athletic programs with poor graduation rates will have the number of athletic scholarships they can offer reduced, providing a significant incentive to make sure athletes graduate. Even if incentives exist to circumvent such rules, perhaps by diluting the academic content of courses to which athletes may be steered, stricter rules do set a standard and significant penalties can deter violations.

A broader concern, however, applies even to elite athletic programs that provide opportunities for and encourage athletes to pursue their education and graduate. The intensity of competition, the travel and missed class time involved in playing a national schedule, the extended length of seasons, and off season training schedules may involve so great a commitment of time that the pursuit of educational goals is severely compromised. Thus, revenue is generated when high profile teams earn national ranking but that requires playing a national schedule, with the scheduling of games influenced more by attractive time slots on television and the need to travel extensively to play other national powers than requirements of class attendance.[5] These factors do raise issues of concern for those who would defend elite high profile intercollegiate sport as presently constituted.

French's defense of elite high profile intercollegiate sports as forms of entertainment legitimately provided by the university does have some force however. It is at least arguable, as he suggests, that provision of entertainment is one of the legitimate functions of colleges and universities, particularly large public institutions. However, such activity is legitimate only if it does not undermine the chances for the athletes in such programs to receive an education, does not subvert academic norms (as would be the case with academic fraud), and, more broadly, only if it does not involve a kind of disdain for the academic mission of the university which comes to be regarded as an obstacle to athletic participation rather than a significant aspect of the student athlete's intellectual and personal development.

There is another issue raised by the entertainment argument and its critics, however, that suggests both sides rely on a perhaps dubious common assumption. That assumption is that athletics and academics are two sharply distinct kinds of activities. However, as we will see in the next two sections, that assumption itself is open to serious challenge.

The University and the Teaching of Skills

French's discussion has called our attention to the point that attempts to characterize the mission or function of the university are normative in character and often contested. In a recent paper, former professor of philosophy and then university president Myles Brand, now President of the NCAA, has pointed out that much of what goes on in contemporary academic institutions involves the teaching, development, and exhibition of skills.[6]

Many such skills can be critical and highly analytic, such as learning how to formulate and criticize arguments, or how to design a double blind clinical trial. Others, however, such as those exhibited in dance and musical recitals, involve performance and exhibition of skills. Brand raises the issue of why the exhibition of some skills, say in dance, is considered within the boundaries of the academic enterprise and often receive academic credit towards graduation, but exhibition of other skills, such as those exhibited by athletes, is considered nonacademic and extra curricular at best. Does this boundary line distinguishing the academic, understood to include intercollegiate athletics, have an acceptable justification or is it arbitrary and unjustified?

Brand's target in his paper is what he calls the Standard View that he claims is held by many academic faculty. According to the Standard View, intercollegiate athletics is an extra-curricular activity, outside the boundaries of the academic enterprise. According to Brand, however, the Standard

View expresses a prejudice against the body.[7] Like French, Brand believes the academic critics of athletics have too narrow a view of what colleges and universities should be about. But where French argues for a pluralistic view of the mission of the university, including purposes beyond the purely academic, Brand argues for a broader notion of what counts as academic than he believes many faculty critics of intercollegiate athletics accept.

Brand starts from what he calls a "seemingly small point," namely that "When the educational experience of student-athletes is compared with those studying the performing arts such as music dance and theater as well as the studio arts, it is difficult to find substantive differences."[8] Thus, like student athletes, student musicians practice a large number of hours, often more than is required, perform with various musical groups, some college sponsored, and often admission is charged to such events. Performance and practices often are intense. In addition, there is competition for places in the performing groups, and for students with the talent necessary for participation. Some preference may be given in admission to talented students in the arts and some may have aspirations for professional careers, although, as is the case with student athletes in the NCAA, almost all go on to careers in other areas of endeavor. According to Brand, "These similarities point to a convergence of educational experiences between student-athletes and others . . . but the activities of the student-athletes alone are not considered to be academic, or to be in conflict with academics."[9] Is there any plausible justification for this distinction?

Defenders of the standard view would most likely reply that it is the intellectual content of academic courses that distinguish them from intercollegiate athletics. However, Brand maintains that in many performance courses in the arts, what is being taught are skills; "knowing how" rather than "knowing that." Moreover, athletics also involves content, such as knowledge of various strategies and the proper responses to them, as well as (this is my own addition) the ability to distinguish between morally acceptable and unacceptable conduct within the sport. In any case, in actual artistic performance, such as a concert or dance recital, it is not the "knowing that" which is most crucial but rather the exercise of skills at an appropriate level of excellence.

Although Brand's position does raise significant issues about the sharpness of the line between the academic and the non-academic, which is perhaps yet another dualism that might be called into philosophical question, it itself faces serious questions. Critics might maintain, for example, that the goal of elite intercollegiate athletics seems to be to win and to generate the revenue produced by winning, not to express artistic or intellectual values, as is the case with performances in music, dance, and theater.

However, while this criticism does not lack all force, it does seem overdrawn. First of all, the overwhelming majority of intercollegiate athletic contests do not involve high profile sports and are not intended to be revenue producing. Second, while artists normally may not aim at "winning," they do aim at excellence in performance. Similarly, although the cult of winning may have gotten out of hand in many area of sports, intercollegiate athletes often can be seen as aiming at excellence as well, with winning the natural by-product of top performance just as acclaim or the earning of an award can be the by-product of outstanding achievement by an artist. So there might be a difference, as the critics argue, between performance in athletics and the arts but perhaps not as sharp a one as the criticism might initially suggest.

Brand's critics also might argue that music and dance are embedded in a long tradition of intellectual development. Performance in these areas takes place in a context of artistic thought and often expresses or illustrates important themes of human existence or basic human values. However, athletics also can be studied as taking place within a tradition and a history. Moreover, athletic competition can express or illustrate important values such as dedication, excellence, and perseverance in the face of adversity. Brand's case would be stronger, however, if intercollegiate athletes not only participated in sports but also studied their history, social significance, and the ethical dilemmas that arise within them, just as artists may not only perform but also be students of art as well. In other words, Brand's argument would apply most fully when intercollegiate athletes not only participate in sports but also study them within an academic framework just as artists often take courses in, say, the history of music, art, or theater.

In addition, Brand's argument raises the issue of just which skills should be regarded as within the proper domain of a university or college education. If we include not only dance recitals and musical performances but also playing basketball and soccer, what about skillful performance in activities ranging from poker to cooking, to gardening, to playing Monopoly? Must we become so inclusive that no exercise of skill can be left out of the umbrella of the academic? Moreover, should we view those exercises of skill that do seem to be closely related to the academic enterprise, possibly including athletics, to be offered for academic credit or should they be viewed as adjuncts that reinforce a more traditional academic education but which, as Elaine of "Seinfeld" might express it, are not "credit worthy"?

In fact, we might distinguish between a strong and weak version of Brand's thesis. According to the strong version, participation in intercollegiate athletics is credit worthy, at least if performances in the arts also are credit worthy. According to the weaker thesis, participation in intercollegiate athletics, while not credit worthy, is not merely extracurricular either. Rather, it ought to be seen as more closely related to performances that are recognized as academic, and thus as an important adjunct to the academic program.

Brand's argument does suggest that doubt is warranted about where the line should be drawn between the academic and the extra-curricular. The case for the weak version in particular is worth considering and may be reinforced by considerations I advance in the next section of this paper. While those who believe athletics falls on the non-academic side of the line would probably still maintain that it lacks the intellectual content and association with traditions of high art that are the hallmarks of the truly academic, it may be quite difficult, as we have seen, to articulate these notions in a way that clearly and effectively undermines Brand's approach.

Rather than pursue these points here, I want to explore the question of whether intercollegiate athletics might have educational value from another angle, by focusing not on the skills exercised in performance but on what might be called the cognitive virtues presupposed by the pursuit of excellence in athletics.

Athletics and Cognitive and Moral Virtues— An Assessment

To begin this section, I want to describe a theory or model of competitive sport, one I and others have defended elsewhere, that I believe will prove highly relevant to our inquiry into the relation of academics and athletics.[10] This theory, which might be called sport as a mutual quest for excellence through competition, not only helps to explain why so many in fact find competitive sport so fascinating but also provides an ethically defensible account of it as well.

According to an important analysis of the nature of sports by the philosopher Bernard Suits, sports are a sub-class of games.[11] Games, in turn, are defined by rules but the rules have an unusual feature. The constitutive rules of games create obstacles to achieving the primary task of the game that to an outsider may seem unnecessary. In one of Suits's examples, a bystander can't understand, if a person to whom he is talking wants to get from point A to point B as quickly as possible, why he doesn't drive there. However, the person in question is a runner in a marathon and must conform to the rules of the race, including starting at a certain time and running the course rather than taking short cuts or using alternate forms of transportation. Similarly, the rules of checkers create obvious obstacles to removing the opponent's pieces from the board; for example, they prohibit simply knocking them to the floor. Games, Suits suggests, are activities that involve overcoming unnecessary obstacles created by the constitutive rules. His suggests that games, including all or most sports, are fascinating and interesting because they involve the participants testing themselves against these artificial but challenging barriers to success. More specifically, in competitive sport, the participants challenge themselves to meet the test created by the rules, overcoming the special obstacles that are sport-specific, including the moves and strategies of the opponents.

Of course, it is debatable whether Suits's analysis, as he more fully develops it, provides necessary and sufficient conditions for an activity being a game.[12] Rather than pursue that issue, let me turn to how this account, which only has been sketched here, might apply to our inquiry.

First, but not most important for our purposes, this account explains a good deal of what makes competitive sport so fascinating for participants and spectators alike. It is interesting to try to meet challenges that are well designed to bring out the best in us, and also interesting to see others attempt to do so. Over the course of a full season, or athletic career, a narrative is generated with high and low spots, chances for improvement, failures, and successes. Tiger Woods' lifetime quest to surpass Jack Nicklaus's record for the most number of major championships in golf is one such story. So is the story of the basketball team that starts its season with a string of losses but is able to turn things around to win the rest of its games, as is the story of the talented team picked as the best before the season but which loses many of its games, even to inferior opponents, due to the inability of its members to overcome differences and work together. Failures, and what can be learned from them, are just as much part of such narratives as are successes. Even if the participants on the team that loses because of lack of cooperation do not learn from their experience, observers may draw accurate conclusions about the need to overcome differences in pursuing common goals. Clearly, these conclusions can be important outside as well as inside the world of competitive athletics.

Second, as the last example suggests, athletic contests also have a normative structure. This structure has several levels. One is the level of identification and cultivation of personal virtues that lead to success in meeting the challenges of one's sport. These can include the familiar ones of dedication and commitment but also might involve honesty about one's abilities and those of opponents, willingness to accept criticism and to strive to overcome weaknesses, and respect for the challenges set by the constitutive rules of the contest. What is not always noted, however, is that in the good athletic performance, such values are also expressed and revealed to a wider audience; for example, the audience may appreciate the virtues exhibited by skilled athletes and even hope to emulate them in their own lives. Finally, such norms may provide grounds for criticism, as when athletes do not show respect for the deepest values of their sport or when they avoid playing worthy opponents simply to rack up win after win against deliberately chosen inferior opponents.

Athletes often are called upon to make moral choices concerning fairness, sportsmanship, and respect for the values implicit in the traditions and structure of their sport. Indeed, the model of the athletic contest as a mutual quest for excellence suggests that opponents not be regarded as mere things, obstacles standing in the way of one's own victory, but as facilitators who make the good contest possible. Thus, David Duval, once ranked the number one golfer in the world, expressed this attitude, and showed respect for his sport, when he remarked about competing with Tiger Woods that "If I come head-to-head against him at, say, the U. S. Open, I want him to be playing as good as he can play because I want to beat him when he's playing his best. It would be a heck of a lot better, if you know he gave you all he's got, and you beat him."[13]

Indeed, such a view of the athletic contest shows why winning is a significant but nevertheless imperfect indicator of athletic success. A winning record is a sign of excellence at meeting the challenge of a sport only if attained (at least for the most part) against worthy opponents. Right now, I happen to be the best basketball player on my block, which considering my age and declining skills might be thought surprising. Of course, the next best player is four years old and cannot shoot the ball high enough to reach the basket. My string of victories against her, unfortunately, lacks all significance, since the element of challenge is missing.

In fact, as several commentators have argued, athletic competition has many parallels with dialogue in critical inquiry.[14] In sports, each opponent reacts to the choices and skills of the other, tries to anticipate and respond to strategies, and over time to overcome weaknesses so as to mount a better challenge in the future. Similarly, in critical inquiry, we respond to the challenges of intellectual critics, try to anticipate their strategies, and consider how best to overcome weaknesses in our own position. In each case, we can learn a great deal about ourselves and others through subjecting ourselves to intellectual and to sporting challenges, so both can contribute to the process of self-examination and intellectual and moral growth. And just as Duval wants to beat Woods when Tiger is playing at his best, participants in critical dialogue should want to address the strongest version of alternate positions rather than formulations made of straw.

Of course, we need to be careful about reducing competitive sport to an alternate form of inquiry or assigning it a monolithic function or goal. Competitive sports can be played or observed purely as a form of amusement or entertainment, or pursued for reasons of health, friendship, or engaged in to achieve external rewards like fame and fortune with little regard for the internal values of the practice. However, it also is important to note that these other functions or goals often are parasitic on the idea of pursuing excellence through challenge. Thus, if we were only interested in health, we could simply exercise and not play sports competitively or even watch

246 • INTERCOLLEGIATE ATHLETICS

them. Moreover, much of what sports audiences find entertaining about sport is precisely the pursuit of excellence in the face of challenge.

What all this suggests is that competitive athletics can and often does have a relationship of mutual reinforcement of academics in intercollegiate contexts. This is most likely to actually occur and probably can best be fostered in the atmosphere of Division III of the NCAA, and in Division I conferences such as the Ivy League which at least make attempts to integrate athletics and academics (although even they may improve their effort in these areas), but perhaps with some modifications can apply to other areas of intercollegiate athletics as well.

In particular, if many of the values involved in intercollegiate athletics, conceived of along the lines of the mutual quest for excellence, have parallels in intellectual inquiry, emphasis on commonality of virtues necessary for success in one area can help promote development in the other. Of course, the nature of any causal link surely is complex and highly dependent on contextual factors. For example, it is likely to be stronger the more attempts are made to integrate athletics and academics and weaker the greater the emphasis on generation of revenue for the institution and competitive success at the most elite levels of intercollegiate sport. Now, some skepticism about causal links between development of athletic and academic virtues may be warranted in some contexts. However, general skepticism about whether development of cognitive and moral virtues in sports sometimes reinforce parallel virtues in academic endeavors may have little more pre-analytic plausibility than general doubt about whether promotion of critical attitudes in philosophy classes can promote critical attitudes elsewhere, say in considering speeches by politicians.

Moreover, even if the causal thesis is problematic across the board, the thesis of mutual reinforcement, as we have seen, has non-causal as well as causal interpretations. For one thing, the exhibition of such values in actual contests may illustrate, express and reveal values common to athletics and academics to a wider audience. Thus, a team in which players work together to improve after honestly analyzing team weaknesses can illustrate how critical analysis of one's skills, coupled with the desire to improve and a plan to do so, can lead to improvement.

In addition, cognitive and moral virtues critical to success in the mutual quest for excellence may function as standards that can be used to critically appraise behavior both within and outside of athletics. Thus, a professor can say to a student, "if the basketball team can keep trying to overcome its weaknesses in spite of repeated failures, you can keep trying to overcome your writing deficiencies as well." Or a professor can say to a student athlete, "in effect I'm your coach in this course and if your coach in athletics expects you to pay attention when you are told where and how to improve, I expect the same." Similarly, student-athletes can say to professors who may have negative stereotypes about them something like, "Look, I've worked hard to overcome obstacles in my athletic career and you shouldn't just dismiss my ability to improve in this course just because you assume football players aren't good students."

All this suggests that it is a mistake to regard academics and intercollegiate athletics as totally independent practices that most often must be in conflict. Rather, when properly conducted, these practices can be mutually reinforcing While some conflicts may be unavoidable, e.g., traveling to a contest may take up time that can be used to prepare for an examination or may result in a missed class, there may be gains for both endeavors by emphasizing the parallel values that lead to success in each.

NOTES

1. James L. Shulman and William G. Bowen, *The Game of Life* (Princeton: Princeton University Press, 2001).

2. A number of philosophers of sport have defended different versions of the idea that academic and athletic values can be mutually reinforcing. For example, see Peter Arnold, *Sport, Ethics, and Education* (London: Cassell, 1997) and Robert L. Simop, *Fair Play: The Ethics of Sport* (Boulder: Westview, 2004) especially Chapter 6. The present paper is an extension and development of some of the points made in that chapter.

3. Peter French, *Ethics and College Sports: Ethics, Sports, and the University* (Lanham, MD: Rowman and Littlefield, 2004), 115.

4. French, *Ethics and College Sports: Ethics, Sports, and the University*, 116.

5. A significant number of studies have raised doubts about whether many (or even any) Division I athletic programs actually generate a profit. For one discussion of this issue, see Chapter 11 of *The Game of Life*. What remains controversial, in my view, is how to correctly estimate both expenditures and income. For example, how should we count enhanced visibility of a university with highly ranked teams and the effects of such visibility, if any, on admission?

6. Myles Brand, "The Role and Value of Intercollegiate Athletics in Universities," *Journal of the Philosophy of Sport*, Vol. XXXIII (2006): 9–20.

7. Brand, "The Role and Value of Intercollegiate Athletics in Universities," 14.

8. Brand, "The Role and Value of Intercollegiate Athletics in Universities," 10.

9. Brand, "The Role and Value of Intercollegiate Athletics in Universities," 11.

10. For elaboration, see Simon, *Fair Play*, Chapters 2 and 3. For a similar view, sec Jan Boxill, "The Ethics of Competition," in Jan Boxill, ed., *Sports Ethics: An Anthology* (Malden, MA: Blackwell, 2003), 107–115.

11. Bernard Suits, "The Elements of Sport," in Robert Osterhoud, ed., *The Philosophy of Sport: A Collection of Essays* (Springfield, IL: Charles C. Thomas), 48–64. This essay is widely reprinted, for example in William J. Morgan, ed., *Ethics in Sport* (Champaign, IL: Human Kinetics, 2007), 9–19. Interested readers would do themselves a favor by exploring Suits' brilliant and humorous but not widely known book, *The Grasshopper: Games, Life and Utopia* (Toronto: University of Toronto Press, 1978) reprinted by Broadview Press of Peterborough, Ontario in 2005.

12. Suits' fuller account includes the important element of the lusory attitude, or acceptance of the constraints set by the constitutive rules just to make the game possible. See the references in the previous note for discussion.

13. *The New York Times*, Feb 3, 1999: D4.

14. In particular, see Drew Hyland, *The Question of Play* (Lanham, MD: University Presses of America, 1984): 148–151.

STUDY QUESTIONS

1. Is the university's fundamental mission purely academic?
2. Do intercollegiate athletics involve abuses of academic ethics not usually found in other activities of the university?
3. Where should the line be drawn between academic pursuits and extra-curricular activities?
4. What lessons about the value of intercollegiate athletics can be drawn from the importance placed not only on students participating but also on their winning?

CONTRIBUTORS

Scott F. Aikin is a lecturer in the department of philosophy at Vanderbilt University.

Derek Bok served as president of Harvard University.

William G. Bowen served as president of Princeton University.

Myles Brand (1942–2009) served as president of the National Collegiate Athletic Association (NCAA).

Steven M. Cahn is a professor of philosophy at the Graduate Center of the City University of New York. He is the author and editor of more than 40 books, including, most recently, the 25th anniversary edition of *Saints and Scamps: Ethics in America*.

Richard T. De George is a professor of philosophy at the University of Kansas.

Paul D. Eisenberg is a professor emeritus of philosophy at Indiana University.

Leslie Pickering Francis is a professor of philosophy at the University of Utah.

Martin P. Golding is a professor of philosophy at Duke University.

Philip Kitcher is a professor of philosophy at Columbia University.

Charles R. Lawrence III is a professor of law at Georgetown University Law Center.

David Lewis (1941–2001) was a professor of philosophy at Princeton University.

Paul J. Olscamp served as president of Bowling Green University and Western Washington University.

David Shatz is a professor of philosophy at Yeshiva University.

George Sher is a professor of philosophy at Rice University.

Robert L. Simon is a professor of philosophy at Hamilton College.

Robert B. Talisse is a professor of philosophy at Vanderbilt University.

Abigail Thernstrom is a senior fellow at Manhattan Institute.

Stephan Thernstrom is a professor emeritus of history at Harvard University.

Laurence Thomas is a professor of philosophy at Syracuse University.

Nancy Tuana is a professor of philosophy at Pennsylvania State University.

Robert Paul Wolff is a professor emeritus of Afro-American studies and philosophy at the University of Massachusetts, Amherst.